Collected Poems

ALSO BY SEAN O'BRIEN

Poetry
The Indoor Park
The Frighteners
HMS Glasshouse
Ghost Train
Downriver
Cousin Coat: Selected Poems, 1976–2001
Dante's Inferno: A Verse Translation
The Drowned Book
Night Train (with Birtley Aris)
November

Essays
The Deregulated Muse

Plays
Aristophanes' The Birds: A Verse Version
Keepers of the Flame
Laughter When We're Dead

Fiction
The Silence Room
Afterlife

Sean O'Brien

Collected Poems

PICADOR

First published 2012 by Picador
an imprint of Pan Macmillan, a division of Macmillan Publishers Limited
Pan Macmillan, 20 New Wharf Road, London N1 9RR
Basingstoke and Oxford
Associated companies throughout the world
www.panmacmillan.com

ISBN 978-1-4472-1735-0

9 8 7 6 5 4 3 2 1

A CIP catalogue record for this book is available from
the British Library.

Printed and bound by CPI Group (UK) Ltd, Croydon, CR0 4YY

To Gerry Wardle

Contents

The Indoor Park (1983)

The Snowfield   3

Walking   5

Air   7

Station Song   8

Le Départ   9

The Park by the Railway   11

Stories   12

Anne-Marie, the Flower Girl   13

Victorians   14

The Disappointment   15

The Police   16

The Name   18

The Brochure   19

Clio   21

William Ryan's Song in July   24

In the Head   25

Jazz   26

For Lowell George   27

The Beat Goes On   28

The Next Meeting   30

Midsummer's Eve   31

Not Sending Cards this Year   33

The Widower   34

The Seaside Specialist 35

Gun Law 36

Heatwave 38

Late 39

Quiet Wedding 40

The Lamp 41

Tides 42

Victims 43

From the Narrator's Tale 44

Two Finger Exercise 46

The Captain's Pipe 47

The Amateur God 49

The Frighteners (1987)

In a Military Archive 53

The Dampers 54

Young Howard 55

A Master 57

The Realists 58

Civilians 60

Summertime 61

The Red Hospital 62

The Allotment 64

Trespass 66

Song of the South 67

Unregistered 68

Terra Nova 69

London Road   71

The Mechanical Toy Museum   74

How Ryan Got His Start in Life   76

Ryan at Home   77

Ryan's Vocation   79

Ryan's Rebirth   81

Ryan and the Life to Come   83

Ryan's Farewell   84

Envoi   86

After This Poem   87

Cousin Coat   89

The Yard   90

Fiction and the Reading Public   92

In Madre Maria   95

A Matinee   96

Kingdom of Kiev, Rios das Muertes   98

The Head Man   100

Geography   102

HMS Glasshouse (1991)

Before   105

Thrillers and Cheese   107

In the Other Bar   109

Hatred of Libraries   111

A Donegal Golfer   113

Entertainment   114

Propaganda   115

Boundary Beach   117

The Brighton Goodbye   119

At the Wellgate   120

Mission Impossible   121

Dundee Heatwave   122

Fishing   123

Notes on the Use of the Library (Basement Annexe)   124

In Residence: A Worst Case View   126

Betweentimes   128

HMS Glasshouse   129

Cold   131

On the Piss   133

From the Whalebone   135

Working on the Railway   136

Serious   137

Naughty Ron   139

Ballad of the Lit and Phil   141

An Ordinary Evening in New Holderness   146

A Corridor   147

To the Unknown God of Hull and Holderness   149

After Laforgue   152

Ghost Train (1995)

Somebody Else   157

Revenants   160

Interior   161

Special Train   163

The Politics Of   166

Autumn Begins at St James's Park, Newcastle   167

A Rarity   168

The All-Night Afternoon   170

Rain   171

Poem Written on a Hoarding   173

Essay on Snow   174

House   175

Of Origins   177

Latinists   178

AWOL   179

No One   181

Valentine   182

Railway Songs   183

A Provincial Station   186

The Middle   187

A Secret   188

Le Voyage   189

Paysage   190

Homework   191

Biographer   192

Something to Read on the Train   193

Cantona   195

Paradise   196

On Not Being Paul Durcan   198

Reading Stevens in the Bath   200

Amours de Grimsby   202

R=U=B=R=I=C   204

Downriver (2001)

Welcome, Major Poet!   209

Acheron, Phlegethon, Styx   210

Nineties   211

The Ideology   215

At the Gate   218

The Eavesdroppers   219

Last Orders at the Fusilier, Forest Hall   220

Ravilious   221

A Northern Assembly   222

Baltica   228

Riding on the City of New Orleans   230

Indian Summer   232

Kanji   234

The Grammar School Ghost   236

Cities   237

Songs from the Drowned Book   239

Songs from the Black Path   243

  Beginning   243

  The Iron Hand   244

  Lament   245

Songs from *Downriver*   248

  On a Blue Guitar (Lulu Banks)   248

  Horizontal (Bobby Smart)   248

  Smoke Signals (Bobby Smart and Sailor Chorus)   250

  Time on yer Beer Now (The Company)   251

from Sports Pages   254

   Proem   254

   The Origins of Sport from Ancient Times   255

   The Olympics   256

   Football! Football! Football!   258

   Amerika   260

Noonday   263

Lines on Mr Porter's Birthday   264

Postcards to the Rain God   265

Synopsis   269

Ex Historia Geordisma   271

   from The Go-As-You-Please Songbook   271

   from The Poems of Mercedes Medioca   272

   Seriously, Like   273

Poem for a Psychiatric Conference   274

The Railway Sleeper   277

The Genre: A Travesty of Justice   283

From *Inferno* (2006)

Canto III, The Entry to Hell   291

Canto VIII, Crossing the Styx   297

Canto XIII, The Wood of the Suicides   302

Canto XVII, Geryon; the Usurers   308

Canto XXII, Escape   314

Canto XXV, Snakes and Metamorphoses   320

Canto XXVI, Ulysses   326

Canto XXXIII, Ugolino   332

From *The Drowned Book* (2007)

Dedication   341

The Apprehension   342

Water-Gardens   344

River-doors   346

Eating the Salmon of Knowledge from Tins   348

By Ferry   350

Drains   351

A Coffin-Boat   352

The River in Prose   355

The Mere   357

The River Road   358

Three Lighthouses   359

Grey Bayou   361

The Lost War   362

Timor Mortis   363

Sheol   365

A Little Place They Know   366

Symposium at Port Louis   368

Proposal For a Monument to the Third International   371

Valedictory   376

Fantasia on a Theme of James Wright   379

The Thing   380

Thom Gunn   381

Serious Chairs   382

Three Facetious Poems   384
   Sung Dynasty   384
   Why The Lady   384
   Of Rural Life   384
Lost Song of the Apparatus   385
Six Railway Poems for Birtley Aris   387
   Inheritance   387
   Cherchez la Femme   388
   Yellow Happiness   388
   Bridge   389
   Reasonable Men   390
   Here You Are   391
Railway Hotel   393
Grimshaw   395
Rose   396
Blue Night   397
Transport   398
Abendmusik   399
The Hand   400
After Rilke: To Hölderlin   401
Praise of a Rainy Country   403
Blizzard   405
Arcadia   406

From *November* (2011)

Fireweed   411
Jeudi Prochain   412
The Citizens   414

Sunk Island 415

Salisbury Street 416

Josie 417

Vérité: Great Junction Street 418

Cahiers du Cinema 419

White Enamel Jug 426

Sleep 427

Europeans 428

Elegy 429

The Lost Book 432

Novembrists 436

Counting the Rain 438

The Plain Truth of the Matter 439

First Time Around 440

Sunday in a Station of the Metro 441

Marine Siding 442

Closed 443

The Island 444

Railway Lands 446

Infernal 447

Bruges-la-Morte 448

The Drunken Boat 450

Michael 454

The Landing-Stage 455

Dinner at Archie's 456

Porteriana 458

Leavetaking 459

The Heat of the Day 462

Tables and Chairs 464

Aspects of the Novel 465

   Chapter 16 465

   Want of Motive 466

   The Uninvited Reader 467

The River on the Terrace 468

Narbonne 469

On the Toon 470

   Canto I 470

   Canto II 473

   Canto III 475

Notes 479

Index of Titles 485

Index of First Lines 495

Acknowledgements 505

The Indoor Park
(1983)

The Snowfield

It is so simple, being lonely.
It's there in the silence you make
To deny it, the silence you make
To accuse the unwary, the frankly alone.
In the silence you bring to a park
When you go there to walk in the snow
And you find in the planthouse,
Next to the orchids in winter slow-motion
And sleeping unreadable mosses,
Sick men, mad, half-born, who are sitting
As long as the afternoon takes.
Left there by helpers hours ago,
As if preparing for a test,
Each holds a book he cannot open.

Some days you put together
Sentences to say for them
As you leave to go back to the street.
With work they might be epigrams
Of love and modest government.
And this thought frees you. You pick up the paper.
You eat. Or you go to the library and talk.

But some days there is nothing
You cannot know. You still leave,
But it seems to take hours, labouring
Back to the street through the snowdrifts
And not worth the effort.
It seems that this is all there is.
It happens like snow in a park, seen clearly
After days of admiration, and looking

As if it had always been there, like a field
Full of silence, that is not beginning or ending.
It is so simple. You just hadn't looked.
And then you did, and couldn't look away.

Walking

I am in love with detail. Chestnut trees
Are fire-damaged candelabra.
Waterbirds are porcelain.
The planthouse is the room within the room
And all this is England,
Just left here, and what's to be done?

It does not remember the dances,
Silk stockings and murders and money.
We were not invited. We came late
To trespass on ourselves among the furniture,
Admiring the upholstery of Hell,
Where the talk is the best and you know it.

Adulterous cortège of cars around the park,
Where the couples are solving themselves with despair.
They will die of each other.
They have names, they were born –
If they're held to the light they have souls,
Like little ingots knocking at the heart.

O Vaughan and Geoffrey, Annabel and Jane,
Your time is up, you've gone professional.
You are condemned to live this script
Until the gestures make you retch,
And then for ever, knowing it –
The passive yes, the nominated self,

The grammar till it vanishes
Among these great facilities,
Where she and I are walking, I believe.
We're holding hands. I say, and then repeat,
There is no nightmare big enough to hurt,
Since it fits with the tick of the gold at my heart.

Air

I shall be writing you until I die,
You in your several selves, my friend of half a life,
My girl, my enemy, my judge.

An empire of affection built in air:
The air remains, the context of At Last.
It fills the space between the lives with words —

The last of everyone, through Caesar, Janis, Marx
And Ron McKernan, and from each
A democratic breath of silence

As helpful and useless as drink.
They died, and we diminished proteans
Have died as well, in every second thought.

We drew the map, and gave the place its names
Of water, light, and grass for lying on,
That single summer, standing at its heart.

—We didn't. We were not ourselves.
Nor are we now, when we've concluded
Every variant of hate.

We named each tic of sentiment, or not.
It's called *The Oxford Book of Early Life*,
And here's the long, uneasy supplement

That cannot trust its sources. Air,
And we can only add to it
Our passionate routine,

In case our scholarship should yield
The facts of how we lived and felt
And breathed the air behind the air.

Station Song

I should have seen you all the time, you ghosts,
But I was taken up elsewhere
With getting on, which got me here.
I'm back for good. You are
So patient, like the best of hosts.

Am I your guest?
The girl, is she one too?
You say there's nothing I must do,
That I am not accountable to you.
You wish me nothing but the best.

I try to see if I'll get lost.
I walk the streets. But then a sign
Propped up on bricks explains what's mine:
One door along this line
Of doors that open on to dust.

Le Départ

You've been leaving for years and now no one's surprised
When you knock to come in from the weather.
The crew is past embarrassment:
They can live with their nautical names, and with yours.
So sit, take down your glass, and talk
Of all that is not you, that keeps you here
Among the sentimental stevedores
In the drinking clubs in the dank afternoons
Of your twenty-ninth year. There may be news.

Indeed. Somebody drowned last night, walked sideways
Off a Polish fishmeal hulk. A rabid Paraguayan bear
Was seen among the kindly hookers eating fruit.
A hand-carved coelacanth was found
When the cells were dug out to lay drains . . .

How can you not be struck by these arrivals?
The perfect boat is sailing Tuesday week.
It's heading southwards, way beyond the ice –
Starsailing seems quite plausible by night.
Until then there is querulous Ninepin
(The loss of his ticket for thieving)
And Madeleine's never-secret grief
(Be kind, and ask politely what)
And someone selling crocodiles
And hash from the sump of a jungle . . .
Now even the Juvaro have secret accounts –
Sell them your Service Forty-Five
And get a tape-recorder back . . .
The Amazon's an answering service:

No one's ever really lost. A month ago
Rocheteau, stuck for credit, offered up
The pelvic bones of Mungo Park
In exchange for a fifth of Jim Beam . . .
We always thought that Scot was lying about Africa.

It is easily night: soft boom of lighter-boats
Beyond the fogwall, swung on inauthentic tides
That left you here, that left you here
As the lovesongs go over the warehouse
Among patrolling cats and a lost ARP
With his bucket of sand and his halberd.

You are doped on the stairs on the way to the moon
With Yvonne, who has aged but not quite,
Who knows the words to every song
And places one flattering palm on your spine
Till you move, who keeps a special bottle
For you (but half gone, half gone) by the bed,
A black fire of sugar that says all there is
About travelling. You're halfway there.

And all shall sing until the awful morning
Reminds them of themselves,
Then sleep in early restaurants,
Boastful of such daft endurance,
And then inspect the shipping lists
Until the time is right.

'You talk in your sleep,' says Yvonne.
'So I woke you. All this travelling –
You leave the girls for what?
Are we not always, always travelling?
Let's drink to that, and one before you go.'

The Park by the Railway

Where should we meet but in this shabby park
Where the railings are missing and the branches black?
Industrial pastoral, our circuit
Of grass under ash, long-standing water
And unimportant sunsets flaring up
Above the half-dismantled fair. Our place
Of in-betweens, abandoned viaducts
And modern flowers, dock and willowherb,
Lost mongrels, birdsong scratching at the soot
Of the last century. Where should we be
But here, my industrial girl? Where else
But this city beyond conservation?
I win you a ring at the rifle range
For the twentieth time, but you've chosen
A yellow, implausible fish in a bag
That you hold to one side when I kiss you.
Sitting in the waiting-room in darkness
Beside the empty cast-iron fireplace,
In the last of the heat the brick gives off,
Not quite convinced there will be no more trains,
At the end of a summer that never began
Till we lost it, we cannot believe
We are going. We speak, and we've gone.
You strike a match to show the china map
Of where the railways ran before us.
Coal and politics, invisible decades
Of rain, domestic love and failing mills
That ended in a war and then a war
Are fading into what we are: two young
Polite incapables, our tickets bought
Well in advance, who will not starve, or die
Of anything but choice. Who could not choose
To live this funeral, lost August left
To no one by the dead, the ghosts of us.

Stories

'You can, now that she's qualified.
Let nothing distract you,' he said.
We drank tea in the visiting hour
As if at our own kitchen table.
'Just go, the two of you.' As if we might
Transform your van into a house,
Add river, pasture, children
In one summer, forgetting ourselves
In the country he came from.

I thought he came from Nenagh.
No, he played football for them.
It's been Dublin, Cork and Limerick
And still he won't stop travelling.
'See, Cork is for strangers: it's short in the mouth
So it calls off the questions. But go.
A woman will console a man.'

Suppose we did. He'd never come.
A bad third novel in the sticks
With him wanting tea at all hours
And you delivering the dead,
He left the place. It's stories now
And they sustain no time, no life.
I've come so far from land I'd drown.

Anne-Marie, the Flower Girl

It could be true. There might just be
No outcome. After all the beds,

The halls with unusual prints,
The sculleries with mould that climbs

From teapots, all the headless birds
Left over by the cats, the years

Of unstoppable weather
You would think by now

She might have grown a bit suspicious.
So all the long-haired boys have gone

To India at last, but she
Keeps busy making things to sell.

The one she always wanted lives
Across the street. She hardly hears

His annual excuse for still
Remaining with that other bitch.

The rooms get painted, cats renewed,
And this month's books are all begun.

A miracle is taking place.
So this is time, and time contains

Her history, and here she lives
Her history, from time to time.

Victorians

White heads, white hats, in garden chairs,
Enthusiasts of time,
Adulterous and hopeful men, who met
Their fallen girls at stations out of town:

This day of summer's yours in perpetuity.
I cannot love your manners or your work,
But accidental bravery persists,
In homiletic lilac and your vanity in stone.

We were the epic exegetes
And called religiose.
We are what's left when time retreats,
The syphilitic rose:

How honesty becomes opaque,
The reason drawing on:
We looked into the little lake
And wanted to be gone.

Let this be noon, before the letter comes,
The daughter coughs, the verses are exposed,
Before the century goes black,
And you go blind, and all the doors are closed.

The Disappointment

The sky becomes mother-of-pearl,
A lady's box of trinketry.
The air inside it can remember
Lavender at two removes,
Like someone's love once dreamed about
But not possessed, and longed for now.

In one of these burgherly houses,
Room on room on corridor,
It is someone's finale, unpacking herself
From lint and pins and looking-glasses.
Bland with young 'accomplishment'
Not even the letters are cryptic here,

Valuable only in histories of boredom:
Chat of some dud couple caught
In frames where time stands in for love,
With their backs to a sea to whose ironclad rightness,
Decked with pennants, fleet on fleet,
They bore unthinking witness. They were cold.

All afternoon I trudge around
Inventing tasks. I look and sniff
And find Victoria and Albert
Brilliant white and everpresent.
From windy plinths The Great outstare
The disappointment of their will

As dusk elaborates the park.
A duck-guffaw, a lacy hem of frost,
A salesman reading *Penthouse* in his car,
Pianoforte being taught and loathed –
Its sweet unwarranted effects,
Not brave enough for sorrow but still there.

The Police

No one believes them. Their windows get broken.
It rains in their yards and their kids
Dress in black and are sullen and pasty.
Their wives would like going to hangings:
They knit and they think about crime.

The police, they have allotments, too:
Like us they don't get paid.
But their beans are like stone
And their lettuce like kelp
And black men come on moonless nights
To burn the greenhouse down,
And their windows are broken
So they don't eat tomatoes.
The police, when they pot their begonias,
Press down with both thumbs, like that,
And a fly can be killed with one blow.

They are not jealous, the police.
When they stare at your allotment
They're sure there's a body below.
But if you say, 'Yes, he's a Roman,'
They ask you, 'And how do you know?'
We are all called *Sunshine*,
Or else we are liars, or both.
We would be better off without ourselves,
Or cordoned off, at least.
The world is guilty of itself,
Except the police, that is.

The police are not immortal, though they try.
They are buried with honours and bicycle clips.
But black men come from the allotments
And chop their gravestones down.
Then lots of queers with foreign names
Dig them up and make films of their bones.

The Name

Vlad the Impaler, the torturer's horse,
And the mercantile towers of Asia
Stacked with skulls like death's exchequer.
Something must be done with Sunday:
Florid libraries deputize for God.
When the light has run back through the page
I can hear the wind gathering leaves,
But one name in the cursory millions
Has lodged like a seed in my throat.
Katya, whom Anonymous has praised
Forgettably for being young and his
In summer thirteen twenty-six.
This is only a way of repeating her name,
A charm, that can't believe in time.
The wine my conscience drinks tonight
Can't run as sweet and harsh as hers
Across my tongue. These apples cannot weigh
As firm and cool as hers upon my hands.

The Brochure

Built for bracing airs above the sea,
It shadows half the beach
And mines the sandstone cliff with larders.
Red brick, grey brick, yellow corners, square
And grosser than the national product.
Admire the glass-eyed Nemo-domes
And sawn-off fire-escapes
On the locked heights.
Behind the screams of hooded gulls
The screams of doomed remittance-men:
Behind them both, the rubber tread
Of floor-detectives, rigorously picked
From jails and noncommissioned ranks.
Their doctors' bags are pursed
For pliers, greaseproof packets,
The complete range of fillings,
Toenails and St Christophers,
Postal orders, things in lockets,
Oaths extracted on notepaper
Headed *The Grand*, plus the various
Snifters of morphine, the various
Samples of semen and blood.
Minute attention is their mark,
While lower down in sweating kitchens
Waiters redirect the pipes
To the bottling plant. At the cocktail hour
Fine goblets of urine appear
On silver trays on tables at the doors
Of virgin brides: beneath each glass,
Lubricious propositions, costed.
Following dinner, the dancing with swords

And the drawing of lots for the novelty gangplank,
Pickled parts are raffled, old songs sung.
Be assured that none is excluded.
In case there is an enemy
The highly trained homunculi
Who staff our deep torpedo rooms
Will fire you from sewer-pipes
Across the moonlit bay.

Clio

(for Dave Lewis)

Arcane and absolutist aunt
Refusing access over tea,
You are my private hierophant
And you embroider me.

You say you know me inside out,
This man I haven't met,
And you could tell me all about
What hasn't happened yet.

But nothing happens here at all
As far as I can see.
The missing pictures on the wall
Are how it's meant to be.

You have the leisure to be bored
And so you still trot out
The view that you must be adored,
Which I take leave to doubt:

Your ironies are second-rate,
Imagination nil –
So how do you concoct my fate,
And what about this will?

You smile that smile and preen yourself
And ply me with a bun:
You were the first one on the shelf
And all you've ever done

Is recognize my vanity,
And tease it till it screams,
Whilst feeling up my sanity,
The small coin of my dreams.

Gentility's as impolite
And secretive as cancer –
Both kick several shades of shite
From any life-enhancer.

Then I hear, 'Let's try again
And then you can go home.
It takes a little English pain
To build a metronome.'

So I'm reciting day and night
The masters and their grief.
I'll know when I have got it right
If boredom kills belief.

Remote and circular, your place
Evaluates my senses,
Palgrave's Golden Interface,
Dismantler of tenses,

Scholar-Critic's time machine,
Will Travel Anywhere,
Though somehow I have never been
Around when I was there.

So will you? Won't you? Should I care?
Has it ended or begun?
I do not know if I can bear
Interminable fun.

But I don't think I'll ever die.
I don't suppose you'll let me.
Every time I say goodbye
You threaten to forget me.

William Ryan's Song in July

Summer for me has always been August, no other.
I shall travel to no island
For Ryan is not to be fooled. Give me August
Or nothing. Can you understand?

Some fools that I have known have laughed
And cared to demonstrate
That August is the end and not the middle.
Yes, says I, for I chose in that knowledge.

The heat is blackened, full of dust then, Ryan
—*I could have told you that.*
The trees of an awful non-fighting weight
—*Which is lost in a week. I had heard of all that.*

August, let me say, is situate
Between July
And sonorous September. It's a sort of middle
For the scary, no place to be in. *Have you heard?*

I shall give you July, for a gift.

In the Head

I watched her coming through the park
And wanted that black hair, that shape,
That curved voice calling me my name,
And as I wanted this I saw
Her life could not be touched by mine.
I know that she is real somewhere,
Her set of rooms and obligations
Owned impossibly without
Me coming up in dreams or talk,
Her earrings, postcards, clothes and love
Invisibly acquired and lost
With birth-certificates and keys:
A life imperial in scale
If I alone could enter it
To map its rich confusion and desire.
You could not count the theories
Aroused and then discredited
In this place in an afternoon,
The shadow pastorals performed
Inside the mind as summer throws
The switch on brick and grass and skin,
And no one minds or needs attend
This conference, and no one dares.
The earth could not support the weight
And raw perfection of despair.

Jazz

It is to you, my dear, I owe
This love of the soloing saxophone.
You are going away, for a while.
I have borne that before.
I am only afraid
Of the highly-strung bass
Like a clock in the groin.

For Lowell George

What fills the heart is felt to make amends,
Until the flooded heart can no more choose
Release than never sing its staggered blues.
I wish you had not found such special friends.
At thirty-four, at three a.m., in bed,
Of overweight helped on by dope and booze,
Before your talent bored you you were dead.

The Beat Goes On

(for Jerry Kidd and John Rowley)

The radio's remembering
Piano-shifting brutalists
In suits of whorish pink, who vocalise
Bluenote-bayous of razz and grief; remembering
Mulatto chords and Mama Roux,
The currency and then the price
The stovepipe-hatted obeah man exacts
For stealing shellac masters
From the tombs of Creole Pharaohs
Still cool in their coke-filled sarcophagi
Under the boardwalks of Hell; remembering
The life we never lived
Again, a riding cymbal-shimmer
Stroked with a hickory Premier C
As the horns stand up in the key of real sex.
Encyclopaedias of air encode
The glamour of the singing poor.
We learn them like a second heart.
They gave the mirror all its moves:
Tonight it will not even laugh –
And for this I have drummed out the grease
From a lifetime of antimacassars,
Nagged by good taste and a future
That looks as high and lonesome now
As a busload of drunks and their delicate axes
Marooned in the snowy Sierras.
There's no cenotaph for those
Who try to cut the cost of touring,
Who go in derailments, in cropdusters' biplanes,

To Klansmen at crossroads,
Shot by their mistreated girls
Or drowned in concrete by the Mob,
And they cannot now honour their contract
To make us a language of passion and style.
But this evening the Sixties,
This evening the King,
So bored he even broadcasts hymns
To the wives of Nebraska and Kansas
Who sweat at the prospect of leisure
And choke on their sociables, feeling Him move
In the air over wheatfields and highways.
The King keeps his class in the bathroom
With the whips and methadone.
He turns the Baptist Gospel off
And hears the princes practise down the hall.
They are harder and blacker and closer to jail
And the heartbreaking four forty-nine.
Tonight the trailer park gets drunk
Beneath a moon of impotence
As someone seminal awakes
At the wheel of a stolen Chevrolet,
To search the airwaves once again
For something that could make him dance,
With whisky freezing on his shirt
And a writ for his skin in his pocket.

The Next Meeting

Tonight's the turn of Mrs Mac
To address the bereaved
At the Spiritualist Church.
Too cold for snow, the punters say,
But nurse their cars around the park.

She will speak of the comforting aether,
Where voices in a loop rehearse
Their sentence to infinity. Outside
It snows a silent alphabet
That vanishes on contact with the ground.

Midsummer's Eve

A blue light is hung in the house
On these nights in the middle of summer,
When dark never comes, then comes at once,
As if this were no time of year
But time for real inside the head.

There is this half-surprise, the hand
Half-visible before the face,
The softened mirror like a door
To the house where the prizes are given
For coming at all, but you don't move.

When the trains are asleep
Between here and the sea, when the one boat
Is rocked on a slick of the moon,
When the last lamp swings off up its track,
You will always be elsewhere,

Sitting it out on the edge of the map
And rehearsing your book of improvements.
The lamp should be meeting a girl about now.
There she is, on the bench, with her face turned away,
As the cold-eyed crew of the M.V. *Moneta*

Play Cheat and look out for a flame on the cliffs.
They are fools. At this moment their man's
In a room full of smoke with the railway police,
Denying it all but with no cigarettes,
Till the heavies arrive; although the girl

Could change it all, were she awake.
But then, who wants an outcome? Who needs it?
You make your offer to the night.
You say you want no recompense.
The night will take you at your word.

Not Sending Cards this Year

Consoled by the dead with their tea-things
In somebody's lodge in the snowed-under forest,
We listen with them as the end of the world
Comes six months late by pigeon post
As the roar of silk thread and a note
On the death of the definite article.

We watch them tune their metres down –
Revise. Revise. Is it enough
To say the end is like the end?
And we admire such
Intensities of indolence
And call them the point of discomfort.

The best to be had is a biro that works
And some milk left for morning.
Let's go out now, to where we live,
The dead harbour, the pub and the station buffet,
North of the Word, where it rains in your face.

The Widower

Most men hire out their lives
To finish off with nights like this,
The blue from which the darkness pours
Upon the knotted apple tree
To simplify the shape of long neglect,

And some of them have stayed in love
A lifetime with intimate strangers,
Discovered a talent for taking a walk
Or for blether begun at the table at noon
And kept through sleep and next day's lack:

But half will meet the end alone
And from a cramped obituary spell out
A name that cannot now be learned
Though it is said like rosaries
And written down the margins of the page.

I've seen my elders pad their gardens
Uselessly and try to read.
Now there is only leisure to exhaust,
And a tree by the builders' default.
It bore no fruit I ever saw.

But let there be one widower
To see one yellow apple wax
Towards its perihelion
And have his solitude precise
And rich until the tree is dark.

The Seaside Specialist

As every mag along the front reveals
It is the festival of skin,
So if your own is grey or loose
Lie down with a gatefold and wank
In the sock-smelling fug of your choice,
At which only the mirror will look.
Then read of how the Anabaptists,
Choosing to go naked, played
With nuts and berries and their friends
To be as little children; how
These heretics were brought to book
And burnt in the sociable squares.
It will look like a posture
Supportable only in summer,
Like those embarrassed couples racked
On postcards in primary colours
Of nuptial malfeasance and loathing,
Sent to prove a holiday was had.
Extended families of pain,
They float in batches to the shore
You reach beyond your book at night.
The sea, the blue comedian
Who rolls the drowned along the aisles
Of an interminable act,
Has autographed each card with love.

Gun Law

I wrote a cheque out in the snow
For money in its element.
More white than I was happy with
And cold enough to weld my hand
To the seat of the bike I had bent.

They did not love me at the bank,
Nor would they give me money.
Then I wished I really had
A murder in my heart,
A Gladstone pocket
Equipped for spectacular slayings.
Hey sucker.
Suck on this. Boom-boom.

The crippled bike bore me away
Down drifted tenfoots, over drains,
Around imaginary housing schemes
Into the sleeping sickness of the archives.
With everything in black and white
I am simply awaiting the dogs.

In the tabloids that I dreamed,
I saw the murdered teller rise
Like an overdraft, wearing a smile
Of such inane complacency
It nearly matched his Christmas shirt
And made me want to cry.
He wiped his lips and offered me
His blinding handkerchief.

Out here in limbo in the snow
In a tanner's yard in Wilmington
At dawn I clear the midnight's drift
From stacks of frozen currency.
A wad of burning Zloties heats
My pan of ice, and here, at least,
Though I lie in the arms of the dollar,
The coins on my eyes are my own.

Heatwave

The chestnuts take their shadows in
Like women bearing winding-sheets.
I hear, though I'm not listening,
The night's held breath of fruit and meat,
And all around my skin I feel
The long day's thick residual heat,
Erotic, inescapable.
Someone is dying on our street.

Late

In the rented rooms above the bay
The simmer of epistles was like sleep.
Old men grow bored with young men's books,
But still they followed and were sold
At the stall that an uncle had kept.
His landlady found roses in the hall
Without a note, and for the afternoon
There was the itch of Sundays at the Spa:
Band-music, marble, heat and wickedness.
He did not have to work, she thought.
Eat greens for the conduct; wear sensible shoes;
Keep up with the journal; walk out to the light
At the pier's end, a mile in the ocean.
Look back for the window seen only from here.
It is only a place you can see.
It survives you. It makes you a ghost,
Where she lived, where we both lived once.
I am embarrassed to have stayed
So long and on so little and for this.

Quiet Wedding

This isn't the way to the airport.
No, this is the way
To the backlots of our family romance.
We are sure of a lavish reception,
Warm black wine in every cup,

In the loved setting
Of sofas and grey, guilty light
That their years in the business of hoofing and hating
Have made them the mistresses of.
Miss Crawford, Miss Davis. Miss Davis, Miss Crawford.

The Lamp

Slowly, these evenings, it warms to its business,
Adding its ivory miniature wattage
To headaches unbidden or begged for;
To love doing overtime, vicious or civil.
A simple but brilliant composure
Of levers and springs, with a bulb and a flex,
It should be an eye but is not, and should know
But does not, and should feel but cannot.
It squats at my shoulder and silently stares,
Giving nothing away of the dreams it can't have.
These dreams concern high cold
And long views from a clinic to Europe
Set out beneath its haze of sun
And politics. No loneliness, no cry,
Can climb to the terrace where money is dying,
In rarefied purple, with desperate good humour.
The lamp is in place by the notes on the desk
In the room that is kept at the dry heat of health
And has four walls of medical journals.
Nobody lives here and no one is missing.
Strange if when some modernist made this
He failed to see its perfect sex. Plug in, turn on
And leave alone: blank ecstasy
Unbounded by the mortal physics.
An anglepoise lamp done in white.
If you were to ask me that now I should act
In reasonable faith to find a name
For what it does, then I would have to say,
You asking me, you being you, and reason being
What it is, and the lamp being here,
A prosthetic of dark in the room,
It sheds light, I suppose. It depends what you mean.

Tides

For Peter Didsbury

There are tides in the paper that lies on the desk.
They are slow. They are burdened with junk,
The circular diaspora
Of piracy and empires, on the Middle Sea.
They are bored with the half-life of scholarly myth,
Bored with the gaze of the sunblind student
Attacked by nausea on a bus to the Gut,
Where adventure appears in a glass of anis
As a species of maritime fraud
At which the police can only smile
As they sit by the fountain comparing their guns.
There are tides in the inky compartments
Of every such homecoming briefcase,
Tides on every desk. They are waiting
For fools to afflict with the notion of time
As a pool of salt in a frame of sand,
To afflict with the index of names
And the index of those without names,
Which is bigger and harder to freight,
And will turn in its leather-and-brass-bound sleep
And despatch the most scrupulous craft to the bed
On the calmest evening, miles from nowhere,
In waters turned milky by moonlight,
That riffle like ream upon ream of octavo
Spread over the floor and left blank.
The boat is rigged. Someone ships out
Across a sea that never breaks,
Whose storms are always submarine,
Where sinking leaves no watermark.

Victims

Some of them like zealots seek
Asylum in the dictionary
And hope that they will not be missed.

Others surrender in public.
They ask a quick death
At the hands; on the tongues,
Of indifferent captors.

Both want to be rid of the future.
There is no escape. They will finish up
Strapped to the big wheel of syntax,
Their names being taken
In vain by the ignorant gods.

From the Narrator's Tale

Whether it happens upstairs or on Pluto
You hear it, but not what it means.
It's the art of narration. You notice
A singular absence of motive.
The pace is a killer. The names are absurd.
A storm of clues among the stars
Comes adrift of its questions
And moves among us now like facts
We can't buy or dispose of. Clear?
A model must be bigger than its source
And most of it be out of sight,
Like Africa from here. Yes, Africa,
Where Hagenbach attempts to con a sheikh.
The world's long curve! Here comes the prose
On paper wings, our Omens of the day.
We hear him fried in Essoline
Before admiring crowds. They love
Their country and the testy Will of Allah.
So tell me, how long is it now
Since Haggers embezzled the Junior Pie?
Of course we always wished him harm –
We did it for the future's sake –
But if that shit can own a soul
That smoulders afterwards, then what,
I ask you, will be made
Of those who really matter here
In this too-long-neglected, imperfectly rendered
Chunk of the whole inadvisable project?
        I sit in the greenhouse and watch
The tomatoes expanding like suns.
Along the heating pipes I hear
The couples and their marriages,

So bored they have even turned back
To the partners with whom they began
For punishment and company. All afternoon
The rows elaborate themselves,
Deranged bureaucracies of noise,
A dire choral symphony
I shall not find the time to write,
Whose theme is custody of pain.
Midsummer's Eve. Tonight's the night.
The template of authority
Is matched against the air. The heat
Rests its gun in the shade of a wall.
And I, as ever, come too soon,
For how else could I tell you these things?
             Now Endean hangs the paper lamps
Around the arboretum, sullenly
Dreaming a drink to his hand.
His boy rakes leaves across the pool
And by a gift of physics finds
Jane's beckoning reflection there.
Her tongue upon her lips welds his
To the cleft in his palate. His mother
Goes down to the cellar with Simpson.
The vol-au-vents wink into flame.
The cat lies more immobile by the range
As ash flakes down upon its fur.
             I am tired of telling this prickteasing truth
That I cannot invent or abolish.
How much we resemble the humans we read of.
Attending the party that calls us to meaning,
Finite but unbounded fools
With all our permutations done,
Interred by accident of birth
Among the blazing nebulae,
We'll crowd the balustrade, and looking down
We'll see us dancing, looking up.

Two Finger Exercise

I play my last arpeggio,
Then shut the dummy keyboard and sit back
To listen as the note decays.

It takes its time. It takes mine too.
It's numbering the ruches on the gowns
Of all the roses on this hill

Where England sprays her armpit
With a subtle distillation
Of hypocrisy and bullshit.

The keys are worn with locking nature
In the inventory of air. Let us be human,
Say critics who need a new interest.

They live somewhere else, counting coal
In the virtuous baths of the North
To build a thesis lumpy with endeavour.

This is where the English live.
And we are foreigners. The bus to work
Braves Congos of complacent tat . . .

The evenings, though, are 'personal'.
I count the rooms. I count again.
I try to sit in one of them. I fail

And imagine pianos instead,
A Bechstein warehouse, grand and dumb,
With teeth as white as privilege.

The Captain's Pipe

Before the poor are working I am here,
Before the air is used or the first kiss planted
Or the heat of Kundalini blooms
At the base of initiate spines.
I dislike the cities, the plains
And this olive drab sweatbox,
The jungle, in one of whose inlets
I anchor and watch without interest or boredom
Green ocean contending with dun yellow river
For rights to the seasnakes, the Lascar morsels.
Left to me, self-interest looks like fate.
Tending the bowl with a fragrant brown thumb
I denature the Buddha: look
How he diversifies in smoke.
A million tawdry gods appear —
Damp earth and bamboo, stuck with feathers,
False dawn's birds of paradise.
Let them declare
That man too is commerce,
Like opals and copra, like gold.
Let exiled bureaucrats
Have cold clear dreams of this
As they twist on starched beds
In the nervous cantonment,
A mile from my imminent pleasure.
Happy the man with a pipe to his name
As the sun steps smoking from the sea
Like a worthy untainted by trade.
On his breast he displays
The gold disc of exemption,
From which all the money was anciently copied,

According to one of the poets I hanged.
I take a lens and polish it,
The first rays warm to the map at my feet.
The first cannon cracks, the citadel chars,
And by evening the gold in its cellars
Will melt like the sun in the water.

The Amateur God

Like sluggish electrons
The first gnats of April
Are cruising the visual field.
The kingfisher's moulting its plaster of Paris.
The cherub is moulting his head.
The goldfish stare upwards from cushions of weed,
Rehearsing blasé vowels at the sun.
The Peace Rose,
Pruned to a barbed-wire paradox,
Stands with its label, as if on a platform
Awaiting the slow train of summer.
The gardener beats a new path out of cinder.
The brazier rolls its crimson eyes
Like Argus. There's nothing but detail
And leisure to name it, with one hand
To cool in the pond, and the other
Rubbing moss into my jeans
Wholeheartedly at thirty as at three.
The afternoon is permanent.
My father, my uncle, in suits of pale ash,
Are still sinking the black in the shade.
The voices of their politics
Are softer than the fountain's voice.
The afternoon is permanent.
The amateur god of this garden is me.

The Frighteners
(1987)

In a Military Archive

The mirror on this corridor
Detains them in its waiting-room.
Sporadically the backward clock
Remembers its authentic boom
And flings the dead men to their knees.
They rise. They smoke. They watch their hands.
They mend the furniture and read.
The King's Own ——shire Ampersands,
Preserved as footnotes in the texts
Of Hockley, Blunden, Hart et al.,
At ease in the grave-geographies
Of Arras, Albert and Thiepval.
Now literature is sent, as once
Were razor blades and letters,
That the dead may study suffering
In the language of their betters.

The Dampers

Damp weather wrings its yellow hands,
Staining the lungs as it fingers for lesions.
It's here, with a velvety flourish,
Liver-spotted pillowslips. Now leather smudges,
Jackets wear the badge of dissolution,
Rooms burst sickly into flower.
The bubbling voices of radio liars
Drift on drowning frequencies.
Damp nineteenth-century music parts
The cardboard necks of violins.
Damp literature, damp diaries,
Damp biscuits, damp regression:
At home, in the damp stacks of *Tiger* and *Wizard*,
With four-colour heroes whose red, white and blue
Has survived on your lack of belief.
Roy of the Rovers? The Wolf of Kabul?
They have sunk through the page and congealed
On the air-raid shelter's floor
In an adipose mixture of ink and ambition,
The ultimate mimetic act.
Why, even the coffins are damp
On their blocks at the makers, awaiting,
As midnight approaches with revels and vows,
Those punters whom the damp detains.
Goodbye. There are more missing faces
Condensing the wrong sides of mirrors,
Or staring back blankly from photos
And shell-holes, still mouthing their names
In the silt of all cancelled intentions.
To drain from the outline and vanish:
You melt, when the offer is made.

Young Howard

Two aunts in garish rosy prints
Sat waiting in the head man's room,
Intent on their vocation; there
'To take me home'. They called me in
From cricket to my life, my life.

They worked in shifts. I dreamed
They stroked my arm until it bled.
Their eyes reflected me alone
With the trust fund of grief I have
Never been able to manage myself.

Today the rear window flashes
Summons to its madman, me.
I'm better now. I know they'd say
It's best indoors. It's getting cold
And no one wants to see you there.

Born just postwar, I live there still,
Young Howard with his special pain,
Largactil crust across his mouth.
I watch the dead in photographs.
My drunken flier with his charm,

My drunken blonde with her estate,
Both shovelled off the road in bits
Along with the MG, kept me
In shorts between the knees of aunts
Equipped with love, with metal combs.

I'm sick of all my annuals,
But every Sunday as I count
Each piece of gravel on those graves
I live my life. I stand erect.
They tell me I am feeling proud.

A Master

For half my life I tried to learn from you.
You gave me cities, voices, other books
And space to make what might at last be mine.
I know now I won't match what you can do:
Who else could show how disappointment looks
When honestly persuaded into line?

The Realists

The rows. Remorse. The birthday guilt
It seemed we'd always waited for.
How quickly childhood makes itself
The subject of all pain. At least
Unhappiness was made to match.

We can talk of the fear on the landing,
Empty shops and lightless Sundays,
Bare legs and cold knuckles. The voices
Transmitted their coded distress
From room to room, half-audibly.

Conspirators in adult hurt,
We were given an atlas to look at.
The globe like a clockface described
Its true circle and all the routes
Guided us back to this room

Where we share an impoverished tongue –
What's wise, what's best, what shan't be thought
By persons whose business is penance
For lives that were never begun.
This evening is an afterlife:

Looking and carefully looking away
We rehearse the responsible half-truths
Like adults, with habits of fiction.
The words will be all we can make,
So that meaning deserts them, then self,

Until only the voices are left
For the listeners awake on the stairs,
Who have learned to believe this is how
These affairs are conducted, and think
Of a day they will speak for themselves.

Civilians

After eating with friends, after music and wine,
The citizens lay down. Some dreamed
Of subways to the oven's mouth.
All took their passports to the flames.

In the cellar's cellar
People wrote journals. The pardons
Awarded to God were so many.
Now we own the manuscripts.

Brave to have needed a coat,
To have paused in the hall at the mirror,
To brush away dandruff,
To check for a pen.

Be lyrical and serious, they say,
And try to think of history as home.

Summertime

For Richard Richardson, Kent NUM

The news is old. A picket line
Is charged and clubbed by mounted police.
Regrettable. Necessity.
You have to take a balanced view.
That kind of thing can't happen here
And when it does it isn't true.

Adore yourself and in the body's
Shrivelled province bask and breed.
Indulge your fudged affairs and lust
For what your terror says you need.
It's hot. Lie down and vegetate.
There are no politics, no state.

At noon on Brighton beach it's clear
Why heatwaves make the English glad.
Beneath that burnt imperative
In oiled, obedient ranks they lie,
To forge a beachhead close to home
And found the final colony.

You have to take a balanced view.
That kind of thing can't happen here,
And when it does it isn't true.

The Red Hospital

For Steve Johnston

The train stopped this evening. I looked
And the place still had flames in the windows.
I knew what they meant about cold.
The Victorians wanted a hospital
Bigger, more 'moving' than death,
As elaborate as empire, as law.
It unmarried the poor, since it could,
And they came out in boxes.
It stood at the street-end, a red-brick
Cathedral of cold, like a court or a jail,
And the terrace was cold, in its mock-Gothic shade.
I could feel it by thinking *red hospital*,
Watching the clock to learn by heart
The tables of its endless afternoons,
While grandmother slept and the fire
Decayed to red rubble. The phrase was stuck
Like dirty language in my mouth –
Red hospital, like *fuck* and *cunt*
Repeating themselves on the walls.
The cold came through the door by right.
The only good was punishment.
But the old men were angels, or almost –
My grandmother said – in blankets
On balconies, nearer reward or relief,
And because they were counting the hours
Were free of their sins. They could die.
It's thirty years on. The wards are shut,
The terraces ash and the workhouse
A word you explain. My grandmother's

Vanished with empire and sin, and there's only
This place between places, made over
To carparks and lights. But it's home.
I can tell, when I loyally shiver,
Go over my tables and swear.

The Allotment

The cold eases over my wrists. I'm at home
With the details, at dusk in October.
My Grandad's allotment's an ashtray
Crammed with herbal cigarettes. The red coals
Fade in the cucumber frames and there's sure
To be frost in the brazier by morning.
Around us the other old men on their plots
Have knocked off for a smoke before home.
They wear their breath in grey balloons
And have fireproof hands and no lungs.
I should mention the moon with milled edges,
The roar down the tunnel of air
That means somebody's scored. But I can't.
I'm the future, a gaberdined dwarf
In the cap of the privileged school
You could see past the willows and sidings.
The spire denoted Victorian money
And officers honoured on plaques,
The names that had employed the men
I stood among. They did not mention this
Or speak to me at all, but went on
Coughing expertly and waiting. I should say
What's not true, that I saw how the ice
Would step into the footprints they left
On the cinders while saying goodnight.
I should find an impersonal manner
To dignify Garbutt and Doonan and Briggs,
The wide-suited utility scarecrows,
War veterans all, who said nothing
Of what they had been, but persisted
In tending their plots and choking to death,

Which was none of my business
But comes back this evening as guilt,
Then as anger, to stiffen my hand
While I write, to remain when the poem
Refuses to end or forgive, when the cold
Has come home and the old men are waiting.

Trespass

The downlands, private under drizzle,
Hoard their woodcut oaks for those
Who own them, who are England.
Horse-commanding wheat-haired daughters
Natter down the gated lanes
Beneath a roof of hawthorns.
Mist admits them, phantom *politesse*.
You take the smugglers' road beneath the fields,
Dead ground without the government,
And as you travel, wonder
What conspiracy this is
That needs a mask of leaves and rain
To find its right of way, and how
You know this hidden route so well.

Song of the South

We change our cars and eat our meat.
There are no negroes on our street.
Our sons are sailing with the fleet.
We keep our mania discreet.

We take our secretaries on trips.
We have a taste for furs and whips.
We look to Panama for ships.
It hurts us when the market slips.

We place our cash in Krugerrands.
We rule the waves, so say the bands
At Brighton, where we own the sands.
You won't find blood upon our hands.

Conservative in politics,
We have no time for lefty pricks
Who sympathise with wogs and spicks.
We print the kind of shit that sticks.

We even bought a moralist.
We fund his comic, keep him pissed.
Just now we need him to exist,
The sweaty little onanist.

It is of property we dream.
We like to think we are a team.
We think that poverty's a scream.
We're still more vicious than we seem.

And speaking of the next world war,
The bang we've all been waiting for,
We will survive: We are the law
That shuts and locks the shelter door.

Unregistered

Six cranes where Baltic vessels come
As if home to the flatness of the land
Which is only not water by virtue
Of no one agreeing to drown.

Six cranes for which nowhere
Is far too precise, with low sheds
And the minimum bollards
And seemingly nobody there.

Six cranes where the ballet is off
And no one jumps ship.
That's the street, that's the pub
And the poster of Showaddywaddy.

Six cranes where Baltic vessels come
With coal to break the strike.
Does Mr Scargill think we think
The revolution starts like this?

Terra Nova

In late afternoon, when the snow began,
The sirens of craft on the river,
Bound outwards from elsewhere to elsewhere,
Reminded the city of sailings –
North Cape, the Baltic forests, Arkangelsk.
No lines of mileage link us now.

And the footprints all over the shoreline
Were only historians, out
For a blow in the shipping museum.
Trespassers who do not drown
Will suffer prosecution, said a sign
On the dockside. No pleasuring now,

No stink and no electric suits,
Just De La Pole coated in white,
Facing inland, his arms by his sides,
Like a man among men in the queue
For the card, for the insult called
History, that won't pay the rent.

The snow fell, like the waste of a subject.
It fell on grids of terraces,
Abandoned quays and stray containers,
On boarded-up windows, in doorways,
In tenfoots, on flame-blackened landings,
Steadily out of the burnt-orange night.

It fell on the tracks behind houses,
On sheds in the vandalised goodsyards,
On scrub and the river and even

The decks of the sea-going shipping,
Which left us the one consolation
Of knowing it snows on them too.

Then I wished the whole place would embark,
The schools and mills and hospitals and pubs
In a team of all talents, a city of lights
Singing *Sod you old England, we're leaving*
For work, heading out on a snow-boat
To sail off the compass for home.

London Road

As I walked out on London Road
Towards the close of day,
I grew confused, and it appeared
I must have lost my way,

For when I stopped and looked around
The hills of Housman's blue
Had ceased to be a colour
And become a point of view.

It matched the spanking outfits
Of the cops who blocked the road.
The only things they seemed to lack
Were bucketfuls of woad.

One said, 'Now son, what business
Takes you out beyond the pale?
Are you quite sure you're what you seem,
A blue Caucasian male?

'You wouldn't be a picket
Or a dike from CND?
We've orders from Her Majesty
To round them up, you see.'

'I'm going down the pub,' I said,
'Like every Friday night.
If it's OK with you, I'd like
To exercise that right.'

Apparently this angered him:
He took me by the balls.
His breath was acrid in my face,
Like bullet-holes in walls.

'We're here tonight rehearsing
For insurgencies ahead,
And if you breathe a bloody word
We'll beat you nine parts dead.

'We'll ask the questions afterwards
And charge you for the mess.
There'll also be a list of crimes —
You'll find that you confess.

'There'll be no point in asking
For the date of your release:
These days we throw away the key
When folks disturb the police.

'Take our advice: get off the street.
Stay in and watch TV.
Unless the law is absolute
The people can't be free.'

I turned and passed a barrier
In fear of an attack.
It isn't safe on London Road
And I'm not going back,

For in that land of lost content
Where facts are redefined
I've seen the enemy within,
The ones I left behind,

And as I walked I heard a song
Stage-whispered on the air,
Subversive in its sentiment,
The sound of no one there:

You poets of the little songs
Devoted to the Muse —
You shouldn't be surprised, my lads,
To find you sing the blues.

The Mechanical Toy Museum

In the mechanical toy museum
At the end of Brighton's Palace Pier
Ten new pence will buy five old,
For history suffers inflation as well

And Jean Boudin might not believe
How big the smudged brown coins appear,
Designed to fit a pauper's eyes
Or the Jolly Nigger's thrifty tongue.

But no one is short of a penny in here
And that crimson-lipped, liquorice
Cast-iron slave is not one of the relics
Preserved in this tomb of Amusements.

Take care. These are delicate engines.
The pin-table predates the tilt,
Two threadbare teams stand riveted
In goalless extra time and the girls

In the peepshow must never be still
Or their bones will step out of their skins.
It keeps you fingering your change,
This taste for proofs of entropy.

Best of all, watch the beheading.
'Madame Guillotine est morte,'
A visitor carefully tells his son,
Who is keen to observe the procedure again.

But when the Bastille springs open,
Why, every time, does it seem that the corpse
Will pluck the straws from his spouting neck,
Take up his peruked head and walk

With absolute confidence back
Down the mad-mirrored ormolu halls
Of the *ancien régime*, as if we had
Never existed, still less eaten cake?

How Ryan Got His Start in Life

The clank of supernatural machinery
Awoke me. So this was the life.
There were galleries, catwalks,
Stopcocks and sumps. There were beam-engines
Sinking and rising and sliding
In coats of gold oil, like a theory
Made fact and abandoned to beauty,
To prove itself over and over to no one.
A roof, I proposed, was obscured by the steam
Which was all these endeavours produced.
Some small high panes shed snowy light.
I left, down humming lanes of plant,
Stepping out on a street near the river
I still haven't seen, by a half-silted dock
That was swallowing snow without let.
A gull came gliding through the flakes
And then posed on a bollard. Was this
A bureaucrat? It worried me,
This life without a form to fill.
A clock on a black church said morning –
I looked for a drink and am doing it now,
At this bar where the eggs have been pickled
As long as the taciturn punters,
While afternoon drains out of lunchtime.
My liver is damaged already. I write this
In Stingo on blood-red Formica,
And wish you were here, whoever you are.

Ryan at Home

Contraceptives crisp with frost
And turds gift-wrapped in yellow pages,
The glamour-girls' *membra disiecta*
Shedding their gloss with their papery skins –
They lie, as if only a moment ago
The monsters' working lunch dispersed
At the terrible news: this is home.
It's Saint Crapula's Square
And the knee-trembling district,
Whose sensitives want to be Rimbaud
Or Hitler, where sound drains away
Through a grille to the sewers
And all the Victorians said
About wanking turns out to be true.
Sweet home: the slab of sluiced grey hearts
And the church with its sensible hours.
The maps are discreet and the texts
Where a marginal reference is scented
Are shelved in a library not even the Pope
Could unlock nor a Frenchman imagine.
A town without transport or drink,
Where the papers are vetted
Of all but the innocent a's and the's
Like stammering youths in a chemist's.
Though counsel dutifully phone
Locked offices where flies are wintering,
The torturers keep to their punishing schedules.
The screams of the random arrested
Are stretched beyond all recognition.
Their answers could only be wrong.
Eccles or Eichmann or Ryan himself,

Everyone has to be somewhere,
And this is the place I was thought of,
My mission to hand out the shits
By declaring it Sunday for ever.

Ryan's Vocation

(for Steve Knowles)

The yellow lamps hang underneath the smoke,
Expensive moths that should be somewhere else,
Discreetly overlooking the affairs
Of those with style and more than one address.
They worry us. We're torpid devotees
Of Scampi Crunch and torn and worried mats
Inscribed with inkless biros by the daft.
Those fittings nag our long bad faith
By promising elsewhere. Our articles
Are habit, disappointment, anomie,
A taste for muddy beers and pubs like this,
Whose tedium we've trained to share with all
Like-minded punters disinclined to speech.
There are no names, no other lives in here,
No talents or good ways of killing time.
What links us is the way we sit and brood
On all what little happens cannot mean,
Like revolution, money or free Bells.
The landlord polishes away the light
Along the bar, then gives it back and stands
Remembering the faces it contains,
As if they'd had the sense to up and go
And weren't observing him observing them,
The ornamental critics of his style,
His clothmanship, short measures and the ban
He hopes to universalise one day.
And we for our part labour to achieve
Paralysis, to save us going home,
Aspiring to the stillness of our gods —

The toucan doomed to reproduce our thirst
Forever with a dry glass at his beak,
The girl from Babycham who promises
That sex was good in nineteen fifty-eight.
Tonight, dear gods, may I donate my tongue
For polishing, to join you on the shelf,
To wear the speechless look of long disuse
And sit among your sacred cack, the plates
From Lowestoft, the green glass cat, the Queen,
That paraplegic octopus, those caps
Whose frigates' names outlive their crews. Let me
Give up the ghost of all action and stay.
Let traffic shudder me, time dust me down
To perfect disregard, a curio
No one would steal or even care to break.

Ryan's Rebirth

I step from the wardrobe unblinking.
My coat wears the contours of sleep
And my mouth has been pissed in by goats,
But otherwise I am unchanged,
Unaged, unloved, unspeakably myself.
The names and rooms are new,
Like the speed at which damage approaches
To offer its tongue to your mouth.
I am hired to suffer, you tell me,
To remake your language, erotic routine
For when love has a stammer; to offer
My dick in good faith to the night
And the outcry inside it; play
With pillowed hair and find
A handkerchief for pain — all this on behalf
Of the cackhanded god of my metre,
And I in return am unburdened by feeling.
I love it. I love it to death when the leaves
In the calendar fret for a crisis —
Those phone calls and notes, getting hard
During meetings, not catching the eye
Of the other whose clothes will be mixed
With your own in the morning; the effort
Of marriage, in which case the penis
Goes home like a coward for money,
In which case its agent gets up for the papers
With one girl asleep and the other on pills
And enquires too late if this shuddery complex
Of adult emotion and juvenile crime
Is not after all less seductive than boredom
And merely a means of election to pain —

But the whole transformation from lovers to clients
Is simply a process that needed to happen,
Which none of those lyric perfections
With her under trees and her hand down your pants
Can arrest at this date or at any to come.
I am your creature and I know the answers
You want but would rather not bear to be told.
Now I sit at your desk and transcribe the grey details
Exactly in agony's order and know
For the length of this business I'm back in the world –
And if in the midst of the labour I tell you
A job that's worth doing's worth doing for ever,
Then that is my nature, which does not exist,
Except when you want me: so make up your mind –
There is work to be done while you ponder on that.

Ryan and the Life to Come

There's ground you cannot farm or build on.
It's found after sidings and prefabs,
All tussocks and halfbricks, with sheds
Like the bases of doomed expeditions.

Left to myself I should gravitate there,
At home like the madman of Hessle,
With his orange-box encampment
As lavish with signs as an airbase –

No sneakers no creepers no polices
In ten-foot-high letters to advertise fear.
Woken at dawn by my bubbling chest,
With the fog close up and the river

A funeral *tong* from the lightship,
Perhaps I would come to consider the rest
As an indolent meantime, a waste
Of the chance to know nothing, claim all

And to speak my own trivial language –
Its jabbered ellipses and sly repetitions,
Unbreakable meaningless code.
And then I suppose I would die,

Gone out like a sheep by the hedgerow,
My fame the discomfiting feeling
Of aimless appraisal, politely endured
By any unfortunate visitor there.

The gods are not perfect. They hate us.
I might have to be one myself.
If so, make it earthy, a no-name,
And mindless and truthful as well.

Ryan's Farewell

Tonight the summer opened like a park
Seen distantly, a blue-green reservation,
Lamps flicked on among the woods,
On lake and lawn. RSVP.
The moon hung like a furnace-mouth
Where all the names of heaven burned
A lengthy correspondence with your kind –
Or I'd gone past believing that sense
Could be decently made of the place,
But I had a last look at the details.
Luminous cricketers quit the pitch
Like heroes blessed by radium.
In afterlight the rhododendrons
Shed themselves and lime trees twitched
Like mummers with too many lank green hands.
Beer seethed in jugs. Beside the road
The drowned man in his standing pool
Turned over and his shoulder whitely tore
The cloth-of-green that heat and rot had woven.
The clawfooted beeches furnished the woods
To a nursery's comforting scale,
Like the cretin-sized 'A' meaning Abergavenny
Engraved in the gamekeeper's lintel.
So much to announce the mere self
With its dim little claims on tradition,
To land given shape by possession, by charm,
By the snivel of chords from the organ,
Entwining the bellrope and fading
But never entirely meaning to go.
These people would tear out your eyes
And buy gifts for their mothers, then bore you

With both as they stood the next round.
I'd failed. I was free to abandon this life
Without once understanding the facts
That could never be trusted or altered,
Or grasping what 'sensible' meant.
On the hilltop I listened: the ocean
Unpicking, restitching its border. Not there.
And the keyhole of light on the forest was someone
Believing they'd made me already. Not there.
I would step through myself like a mirror,
To enter the index of air and have done.

Envoi

Or else on a road between roads in warm darkness
Corruption was waiting, a drench of cut roses
Left out in a guileless tin bucket –

A tremor of pastoral weakness
For things in themselves,
Meaning sex, meaning state, meaning here –

And that was me finished, believe it,
Caught out with my pants down in Sussex,
Bone-thirsty and craving for skin.

The chestnut's candlepower lights me home.
Another wife is waiting in her house
With strong tea and clean sheets and my new name

Tucked into her cleavage. The police
Are just putting the drunkards to bed,
Having mastered their nicknames. The ocean

Is crooning at Brighton and if you say money
It's something we'll have to regret
And make do with. Believe me. I'll promise

It's just until morning, I'll tell you
Tonight I could almost believe it myself,
But do not be misled by these tenses:

Suppose I agree to this pleasure: remember
I'm nowhere near finished with you,
So expect me, be sleepless and listen
For what I might mean when I stop.

After This Poem

After this poem, perhaps it is evening.
Perhaps I am pleasantly tired?
More likely I'm knackered. Perhaps
The near ocean resuming its sound
Like the endless unzipping of silk
Will incite me to bed, or perhaps
I will feel like a drink: but in fact
It is simply a walk I require –
A mile down streets the effort seems
To have rinsed of its language for once,
To replace it with breathable air.
Across cool mats of sodium
Spread by the streetlights, I drift
Past benches upholstered with shadow,
The drivers asleep in their whispering cabs
And the girls who are tired from dancing,
Who lean under trees holding shoes,
And I find I am glad when the facts
Can be empty of all but themselves:
Which is when I remember the others.
Indoors and unlucky this evening
They shout at the walls through the smoke
As the paper goes blank on their desks.
Some have given up, and staring out
Could see me as I pause below,
A character the yawning moon
Declines to animate tonight,
While others burn the dictionary and drink,
And the rest persevere through a dead-shift
Attended by coffee and heartburn,
Afraid after all they have nothing to say,

Afraid that tautology rules, OK.
They'd never believe it if I
Were to offer this alingual walk
As a proof that the thing will emerge,
The mad cousin of what they imagined,
Imperfect, but able to tell you its name
And blessed, it appears, with a personal cry.
They'd never believe it. Me neither.

Cousin Coat

You are my secret coat. You're never dry.
You wear the weight and stink of black canals.
Malodorous companion, we know why
It's taken me so long to see we're pals,
To learn why my acquaintance never sniff
Or send me notes to say I stink of stiff.

But you don't talk, historical bespoke.
You must be worn, be intimate as skin,
And though I never lived what you invoke,
At birth I was already buttoned in.
Your clammy itch became my atmosphere,
An air made half of anger, half of fear.

And what you are is what I tried to shed
In libraries with Donne and Henry James.
You're here to bear a message from the dead
Whose history's dishonoured with their names.
You mean the North, the poor, and troopers sent
To shoot down those who showed their discontent.

No comfort there for comfy meliorists
Grown weepy over Jarrow photographs.
No comfort when the poor the state enlists
Parade before their fathers' cenotaphs.
No comfort when the strikers all go back
To see which twenty thousand get the sack.

Be with me when they cauterize the facts.
Be with me to the bottom of the page,
Insisting on what history exacts.
Be memory, be conscience, will and rage,
And keep me cold and honest, cousin coat,
So if I lie, I'll know you're at my throat.

The Yard

White overflow, white wall.
The frosted window, framed in black.
A plantpot long abandoned by the classics.
All the other sleepers here
Who made this doorless yard their own,
A vacancy where fiction writes
Its memoranda to the world.
No ins, no outs, but here we are.
The Belgian sensualist Van Loup
Abandoned wit as well as sin
To embark on his journal of light.
He would climb from this window
To crouch with a campstool,
Awaiting ten minutes a day
When the yard was engaged by the sun,
And then watch as his shadow
Was formed and absorbed by the wall.
Veronique, who sang and danced,
Was aware of the yard in her mirror
But mainly concerned with how best
To fit wardrobes enough in the room
To conceal all her lovers at once
From each other, and pondering this
She failed to see the murderer,
Attired as an acrobat, step down
Inside the yard and don his gloves.
Group Captain Flack conceived the walls
As a chamber in nimbus. Awaiting Von Zundert
The Camel could circle, secure
In a gin-engined terror, forever.
And others are only disclosed

By the rustle of visiting cards,
But the distance that cancels their voices
Can never dispose of their absence.
They never ate, or washed, or loved
Or read, or were ruined, or kissed
Or killed, in private or by process of the state,
But all of them offer the relevant postcards
Of cities where none of this happened.
They show you cathedrals, casinos and brothels,
The fleet still at anchor, the news
And the hemlines arrested, industrial ghettoes
And graveyards according to station,
Cuisine and critique and the way to bribe policemen,
The jails and the libraries, barracks
And monasteries, map-rooms, asylums,
The price of their pleasure and how it was paid.
What you hear is these people insisting –
Not written in Latin or Teuton,
Not written in Volapük, algebra,
Enzyme or semaphore, braille, blood or code,
But in breath on the windows of trains,
In invisible ink on your lover's back,
All from the viewpoint of Proteus
Now, in a language that does not exist,
In the tongue the yard speaks
To the living, the dead, and all those
Who are neither but cry to be heard.

Fiction and the Reading Public

You read, and then you go to sleep:
That's work's permission to be dead.
And while you sleep you watch them pulp
Whole libraries you have not read.

They make you read what money writes,
A thing left in a carriage,
Spine unbroken, loud with secrets,
Fifty Ways to Wreck Your Marriage . . .

Dexter had to give up reading –
Lulu said it wasted time
When he could give himself to money.
Dexter planned the perfect crime.

Dexter stunned her with a bundle
Of old *Partisan Reviews*.
The arm discovered in Death Valley
Livened up the evening news.

If Lulu stands for capital
And Dexter stands for wit,
If Lulu's in the mortuary
And Dexter's deep in shit,

Then what's required is a book
Psychosis in a Trailer!
Someone put the money up
And sent for Norman Mailer.

Mailer worked on it for hours.
The plans he made were vast,
And though in fact no text appeared
He spent the money fast.

When Dex said, Norm, I'd love to read
My life before I vanish,
Mailer shrugged, I'm sorry, Dex,
I just can't seem to finish:

My novel need not terminate
Because its hero fries.
Remember, fiction's fictional,
And therefore never dies.

When Dexter hung his head and cried,
But Norman, wait a minute:
What kind of story stays alive
Without the hero in it?

Mailer punched the grille and said,
You've got me beaten, Jack.
Go shoot the Pope. Read Wittgenstein.
But just get off my back.

Of that of which I cannot speak
I am condemned to silence,
Plus *you're* condemned, let's not forget,
For readership with violence.

As Mailer left, he did not mourn
The book he had not made:
He only muttered to a guard
That art had been betrayed.

They came to Dexter on Death Row
And asked his final need,
And Dexter said, I don't suppose
There's anything to read?

They brought him *Fonda's Workout Book*
And *How to be a Sucker*.
Here Dex, these ought to shut you up,
Pretentious little fucker.

In Madre Maria

(for George Charlton)

The priest and the police chief are in the back room.
They consider elections, the drought and the war.
When their glasses are smashed they are deaf to the boom.
There are more in the cellar. It's happened before.

Since Marquez, men say, there is nothing unique.
There is no one to witness what no longer boggles.
The runway is short. The pigs do not speak.
But soon, as one pig, they will put on their goggles.

A Matinee

The shops, the banks, the bars are shut.
The square smells like a cinema,
All breath and chocolate and sweat.

The islands' washed-out distance
Means the Fifties' rotten movies
Where I learned how to be bored

With love and money on location,
Postcard Europes, plots I couldn't grasp.
The starlets in their wide white skirts

Were always speeding on the cliffs
Or flinging into rooms to weep
At letters or the lack of them,

While stationed in the cypresses
Their leading men would smoke and stare
At nightfall, as the orchestra

Cranked up its fatuous claims
That the issue was passion,
Which seemed even worse than the adverts.

The stylists of never and nowhere
With nothing to do but rehearse
To the vacant plush darkness

And me with my headache and choc-ice.
Tedious wealth, I sympathized.
So when today I'm dull enough

To be Rossano Brazzi, let me sing,
Desert you, loom in archways, ask
About the past or unctuously show you

How the fishermen eat fish, then pose
Beside the ocean, signifying grief.
White girls in white skirts

With invisible legs and no sex,
Sealed in your villas being old,
Since all that I can manage is

To run those afternoons again,
I've left my number at the desk:
What better offers are there now?

Kingdom of Kiev, Rios das Muertes

All afternoon, the streets are deaf with snow,
Its dripping dud piano muted,
The fire in the garden silently burning,
The visitors visiting others. Midwinter.
Words grow from each other to conquer the board
With childhood's careful mania.
The Kingdom of Kiev is colder than Hell
And Los Rios das Muertes are many –
Lies concerning geography,
The inexhaustible resource
From the era of General Knowledge,
Where Tupper and Wilson still circle the track
And an amateur Norwegian goalie
Whose name I'm afraid I've forgotten
Has kept a clean sheet for three years.
Consider the baking of salmon
In riverbank mud, and the means of ensuring
That wells dug in marshland run clear,
The feathers, the lead, how high the moon
And what precisely Grant had drunk
At Appomatox – useful stuff,
Assuming six times six will still
Fend off the nuns and chewing-gum
Enfolds the heart, and the air-bubble
Trapped in the co-pilot's molar explodes
At twenty thousand over Skaggerat . . .
If the Kingdom of Kiev is colder than Hell
Take furs to exchange and be careful
To sip the right side of the fiery bowl,
Not forgetting the boxes of Dickens.
If Los Rios das Muertes are many,

Choose one and remember your journal:
Observe how it breaks into leaf.
Slip a hand in the wet-velvet blackness
By night, in the squamous dun khaki by day.
Honour your dad on his moped,
Come home bearing gifts from the blizzard –
In Muscovy, *The Fawcett Expedition*,
Marrying tundra and tropic
As suitable places for anyone versed
In the pointless collection of facts.
The telephone won't ring, but if it does
I'll know until I pick it up
That the atlas has finally called.

The Head Man

For Margoulis Grolsz

You say you've been back for a look.
You're struck by the impressive podium,
The throne in which the Head Man sat
And ground his teeth with gout,
Dispensing justice and the lash
To the 'conference of funeral directors'
Who listened in pustular torpor
From the Main Hall's fog of breakfast farts
To the news that we could not speak English
Or read it, and ought to avoid it,
And worst of all ate in the street
Without caps on. Ah yes,
I remember it well, being frightened and wrong
On a permanent basis, secure
In the knowledge you'd never be short of a row,
And the lesson remains,
In this world of strong women
Who put me in mind of that pantomime demon
Revolving the dice in his head to decide
If today was for charm or for excoriation.
I stuck to my books, but my verses were proof
That the Russians had sent me
To fire the Hall, snog Edna the typist,
Abstract the school fund and be famous
And not know the value of money.
In fact all I stole was a copy
Of *Culture and Anarchy*. Touchstone, indeed:
It retains its original boredom,
Safe and stale in custard covers.

I read it last night when you'd rung,
Fell asleep and then dreamed of the journey
We'd talked our way out of for years –
By Araguaya, Negro and Las Muertes
To the utmost Amazonas, by canoe,
Our only plan: escape the map!
In the feverish heaven of jiggers,
Long after the final dry sock and the whisky,
Sick of mandioca, sick of fish,
Where the river runs into the sky and the trees
Form an endless and foetid arcade
With the promise of nothing beyond it – lost,
With the whole undertaking distinctly
Like something in Conrad gone wrong,
We arrived in the clearing, in which stood the hut
With its trellis of head-sporting poles.
When we ventured inside he was there,
Drinking port from a skull, reading Arnold
And saying, 'Late again. Explain yourselves.'

Geography

For Gerry

Tonight the blue that's flowing in
Beneath the window gloves my hands
With coolness, as indifferent as a nurse.
The ridge of forest wears grey smoke
Against grey pink, then deeper blue
Discloses what I cannot see,
The channel's distant bays, their sands
Drawn into shape by bows of surf,
Then further capes and promontories,
Sea-pines and isthmuses and island stepping
Out from island, all
Remoter than a name can reach.
Out there is home, a hammered strand
By some unvisitable sea,
Beyond all empire and all sense,
Enduring minus gender, case and tense,
A landfall, past imagining and free.

HMS Glasshouse

(1991)

Before

Make over the alleys and gardens to birdsong,
The hour of not-for-an-hour. Lie still.
Leave the socks you forgot on the clothesline.
Leave slugs to make free with the pansies.
The jets will give Gatwick a miss
And from here you could feel the springs
Wake by the doorstep and under the precinct
Where now there is nobody frozenly waiting.
This is free time, in the sense that a handbill
Goes cartwheeling over the crossroads
Past stoplights rehearsing in private
And has neither witness nor outcome.
This is before the first bus has been late
Or the knickers sought under the bed
Or the first cigarette undertaken,
Before the first flush and cross word.
Viaducts, tunnels and motorways: still.
The mines and the Japanese sunrise: still.
The high bridges lean out in the wind
On the curve of their pinkening lights,
And the coast is inert as a model.
The wavebands are empty, the mail unimagined
And bacon still wrapped in the freezer
Like evidence aimed to intrigue our successors.
The island is dreamless, its slack-jawed insomniacs
Stunned by the final long shot of the movie,
Its murderers innocent, elsewhere.
The policemen have slipped from their helmets
And money forgets how to count.
In the bowels of Wapping the telephones
Shamelessly rest in their cradles.

The bomb in the conference centre's
A harmless confection of elements
Strapped to a duct like an art installation.
The Première sleeps in her fashion,
Her Majesty, all the princesses, tucked up
With the Bishops, the glueys, the DHSS,
In the People's Republic of Zeds.
And you sleep at my shoulder, the cat at your feet,
And deserve to be spared the irruption
Of if, but and ought, which is why
I declare this an hour of general safety
When even the personal monster –
Example, the Kraken – is dead to the world
Like the deaf submarines with their crewmen
Spark out at their fathomless consoles.
No one has died. There need be no regret,
For we do not exist, and I promise
I shall not wake anyone yet.

Thrillers and Cheese

The night has built a district of its own.
Its residents are killers and the law
And a huddle that might become either.
They stoop at a hatch in the roadside
With lamps, in professional silence,
And choose, it appears, to ignore you.
It happens between the last train and the milk:
The viaduct's dripping with echoes,
The cab-rank deserted, the streetlamps and shadows
As set in their ways as a one-party state
When the rumour of elsewhere has failed.
It is no time of night to be walking,
You say to yourself after too many thrillers
And cheese before bed and bad sleep:
But here you are doing your oral,
Intoning the newsagent, takeaway,
Church of the Dozen True Faithful, then counting
The chairs in the busdrivers' clubroom
Attending a stage from which every last echo
Of Waylon has died, like the humour
You formerly brought to a chance of unease.
You'll say you are out for the smell of the sea
And the paper, for innocent details –
The top copy rutted with string,
The blather of two men up early,
A band of late stars in the fanlight.
But those are no part of this caféless hour,
This death of shebeens, this ticktock
Where urns drip on stairwells,
In which there's no sleep and no moral
And fear has come up like a breath from the drains

With the thought of confession and failure
To know what the crime might have been.
As you stand by the urinous callbox
That waits for emergencies only to stick
A black tongue in your ear, imagine
A rat's nest of sheds at the back of the station,
A man at a desk doing puzzles by striplight,
His life, how it is when he sleeps,
What his notion of honour might be.
He turns from his pastime to make a fresh entry
In infantile biro, and rises and yawns
And goes out for a piss and looks up
At the same constellations, the lights on the line.
He knows what he knows, which is secret,
Constructed, installed and maintained
Without meaning or leave to appeal.
This man you compose in his office,
The shade of subliterate, dutiful evil,
Is one of a mass without number: no telling
Who does or is done to, no circuit to break
And no guilt to award, nor any place
Except inside, where you must know
That thrillers and cheese notwithstanding
You're mad and the whole thing is real.

In the Other Bar

Forever a winter too old,
With her manners not quite of the moment,
She's wearing it well, the bad sister of London.

For all that the young are pronouncing
On art and safe sex, they will never belong
Where the numberless theatres are dark,

Where the numberless writers have stalled
At the peak of a small reputation
Caressed in damp stacks of *Horizon*,

Which mingles with *Lilliput*, not to deny
The Fitzrovian marriage of letters and smut.
Here the long honeymoon

Waged from Black Rock to the borders of Hove
Will go on so long as a thimble of gin
Can be traced between now and five-thirty,

Ensuring the casual entrance of someone
Surprised to be here at this ticklish hour.
Beneath the slow wink of the optic there follows

The search for the chequebook, the novel
To rest on the bar while she smokes
And instructs us that boredom requires

A talent before which the proper responses
Are envy, humility, unbidden refills
And goes-without-saying acceptance

That she makes her entrance once only.
Her friends are the footnotes of footnotes,
Her lovers gone down in the Med

Or the annals of Gordon's, and she
Who has posed and factotumed for ever
Could always have been what she chose,

But did not, d'you see, as it happens.
It's almost like love, to be met by a vanity
Nothing corrupts, which is always at home

And has nothing in mind but itself,
The whole lifetime of elegant, objectless
Fucking and fighting, despair as a style

In the district of post-dated cheques
And not-quite prostitution,
Blank beyond judgement and not to be missed.

And when you come back from a pee
She has left you a stool and an ashtray.
Then later when walking through streets

Which can still catch the sun
There is someone who might be an actress
Whose name you can almost remember,

Glimpsed high on a balcony, resting
And staring straight through you
And keeping her looks in this light.

Hatred of Libraries

So here we are now in the library, wasters.
Scholarship passes its notes to the dead
And the immanent hush of authority damns
Our presumption and jokes and mere presence.

For what in the end are a beer and a sandwich,
A lavatory, someone to meet, if not failures
To grasp what this absolute vault
In the latinate centuries means by itself?

True students are early and warming their hands
At descriptions of hell, and in love
With perpetual winter are glad to be humbled
A lifetime by facts and unbreathable silence:

But we lack the rigour and cannot be still
When the world is refined to a rumour
In draughts, in the sighing of doors which have ceased
To be exits but lead only inwards, to fastnesses

Few may expect to survive and to which we shall
Certainly not be admitted. Through chamber on chamber
The second-rate bones are reduced to a dust
In the lost oubliettes of unwisdom, beyond which

Is waiting that whispered (apocryphal?) work
Which is found in no index and has to be read
With both hands on the table in view of a bishop.
It gives us a laugh. But imagine, O friends

Who have run out of funding and loaf in your sweat
In the guttering days of your final extension,
What might be revealed in that innermost text
To the frivolous hope that within its

Unthinkable pages the Word might yet offer
A light to the desperate. For knowing our sins
And our luck we may fairly suppose
We should find there in black-letter fire: NO SMOKING.

A Donegal Golfer

In my book even golf is sinister,
Played solo at night-time by salesmen
With grudges and one club too many.
Their wall-eyed bull-terriers yawn
In the cars, with the radio on, and I watch.

By the harbour, incendiaries drink
With their in-laws, ambitious morticians
Whose nieces they married and murdered.
These men, do they listen, perhaps, for the tide,
For a torch coming on? I know I do.

At dawn, when the ration of floaters is washed
In the wake of those boats without nets
To which golfers will signal while probing
For oil in the sands of the short seventeenth,
I'm going out. I may be quite some time.

Entertainment

In studied southern dialects
By lavatorial viaducts
Threats are passed from hand to hand.
In concrete pillars corpses stand
At permanent attention.

The music slowly claws its way
Through scrublands of conspiracy
Until it finds the keys that mean
The meat hook in the ice machine
Beloved of convention.

Verbals or the freezer, lads,
Or residence in riverbeds,
Or something somewhere in between,
The like of which you've never seen,
A startling invention.

The tide comes in. The trains are late.
The night rubs out another date.
The city puts itself to bed
Beside the bagged-up lately dead
Too numerous to mention.

Propaganda

After the whole abandoned stretch,
The bricked-up arches, flooded birchwoods,
The miniature oxbows and dubious schools,
After the B-roads that curved out of sight
Beneath bridges to similar views,
All the scenery hauled away backwards
While this train was heading elsewhere,
After the threat to our faith in the railways,
It seems that at last we have come to the place
That described us before we were thought of.
We stand on its sweltering, porterless platform
And wait in the time-honoured manner.
The stalled afternoon's like a story
Once left on a train with a chapter to go,
Smelling of oil, of dust and old sunlight.
Here are the canopy, flowertubs, posters for war
And the bum-frying torpor of benches.
Here are the smoke in the throat of the tunnel,
The footbridge a guess in the glare, and the clank
As the points irreversibly switch, and here
Is the perfect assurance that somewhere
Close by it is quietly happening.

It's here that Germany in person calls
By parachute, at first confused to death
By Brough and Slough, by classroom spinsters
Jumping on the hand grenades. Their dull reports
Alert the author sleeping at his desk,
The curate and the mower in the fields.
A bucket fills and overflows, abandoned,
To blacken the stones of a whitewashed yard.
In the brown upper rooms there are women

Attending to letters. We are not permitted
To stand at their shoulders and may not
Determine the date, but the subject
Is things going on as they must, the summer
Still adding fresh months to itself, and the way
You'd never guess by simply looking round.

How easy to know where we stand, within sight
Of the back-to-front fingerpost, certain
That commandeered railings still rust
In the sidings, that somewhere up there
In the ferns is what looks like a gate
But is really a lock on the gelid
Forgotten canal, that its waters retain
All their monochrome heat and exist
For the drenching of constables.
Oh Mr Porter, the convicts are coming,
Ineptly, their suits full of arrows,
Over the dismal, bunkered levels,
Still sawing their irons and shouting.

It's midnight. On schedule, the ghost train
Is failing the bend by the claypits,
And stiff with old service revolvers,
Unsleeping on hard wooden chairs –
The price of this unnecessary trip –
We stare at the waiting-room fireplace and know
That the corpse in its bundle of coats
Will awake and the door be flung open
When Hammerpond enters, no longer a tramp,
To deliver the long explanation
Whose end we will miss when the radio coughs
And announces that all roads are flooded,
The sovereign's in Canada, Hitler in Brighton,
And no one will leave here tonight.

Boundary Beach

Invalids, perverts, and chambermaids born to be duped,
And those characters never awarded a name
Who must pass just before and just after the moment
And never be wiser: they have been here.

And the bad men themselves, stepping onto the grass
With a hum of the sexual magnet, were here.
The bad women whom cash and contempt had enraged
Were seen waiting, the sisters of Ruth, to be hanged

All along the blue border of Sussex and England
Where everything stops, even money, on Boundary Beach.
They arrived in their fugitive tenses, like art.
One would ladder a stocking, another count change

In the torment of not-quite-enough, and the third be on hand
With a wallet to match the occasion, a car
And the promise of waking up changed. They were English
And liked a good murder, the thrill of comeuppance

Achieved in the shelter behind the hotel. The detectives
Were born to the trade. Their exhaustion and fury
Would fill the slow shoes of the law, put its questions
From Volks to the fringes of Shoreham and go

Through the head-scratching, half-sipping migraine,
The grey, overheated minuteness that led
To the tawdry perception – a ticket, a stain – and then on
To a room by the A23 and the motive. Imagine them

Coming downstairs with the knowledge,
The windowless corridors left with their keyholes
And Do Not Disturbs, their adulteries, there at the death
While a constable sat in the kitchen, his collar undone,

As he wiped his moustache free of mustard
And offered his view to a maid and the boots
Who would read the same evening a fuller report
And glance out at the darkness before turning in,

In a hundred hotels that claim views of the sea,
Where the sleepless are counting the waves,
All along the blue border of Sussex and England,
Where everything stops, even money, on Boundary Beach.

The Brighton Goodbye

This is the place we imagine we live,
Where the land slowly stops,
Among streets where the sea is implied
In white walls and expectant top windows
Left open for signals offshore.
The air is as bright as the harbour at noon
In the heat that can turn even cops into punters
And which we inhabit like natives of summer,
As if we had known it must come.
Now everyone seems to be leaving:
The bar-room will empty tonight
And be shuttered tomorrow,
A capsule of posters and still-sticky tables,
Its music absorbed into smoke.
The girl in the shop buying fruit
Has her mind on a schedule,
Her brown skin important with travel.
The old have prepared for a lifetime,
And now as they sit on their doorsteps
And wait to be told or collected
They cancel the hours with freesheets
Whose Gilbert and Sullivans, dogtracks
And fifteen quid bargains are clues
To a culture they've never known
Time or the passion to learn.
It is suddenly late. The afternoon yawns
And continues. A lean-to of shade
In a sunken backyard is the colour
Of Indian ink at the moment
The ferry swings out of the bay,
When the sea has no need to be local
And shows you the colour it keeps for itself,
Which you look at with terror and love.

At the Wellgate

Their speechless cries left hanging in the cold
As human fog, as auditory stench,
The boreal flâneurs donate their stains
And thick cirrhotic sherries to the bench
Outside the precinct where they're not allowed,
And finding they've no stories to tell
And thus no purchase on the Christmas crowd,
Descend by means of manholes into Hell.

Which in their case is arctic and unmapped,
Its every inch the coiling thick of it,
As if the Piranesi of the tubes
Had framed a labyrinth of frozen shit,
In which they wander howling and rehearse
The notion that elsewhere could still be worse.

Mission Impossible

for Bob Hughes

The Corps of The Royal Flying Headers
Dundee Battalion (motto: Get Tae Fuck)
Has once more secured its objectives.

Forbidden in every conceivable boozer
Again, the survivors identify
What must be wreckage and what might be them,

And following one-handed Phal/Vindaloo
Plus the ritual piss in a doorway agree
To go thirds on the taxi. There follow

Some savage exchanges in cab-queues
With coatless and possibly pantless
Young ladies who though they themselves

Have been lately expelled from improbable dives
Are nonetheless frank in their disinclination
To come for a quick one in Fintry.

It's snowing. The drivers are taking
No prisoners, not even the damp-trousered wounded.
And this, the men tell you, retreating

In fairly good order up Hilltown, is This,
Which the averagely slaughtered would not understand,
A civil war that thankless volunteers

Must wage by night from street to street
For pride and the arcane insignia
Of groin and headbutt, glass and bar.

Dundee Heatwave

The rotundas of the mercantile retired
Glint with speculation. Telescopes are aimed
Along horizons sudden heat has blurred,
Where Fife habitually stands.
Low steamers slide beneath the bridge
For the remote interiors. Northern tropics
Sweat in the mind's eye and offer
Their opals and foot-rot and concubines
Round the next bend, or the next,
Or wherever young Hawkins and Hannay
Awake in their hammocks, alert
To the sshh of a dog-end in water.
That was the promise, think brittle old men,
Recapping the lenses and gingerly going
Downstairs to the papers and still afternoons
In the cool of their money, to study
The movements of shadows that reach
For their final disposal, the perfect just-so
That accounts for the rest, like a moral.
That was the promise, of stepping from shore
At the foot of the page, the beginning.

Fishing

On the edge of the light from the tea-bar
Where lorries bound westwards pull in,
With the hood of his anorak up
In the darkening drizzle,
He waits for the river to fill.
His friends are on fire with Samurai scotch,
Their window-cleaning ventures failed
Like stolen paint and threats and promises.
But he was always patient as the dead.
You could restock the Army and Navy
With wellingtons found in the reedbeds
And sell back Ninewells its syringes.
The water, he sees, is a warehouse.
And then there's the human dimension,
The surplus the tide has to try and unload,
Who must still, in this unmythological age,
Come ashore and pay money to do it.

Notes on the Use of the Library
(Basement Annexe)

For John Bagnall

1

The Principal's other edition of Q,
Scott by the truckload, and Fredegond Shove,
Manuals instructing the dead how to do
What they no longer can with the Torments of Love,
Mistaken assumptions concerning The Race,
Twelve-volume memoirs of footling campaigns,
Discredited physics, the Criminal Face,
Confessions of clerics who blew out their brains,
Laws and Geographies (utterly changed),
Travellers' journals that led up the creek,
The verbose, the inept and the clearly deranged,
The languages no one has bothered to speak,
And journals of subjects that do not exist:
What better excuse to go out and get pissed?

2

Here is the body of knowledge at rest
In its cavernous basement of headachy light.
Here lie the unread who were boring at best,
And guarding the door is their acolyte,
Grim Miss McNair with her own magazine,
Which is not the extinct *Vulcanologique*
But her sister's new copy of *Harpers & Queen*,
From which she looks up to forbid you to speak.

She means it. Their case is officially shut.
Their posthumous function is solely to warn,
Via silence and odour and pages not cut,
That they, like their authors, should not have been born,
And hers to ensure, with her book-burner's glare,
That no one will add to what's already there.

In Residence: A Worst Case View

This is the flat with its absence of curtains.
This is the bed which does not fit.
Here is your view of the silvery Tay:
Now what are you going to do with it?

Here are the tenements out at the back,
Die Dundee *alte Sächlichkeit*.
Here are the bins where the carryouts go
And here is the dead of the Calvinist night.

Here is the bandstand, here the wee bus.
Here is the railbridge. That is a train.
And here is the wind like God's right hook,
And his uppercut, and the pissing-down rain.

Next is the campus, brimstone-grim,
In which is the Dept., in which sits the Prof.,
Eyeing you narrowly, taking you in,
Not liking the sound of that smoker's cough.

And that was the tremor of inner dissent –
The colleague convinced he was robbed of the Chair
And his friend who agrees and the spy who does not:
Now button your lip and get out of there.

This is your office. That is your desk.
Here are your view and your paperclips –
Manage the first week, feeling your way,
Making a necklace and watching the ships.

Here is the notice you put on the board,
And these are the students beating a path
From their latest adventures in learning to spell
To a common obsession with Sylvia Plath.

Soon there are Tuesdays, long afternoons,
Letting them tell you what's good about Pound.
You smile and you nod and you offer them tea
And not one knows his arse from a hole in the ground

And then there's the bloke who comes out for a drink,
Staring at legs while expounding Lacan.
It's a matter of time: will he get to the point
Before they arrive with the rubberized van?

Or else there are locals with serious pleasures –
Ten pints and ten whiskies and then an attack
Of the post-Flodden syndrome for which you're to blame.
You buy them another and leave by the back.

And this is the evening with nothing to do.
This is the evening when home's off the hook.
This is the evening for which you applied,
The leisure in which you should finish your book.

This is the point that permits no escape
From sitting in silence and getting it done,
Or sitting and screaming and fucking off out.
And this is the letter, and here is the gun.

To whom it concerns, I'm sorry I failed.
It seems I was utterly wrong to suppose
That by having the time I would finish the job,
Although I have put in the hours, God knows:

Hours of carryouts, hours of rain,
Hours of indolence mired in gloom –
I've tried and I've tried. I've even tried prose,
But the money's no good and I don't like the room.

Betweentimes

There is an hour waiting in between.
In ruined districts, blue light waits.
Wrecking yards and bar-rooms wait.
You can study the dust in the windows
Of incomprehensible premises, guess
At the null carborundum, clamped to its bench,
At all the further streets these streets conceal —

Their distant interiors, pillars of air
Under skylights where somebody stood
For a smoke, at the pin-ups entombed
In the necropolis of lockers, at calendars,
Invoices, indents of chair-legs in floorboards,
At tab-ends in cold stores, and voices you know
Are not talking tonight after work.

No clockface admits it, the in-between hour.
Over the road an old barmaid of thirty
Rehearses a spin on high white heels
And supplies, unrequested, a pint
To the old man re-reading the paper.
You'd think they had built this around him,
Brick and varnish, optics, disappointment.

This is how waiting turns into a life,
In the hour it seems would explain
If the mind could forget what it thinks
About failure and history and money, and watch
How aesthetics takes leave of its senses,
In love with the facts of the matter,
The blue light and derelict happiness.

HMS Glasshouse

At this hour the park offers only
A steam-heated acre of glass,
A sign in fresh hardboard, and somewhere
To wait while appearing to act.

We step inside its vaulted heat,
Its bleared below-decks light. We taste
Its air of rot and counter-rot, attend
Its vegetable politics, and watch

As plants with webbed and shellacked hands
Swarm up the stanchions, offering
The universal shrug of making do,
Like the teenagers painting the catwalks,

Who might once have painted the hulls
Of the frigates and merchantmen sent
To secure the Malvinas for mutton.
Their status as national assets has lapsed

And the registers cancel their names:
They are guilty again, as am I, as are you,
As the glasshouse sweats on
Like the *Unterseeboot* of the State

With its periscope down, its orders sealed,
Its routine a deliberate torpor.
We wake in the very same place
With the curious notion that fish

Have been crowding the glass to peer in
At the items preserved for the voyage –
Cast-iron and Pilkington's finest,
Odd volumes of Oakeshott and Scruton

To kill off the time, in an atmosphere
Soon to be poison. Let's make our inspection
On tiptoe, and listen for cracks
In case one of us throws the first stone.

Cold

They have opened the holds of the trawlers,
The dozen not sold off or scrapped,
And cold has been released into the city.
These are the businesslike highlights of cold.
We're talking Kelvin: this is cold
From the North of the North, in a Russian abundance

Renewed at each corner, as now
When the bus station comes into view,
With its arc lights resharpened by ice
At the point of departure,
Green girders, a warehouse of gallows,
And night like a jeweller's pad.

Such difficult venues are magnets
For those who have nowhere to travel.
They come as if promised a ride way back
And having been abandoned once
Can only circle and return, their pleas unheard,
Grown used to the contempt of the authentic.

The place is a test. Who stays too long?
The man lying prone with his history of bags
Who's just failed in a desperate attempt
To reclaim an old selfhood by vaulting the railings
Provides an example. Forget him.
A cabbie could show you a hundred

In all the right places – the end of the pier,
In the doorways of missions attempting their names,
On bombsites or dancing their solos

Across the new precincts, the comics
Not even their mothers would book,
Too gone to know they'll freeze tonight

On Blanket Row and Beggar Lane, marooned
On the spit where the stream from the city
Goes under the river, unquenchably roaring
Its terrible promise, the one they can almost remember
From childhood, an atlas of oceans
That sounds like a mouthful of stones.

On the Piss

They want it right now, do the serious drinkers.
The thirty-year men with no surnames
Go straight to the throat of the matter
For urgent interior drenching and burning
To keep the toxicity up to the mark,
Scum rimming the bath of the body.
They used to be somewhere quite different,
At sea or in jail or pretending to settle
On spartan estates and be married.
They've no sense of humour about it,
No photographs either. One day at a time,
They imply, looking round from the bar
As if something tremendous they've always been offered
Turns out to be merely the carpet unzipping
To vomit its cellar of demons.
No matter. There's more where that came from
A holdall of shirts and the racing on loud,
The face slapped with alcohol, mouthwash
Reminding the tongue what it wants.
Mirror-balls, mirror-tiles. Where it is brittle
And carpets are crusty, in submarine discos
Now boasting a brand new selection of towels to tread on
And doorbolts designed to rip sleeves and break nails,
The walls good for slumping, no paper,
They find themselves seated in violent laughter
With likeminded women – girls until looked at,
Whose heels keep on breaking, who cannot stop
Screeching or crying or finding themselves being hit
For misplaced and forgotten adventures
With other such mateys because it was Christmas
Or someone had won the St Leger. Their lordships

Keep grazing their cheeks with their watches
While wiping the sweat from their pleasure.
Their voices belong with the shit-stained ceramics
And doors riven off. They deliver uncatchable
Howls from the corridor, make styluses jump
Like a warning to someone not there
Who might suddenly turn into you.
They are seen in the parched red interiors
Long after closing, their hands up the skirts
Of unconscious companions, unconscious themselves
With their mouths still at work, wanting more.
They are ready for anywhere tiled and awash
To abrade and contuse in, for rooms where the furniture
Goes to be smashed or to burst into flame,
And their kids have been lied to and stolen
In some other city they will not go into,
For reasons that never were your bastard business.

From the Whalebone

These evenings I step from the Whalebone
At time-on-your-beer for a piss out the back,
And then stand in the mixture of moonlight and sodium,
Waiting and taking it in.
The powdery blue of high summer
Refires the bricks red and black.
There are gaps in the traffic
Where water runs through. And I'm old.
The fifty-year mild-drinking errand
Has carried me this way most nights,
Over ironclad bridges, past tanneries,
Headstones, the grey river glimpsed
As it roars to itself at the bend
To be done with its name in a mile,
And down at the swingbridge the railway sets off
To its vanishing-point, where the houses
And streetlamps run out and the last bus
Turns back. You get all that from here.
It was only the meantime, this amateur city
That never believed where it was.
Behind it the secretive flatlands
Are closed for the night, for the century,
Minding a dialect, a closeness to water
That water is bearing away.
I shall sit on a fly-haunted coach
While it shrugs off the hedgerows and lingers
At shelters where nobody gets on or off,
And then walk the last bit to be sure how it stands,
Grey-green, coming in, the horizon in place
And the atlas beyond it unopened.

Working on the Railway

You are trying to work but you sit
With the wrong book entirely: *Lost Railways of England*,
Whose dust of the forties, the fifties,
Is making you sneeze. When you just have a look
At the picture of steam as it swallows the bridge
At Botanic, you're going. Then Stepney, Stoneferry
And Wilmington. Flatlands. The vanished resorts
Where the girls run down into the water
Like spies with a half-hour free,
Then back to the baker's, the nightschool,
The sombre saloon of the Station Hotel.
Past the window the *Montague Finnegan*
Pulls away north, and the soldiers are crowding
The corridors, wishing that girls were laid on
To be waving farewell, like the future,
A bed you need never get out of.
From there you could grasp it, the railway,
The sea creaming in at the piers,
And just round the corner the carriages stand
In the first of the heat, with their headachy air
Full of dustmotes, their pictures of elsewhere:
An hour of silence that seems to be England,
The life it was offered once only,
Its trivial, infinite distances –
Promises, promises. Write it all down.

Serious

Let us be serious now, says the teacher,
Inserting a pause in the hot afternoon
As she steeples her fingers and waits.

It's hard not to look at the snow
That prolongs the blue end of the day,
Not to think of it gathered

In alleys and gardens across the flat town
For a footprint, but this is Miss Garvin
And those are her fingers,

And though her long nails are a vanity
None of the sisters approves,
She speaks as they speak, for a power

That means us to answer the serious question
We have not been asked, that we cannot imagine
Or fail to be wrong in attempting:

Therefore we are serious now, as we wonder
Who might be the shameful example
To prove the unspecified point.

It may lie in the fork of a crocus
Or bury a jamjar left out on the step,
Or fall in its passion for detail

On two unburnt coals in the grate,
But the snow cannot help or survive
In the heat of the serious moment,

The void of all content
Where something, as ever, is wrong.
Across the yard the boilers roar.

Good children, we long to be serious well,
To multiply the word on slates,
To raise our voices in its name

And wear its ash with modesty.
We slip our hands behind the pipes
And turn them into gloves of pain.

Naughty Ron

When Naughty Ron said middle age
Began at forty-five,
We grinned, convinced he must be mad
To choose to stay alive,

Considering that at thirty-nine
And threatened with the nick,
He still found little boys inclined
To make him raise his stick.

Poor bastard. If he's still around,
I think I see his room:
Its 'discs', its photos of the Fourth,
Part opera house, part tomb,

With sixty growing plausible
And after that, who knows?
But not much chance of supple lads
To smile and touch their toes.

Conscription took him to the Med
And showed him what was what,
An exiled bookish elegance,
But not how it was got,

So time became a preface
To his coming into style:
He thought — and it's his epitaph —
Of teaching for a while,

And that was where we left him,
Five minutes from the sack,
Dictating notes on *Mansfield Park*
While we sat near the back

Examining our pity
Like a warning from the bank:
Imagine life with nothing left
But Verdi and a wank.

Ballad of the Lit and Phil

When I went in that afternoon
With work that must be done
I should have left the books at home
And fetched a scatter-gun.

For all that things seemed quiet
In the varnished vestibule
The maze of galleries beyond
Was given to misrule,

And the enemies of silence
Were waiting in the stacks
And at a given signal
Commenced with their attacks:

To start with, just the graveyard cough,
The snigger and the snerk,
Then someone bawling, *Mustn't chat –
I've come in here to work*,

But somehow taking ages
To get the one thing said,
And hovering, and fingering
The *Listener* instead.

Thus the hours screamed away,
Distracted into dust,
But there were deadlines to be met –
I worked because I must.

I bowed my head and thumbed my ears
And damned if I'd give up.
One broke a chair. Another dropped
His top set in my cup,

And then the tea-lady came singing
And a-banging of her tray,
So clearly they could keep this up
The livelong bloody day.

Some others murdered violins
Somewhere beneath my feet
And blokes came in with spades and dug
The place up like a street.

But still I smiled and held my peace
And laboured down the page,
Until at last a silence fell
Like acid-drops of rage

Through which there came to sit with me
A leading local bore.
He told me how much parquet
Went to lay the library floor,

And how the old librarians
Would mix the morning's ink
And how much sugar Marat took
In what he liked to drink . . .

This last (alas) was interesting
And took me off my guard,
And glimpsing opportunity
He smiled and came in hard.

Please understand, this is a place
For people who pretend.
If someone tries to work in here
It drives us round the bend.

You think this is a library?
It's the temple of a sect
Whose article of faith
Is simple: Only disconnect.

We view ourselves as guardians
Of ignorance and sloth,
And no one stays a member here
Unless he swears to both.

Everywhere and always, friend,
Since language first was stored,
The mass of membership has been
A vast illiterate fraud.

Bodley, Austin, Pierpont Morgan,
Big UL and old BM –
Oh do you seriously think
That anybody reads in them?

And I dreamed a dream of libraries
Exactly as he said,
Repositories of indolence
Where nothing's ever read,

From Adelaide to Antioch,
From Zanzibar to Nome,
A vast deliberate vacancy,
An overarching dome.

The vision was the weariness
Ecclesiastes meant,
And suddenly I understood
The reason I'd been sent,

And why my hopes of wisdom
Were mere errors in the text.
O reader, can you understand
The thing that I did next?

Tenderly I took his head
And bashed it on the floor.
The next I knew, librarians
Were showing me the door.

They threw me out into the street
Where I am lying now.
They made me give my ticket back.
They said I made a row.

And now I'm banned from every
Bloody branch in town,
But I shall visit them by night
And burn the bastards down.

Oh weep for Alexandria,
That library-lacuna,
But left to me it would have turned
To ash a good deal sooner.

An Ordinary Evening in New Holderness

Suppose that the summer is ending tonight,
As by treaty, that August surrenders the town
On the ultimate stroke of its name.

The heat will run down like a battery,
Spending itself through the windows and flagstones
As far as the sea, where its pulse can be felt

In the sand that keeps drinking the surf
As though to continue would draw the far cities
To rim the horizon with light.

In imperial times there were lamps at this pond,
But this evening a matchflare suffices
To bring the air closer and show us

The remnants of weddings and carryouts
Called to the thick of it,
Propped in the mouths of the shelters

Or sitting out under the limes
At whose edges rooms open on rooms
And then air, and the space above trees

Is domestic, as if out of sight
Must be somebody sitting and smoking,
Not bothered, not needing to talk.

A Corridor

The shoulder-high tiles in municipal green,
The brown walls, the bare lavatorial floor
Which is always about to be damp,
The heavy swing doors we shall not
Be exploring today; the long view
We are taking this late afternoon –
Whose end is obscure
With November indoors, it would seem –
In the Fifties, when we were much smaller
And quickly impressed by the minor displays
Of the State which would aim us
From cradle to grave, you remember:
All this we inherit, a corridor
Built by the Irish for God and the Queen.

We trap our germs in handkerchiefs.
We do not spit when on the bus.
Out where the city once turned into fields
Are prefabs growing permanent:
To each its patch of grass, from each a vote.
And here where the corridor turns in a fury of echoes
My father is leaving the party for nowhere,
The intimate cell where the struggle is waged
Over doughnuts in Lyons, the afternoons hung
With sheets of Players, the talk of betrayal.
It's what lies before us when we are too old
To be sure – which was never his problem.
The problems he had were the world
And his terrible spelling, I'm told.
They have rolled up the speeches, the grass from the park
After Mayday and stored them in here.

Behind the baize door a committee
Is handing the scholarships out –
A regime of deaf butchers and bandit accountants
Rewarded for lifetimes of ignorance,
Waiting to get our names wrong.
In the clinic a sinister lady
Will study my feet and insist
I can reach the trapeze.
My grandfather wheels a dead man
To the morgue for a pittance
And votes the wrong way as a duty
To something the next war was meant to disprove.
We vanish to Mafeking, Simla,
The moth-eaten middle of Ireland
Where Marx is a nightmare
That God isn't having
And people like us are a gleam of prolepsis
In somebody's eye – the well-meaning
Impotent heirs to the corridor,
Pacing it out past the dinner money's chink,
Cries from the dentist and telephones nobody answers,
Incompetent dreaming, corrupt and forgetful,
The cellars of pamphlets for futures
That nobody lived. This is ours. Keep walking.

To the Unknown God of Hull and Holderness

In memory of Frank Redpath

'For that the God abounds in examples'

God of blind corners and defunct commercial premises,
God of altered streetnames and of lost amenities,
God of the shut bath-house and the dry swimming pool, the
        leased-out playing field, the partial view to what lies past
        the railway land,
Go with us.

God of the back way,
God of Felix Marsden's route,
God of the Bear and Top House and Full Measure,
God of the windy bus shelter and the flapping hoarding,
God of the hole in the fence, of the cindery feet of embankments,
God of the flattened penny,
Go with us.

God of rumoured ships and proven stenches,
God of the Woolsheds and the sidings,
God of square scorches in grassland,
God of the marquee's imprint and of yellow grass,
God of the infilled drainsite,
God of the windy corridors of board-schools and clinics,
God of sheds wherever they may lean,
God of the in-between district neither Stoneferry nor Stepney,
God of the district not served by the buses,
Go with us.

God of gutted signal-boxes,
God of aimless Sunday walks,
God of the unrestored graveyards,
God of fallen angels under leafmould,
God of flooded tenfoots,
God of the back bar's spongy, sodden seats,
God of the not-yet afforested quarry,
God of the corrugated echo of the whiteworks,
God of the turntable and adjacent sewage farm,
God of the tracks that divide so that one will be always unknown,
God of the green MAIL and of Queen of the South and Stenhousmuir
God of the teatimes of 1958,
Go with us.

God of dead aerodromes,
God of seamed asphalt,
God of unbearable Sundays that taught us to wait,
God of pits in the clay where the water climbed up,
God of the slow deaths of mattresses split on the waste patch,
God of preposterous stained-glass heraldic imaginings left in the
            house of the barmy Lord Mayor,
God who has room for the nuns in the day and by night for the carved
            wooden heads of Silenus that stared from the fire place,
Go with us.

God of the Third Division North,
God of Chilton, Wagstaff, Houghton, Butler,
Though not (alas) of Henderson,
God of the drains and bombsites,
God of the fathers on forty a day,
God of comics and encyclopedias,
God of Sunk Island, stalled ferries,
God of the sea and its fine disregard of established geography,
God of school dinners and Blackjacks,
God of the snowball and half-brick,
Go with us.

God of the upper back window, the privet, the dark afternoon,
God of the dock-leaf and groundsel,
God of white dog turds not found since the Fifties,
God of the orchard, the sickle, the fountain,
God of all summers, all boredom,
God of the book and the start of the trouble,
God of white paper, of iambs and dactyls,
God who gives all but the transitive verb,
Now and in the hour of bafflement
Before your works and what they mean,
Be hidden and persist.

After Laforgue

In memory of Martin Bell

I have put a blockade on high-mindedness.
All night, through dawn and dead mid-morning,
Rain is playing rimshots on a bucket in the yard.
The weatherman tells me that winter comes on
As if he'd invented it. Fuck him.

Fuck sunshine and airports and pleasure.
Wind is deadheading the lilacs inland.
You know what this means. I could sing.
The weekend sailors deal the cards and swear.
The Channel is closed. This is good.

In the sopping, padlocked, broad-leaved shade of money
Desperate lunches are cooking
In time for the afternoon furies and sudden,
Divorces of debt from the means of production.
Good also. These counties are closed.

Myself, I imagine the north in its drizzle,
Its vanished smoke, exploded chimneys: home
In bad weather to hills of long hospitals, home
To the regional problems of number, home
To sectarian strife in the precincts of Sheffield and Hartlepool,

Home from a world of late-liberal distraction
To rain and tenfoots clogged with leaves,
To the life's work of boredom and waiting,
The bus station's just-closing teabar,
The icy, unpromising platforms of regional termini,

Home to dead docks and the vandalized showhouse.
Home for Mischief Night and Hallowe'en, their little tales,
When the benches (the sodden repose of old bastards in dog-smelling
          overcoats)
Vanish, when council employees dragged from the pub
Will be dragging the lake in the park,

Watching their footprints fill up
And hating those whose bastard lives
Are bastard lived indoors. Home,
As Sunday extends towards winter, a shivery kiss
In a doorway, *Songs of Praise*, last orders. Home.

Rain, with an angel's patience, remind me.
This is not the world of Miss Selfridge and Sock Shop,
Disposable income and Lycra, illiterate hearsay
And just-scraping-in-after-Clearing to Business in Farnham.
This world is not Eastbourne. It has no opinions.

In this world it rains and the winter
Is always arriving – rebirth of TB
And *The Sporting Green* sunk to the drainbed.
Here is the stuff that gets left in the gaps
Between houses – ambitious settees in black frogskin

And minibars missing their castors, the catalogues
Turning to mush, the unnameable objects
That used to be something with knobs on,
And now they live here, by the siding, the fishhouse,
The building whose function is no longer known.

It is Londesborough Street with the roof gone —
That smell as the wallpaper goes, as it rains
On the landing, on pot dogs and photos
And ancient assumptions of upright servility.
Nothing is dry. The pillow-tick shivers

And water comes up through the scullery tiles
And as steam from the grate. There are funerals
Backed up the street for a mile
As the gravediggers wrestle with pumps and the vicar
Attempts to hang on to his accent.

Rain, with an angel's patience, teach me
The lesson of where I came in once again,
With icy vestibules and rubber pillows,
The dick-nurse, the wet-smelling ash in the yard
And the bleary top deck like a chest-ward.

Teach me the weather will always be worsening,
With the arctic fleet behind it —
The subject of talk in the shop, at the corner,
Or thought of when stepping out into the yard
To the sirens of factories and pilot-boats,

There like a promise, the minute at nightfall
When the rain turns to snow and is winter.

Ghost Train
(1995)

Somebody Else

In fact you are secretly somebody else.
You live here on the city's edge
Among back lanes and stable-blocks
From which you glimpse the allegations
Of the gardening bourgeoisie that all is well.
And who's to argue? Lilac's beaten to the punch
By cherry blossom and the spire disappears
Among the leaves. Merely to think of
The ground-cover detail this outline implies,
The seeds and saplings and their names,
The little wayside trestles where they're bought,
The just-so cafés, the innumerable
And unnumbered high-hedged roads
For coming home down sleepily,
For instance – that would blind you
With a migraine, were one possible
In this redemptive climate. Sit.

It is somewhere you thought you had seen
From a train. You were not coming here.
It is something you thought was a striking vignette
By an as-yet-uncredited hand. It is somewhere
In moments of weakness at Worcester Shrub Hill
Or in Redditch or Selby you wished
You could enter. You already had. This is it,
The good place, unencumbered by meaning.
For hours no one comes or goes:
The birds, the light, the knowledge
That this place is endlessly repeated –
Is the known world and the elsewheres too –
Will do the living for you. Were you moved

To halve a gravestone you might find
That *England, 2 p.m.* was written through it.

Long before now you've imagined
A woman at work in an attic,
Applying the back of her elegant wrist
To a strand of loose hair. She was sorting
A life, in a shaft of pale dust
Where a slate had come loose, but now
She is quite frankly reading. Kneeling
By a doll's house full of Guardsmen
She's stunned by what she thought she thought.
In the kitchen three storeys below
Are an unopened newspaper next to the hob
And a cat coming in, going out,
Like a trouper, addressing its bowl
In the permanent meantime through which
You come walking so fluently
People would think you belong.
As to the man in her life,
If you lived at a different hour
You'd see him performing his vanishing act
On the bridge by the station.
The train doesn't come, only noises.
A stiff breeze unsettles the fireweed,
Leading the eye to the drop where the stream,
Which is almost as real as the Boat Race,
Goes quietly down to the bend where it vanishes too.
As to sex, you have gained the impression
That somehow it's meant to encourage the others
Who might overrate or not do it at all,
Either way missing the point, although no one
As far as you know has yet clarified that.
The tree-shadows washing the ceiling,

The damp patch in bed, and her manner,
Both brisk and erotic, of pausing
To put up her hair before dressing,
All these suggest you are here.
What, then, of scholarship?
In the 'history room' whose fake stained glass
Is viewed with that tolerant humour
(What isn't?) are somebody's books
In a version of English you half understand.
You search the catalogue
Of the Festival of Britain
Repeatedly for evidence of you
And think it must have been mislaid.
When will you learn? What could it mean,
Conspiracy, when everyone conspires
Against themselves and does not know it?

Revenants

It's four o'clock, an autumn Sunday,
After a hailstorm and just before dark.
The dead are reassembling,
There beneath the dripping trees
Beside the pond, and more arrive
Continually by all the gates.
In the young middle-age of their times,
Demob suits and made-over dresses,
Men with their hands in their pockets
And women inspecting their patience
In compacts, they're waiting
As if there were something to add.

Friends, we are the unimagined
Facts of love and disappointment,
Walking among you with faces
You know you should recognize,
Haunting your deaths with the England
We speak for, which finds you
No home for the moment or ever.
You will know what we mean, as you meant
How you lived, your defeated majority
Handing us on to ourselves.
We are the masters now. The park's
A rainy country, ruining
The shoes you saved to wear to death,
In which we buried you.

Interior

The fields and 'the wooded escarpments'
Inherit the shades of old furniture –
The dun and could-be-blood and lacks-conviction green
Of sofas jammed up rear passageways
In under-advertised hotels whose afterlife is spent
Not being read about in waiting-rooms.
The date is Nineteen Fifty-X. The residents
Have died but not been told. They jostle bonily
To hog the yellow *Telegraph* through days
In steep decline from gin-and-it
To after-dinner coma. Why detain them further?
As if there were choices, as if on the nod
You could crate them all up in the mind of God.
Deep in the retarded shires whose very
Names have been abolished, they persist,
Clandestinely, immortally defunct.
Now if we took that other turning
We should find them, arrayed in rank order
Across the parterre, stripped now
Of rivers and jungles, all rheumily glaring
As though the prow of our canoe displayed
A threatening announcement
They could very nearly read.
Though we go by a different route
We can smell the old country – a pillow
On a yellow face, the endless nagging corridors
Where damp and dust and gas contend.
It lingers in the senile tearooms
And in the crusty carpets of emporia
Where what's for sale is sentimental horror,
The used-to-be, the bad idea.

We hear the silence in the churches wait
For regiments disbanded on the Somme
To swim back through the mud and give
Due thanks, the ploughmen and the gentry
With their proper limbs restored.
Two Ridings later we come to the sea.
On this neglected coast it rolls
Indifferently ashore, a grey-white swell
Unburdening itself, then sliding back
Across the rotted boulder-clay
And muttering *history, history,* as if
That should explain these haunted roads,
Ancestral nowheres, *proper drains and class distinction.*

Special Train

The service ran only on Sundays,
For free, from the sticks to the sticks
Along lines that were never discovered by Beeching.
From Coalville to Warsop, to Crowle and Dutch River,
The world was still driven by steam —
An apology, forty years late,
For a government exiled to history.
They smiled through the smoke from the pages
Austerity printed, believing it still.
No trouble was spared. Already delayed,
We would ride in authentic discomfort.
The carriages smelled of when everyone smoked.
In the corridors nurses and servicemen flirted,
Incurring the mass disapproval of character-actors
Distracted from *Penguin New Writing*.
The chill at the ankles, the seats unraised!
Soon we were somewhere in England,
Names all gone and shires camouflage,
A home from home in the indifferent
Grey-green that black-and-white made real,
Beneath a clear and silent sky which meant
That somewhere else would get it after dark.
We might think about this for a minute
While raising the eggs to our mouths.
I had my agenda. We all did.
I hoped I would finish up handcuffed
To Madeleine Carroll. Instead,
When I went the wrong way to the buffet
That never existed and found a compartment
So clearly forbidden I had to go in,
You were waiting and this was my fault.

We had to get on to the part where bad temper
Discloses a lifelong attachment
And do so without a hotel. We sat there
Not talking. Perhaps we could own it,
The glamorous boredom of evening.
The drunken stave of wires at the window
Played backwards as we watched a river
Swim its *s* away between the poplars
To the east, where glasshouse country
Flared against the dark. Now name that tune,
Sleep-music with its accents leaning north.
We might have lived like that,
Remote and unhistorical
Day-labourers for idle happiness.
You disagreed. Already, you told me,
Far off, at the unrationed end of the Fifties
A radio played a request to itself
In a room on the street we were born in –
Played at this hour on a similar Sunday –
And we were not listening. You studied your hair
In the darkening glass and I saw there
The matter-of-fact combination
Of scorn and indulgence I'd recognize later
As love. When you vanished you left me
A smoke-ring the shape of your kiss,
And the seats were all taken by sinister troupers
Denying in accentless English
Your very existence. No Madeleine either.
I thought it was love. It was politics,
Even on Sunday. Then when I woke up
We were braking to enter a county
Known neither to us nor the Ordnance Survey,
A theme park of oddments
Where tracks were converging

Past pillboxes, scrubland and hawthorns,
Lamp-posts and slab-concrete roads,
To the ghost of a council estate
Where the fireweed brushed at the sills.
This part, we infer, was unwritten.
We've sat here at twenty-past six
On the wrong side of England forever,
Like mad Mass Observers observing ourselves,
And if we should wonder what for, we must hope
That as usual it does not concern us.

The Politics Of

When I walk by your house, I spit.
That's not true. I *intend* to.
When you're at breakfast with the *Daily Mail*
Remember me. I'm here about this time,
Disabled by restraint and staring.
But I do not send the bag of excrement,
Decapitate your dog at night,
Or press you to a glass of Paraquat,
Or hang you by your bollocks from a tree,
Still less conceal the small home-made device
Which blows your head off, do I, prat?
I think you'll have to grant me that,
Because I haven't. But I might.
If I were you, I'd be afraid of me.

April 1992

Autumn Begins at St James's Park, Newcastle

Homage to James Wright

Under the arc, the Toon Army tsunami,
Under three o'clock's great cry on Gallowgate,
Remember the lost world, politics: cages flying
Up from the pit and disgorging their democrats,
Helmeted, in blackface, by the thousand,
Like the sappers of the Somme.

A seated army of convicts
Will be thundering WOR BALL
At faintheart southern referees all winter.

At freezing dusk the bloodbucket bars are stowed out.
Mortgaged to football, the underclass raises
A glass to the ghost of itself
In a world without women or work.

A Rarity

It's under the X where the viaducts met.
It was round the back and further down
And it isn't that street but a vanished
Identical elsewhere that waits
In a different night with a different accent
Beneath a blue sign reading T I X E.
Kelly's *Apocrypha* offers no entry
But don't let that stop you from wasting
The middling years in pursuit of a number
Whose title escapes you, a band you can't
Even remember or swear to have heard.
Polish your shoes, climb into bed
And breathe in the sweetness of nylon and Bass.
The girls are done up to the nines,
Like raccoons with affective disorders,
Rehearsing three steps round their handbags
And speaking in smoke-rings, a code
Meaning *Fuck off and die* or *Be older*,
Knowing it's to you the management reserves
The right to do pre-emptive violence.
You almost believe in the night you went
In on a whim and came out on a stretcher
With vox back-to-front on your forehead.
Rippling in its skin of sweat
The bar retires to infinity, bulb
After bulb swinging back to the stillness
Your dreaming's disrupted, the night
Before music and after, the night of un-music –
No horn-chart, no thin, underamplified Fender,
No workaday-beautiful backline, no voice
Being torn from the soles of the feet:

No such matrix, no such number.
Everything is afterwards, a dripping jacket
Hung across a mirror, drinks becoming syrup,
A van spitting teeth on its way to the knacker's.
The culture of almost is married, divorced
And has always been forty. Yet now you step in –
The wrong hole, the wrong wall, but at least
It's not there in the hours of business –
To run down a shuddering spiral that ends
In a foyer intriguingly minus a door.
Knee-deep in water and flyers, it smells
Like your big sister's hairspray, supposing
She'd used it or even existed.
Under the dandruff of whitewash and rust,
Behind traffic and ship-engines,
Wind in the stairwell, the pulse in your temple,
What you can hear will be nothing, the space
Made of wishing, the cousin of happiness,
Waiting to comfort the longing to know
There is something you still haven't got.
Why not pick up a leaflet? It mentions
The unnumbered white-label item
Unearthed by a rumour (one copy)
In Belgium. The price is an arm and a leg,
Your entire collection, your job and your marriage
And still you won't find it. It's perfect.

The All-Night Afternoon

Perhaps you are still awake now
In the midsummer half-dark beside me,
Hearing the sealed-in roar of trains
To whose drivers this night may be normal –
The moon on blue fields, the still sheep
Awaiting instructions, the sea over there
And the beams on the headlands revolving,
The ships on their fiery courses.

We ought to be starting a journey
Where nature and art have conspired
A result, but not even those passages
Closer to home have an interest in us –
Not the shush of laburnums and roses,
Not the silence that hangs between trains
After midnight, when summer comes up
For its long afternoon in the different language
We'd know, were we different too,
Having nothing but time on our hands.
The moon beats down. It is teaching us
Not to be here, and we cannot obey.

Rain

At ten p.m. it starts. We can hear from the bar
As if somebody humourless fills in the dots,
All the dots on the window, the gaps in between.
It is raining. It rained and has always been raining.
If there were conditionals they too would rain.
The future tense is partly underwater. We must leave.
There's a road where the bus stop is too far away
In the dark between streetlights. The shelter's stove in
And a swill of old tickets awaits us.
Transitional, that's what we're saying,
But we're metaphysical animals:
We know a watery grave when we see it
And how the bald facts of brute nature
Are always entailed by mere human opinion,
So this is a metaphor. Someone's to blame
If your coat is dissolving, if rain is all round us
And feels like the threats-cum-advice of your family
Who know I am up and have come and will go to no good.
They cannot be tempted to alter their views
In the light of that sizzling bulb. There it goes.
Here we are: a black street without taxis or buses.
An ankle-high wave is advancing
To ruin your shoes and my temper. My darling,
I know you believe for the moment the rain is my doing.
Tonight we will lie in the dark with damp hair.
I too am looking for someone to blame. O send me
A metro inspector, a stony-faced barmaid.
The library is flooding and we have not read it,
The cellar is flooding and we shall be thirsty,
Trevor McDonald has drowned as the studio shorts
And the weather-girl goes floating past

Like Esther Williams with her clothes on,
Mouthing the obvious: raining.
There's no need to labour the obvious, dearest, you say,
As you wring out your nylons and shoot me.

Poem Written on a Hoarding

. . . Novembers, Decembers, you smoke-haunted Fifties: lead me
The wrong way to school, by the drain and the tenfoot,
The rain-rotted gate to the graveyard, the laurelled Victorian
Dark of the ruinous gardens, the fogged-over bombsites
Still pungent with bangers. Here's Josie-without-a-last-name,
The nuns and the dick-nurse. Diphtheria. Football.
And here are the snow and that white, other city
I can't recall leaving, or ever re-enter.

Essay on Snow

We have been here before, but not often,
With the blue snow lying on the shaded roofs
And the city beyond them
Lying open, miles of it, with no one there –

Untrodden parks and freezing underpasses,
The statuary anonymous, the cobbled chares
Like streams of blackened ice.
There is a bird somewhere. Its voice

Is like chipping an icicle,
Damping the note, then trying again.
We have lived in the wrong place for ever,
But now we can see what we meant,

The blue snow-shade behind the house,
The abandoned allotment, the shed,
The rags of willowherb, the one-note
Samba of the bird inside the ice.

House

From the bomb-damaged slates
To the submarine stink of the drains,
From the den in the tall, pithy elders
Up to the crook of the mulberry tree
With its view of the spare-bedroom mirror
From which we looked back at ourselves,
The house, my house, your house,
The general house of that time
And that class, in a district still dazed
And half-empty, arrested, it seemed,
At summer's end, got us by heart.
We wandered for years in its corridors,
Counting the footsteps from corner to corner,
Gazing up into the deadlight,
Inspecting the pictures of Bude and Amalfi
Where no one we knew ever went.
Parked on the stairs for an hour
Like victims of shock, we recited
Our tables, or *the Nidd the Ure the Aire*
The Wharfe the Calder and the Don.
We examined our Flags of the World.
We waited, and then as by magic
We turned up again and again at a door
Left ajar, at a room where one curtain
Was drawn on a chaos of papers
And upended drawers. On the desk
Was a bottle of ink which had set
Round the nib of a pen in mid-sentence,
A letter unwritten before we were born.
It was only the place and the date
In rusty italic. This got us nowhere,

But from it we learned that the question
Was not one of meaning but habit, a way
Of being there those off-white afternoons
When someone was always about to arrive
To claim the greatcoat flung across the chair
And fold the page and gently shoo us out
Before forgetting us entirely,
Going downstairs to start shouting
In Latinate paragraphs, hours on end,
About women and history, a problem
Whose cause, whose effect, we are pondering still.

Of Origins

The middle-distant roar of trains
Maps in the miles of railway land,
The scrub-and-hawthorn nowhere-much
That murderers and children loved.

Garden of industrial remembrance
Plus an unexploded bomb, its obelisks
Were sheds and switching gear.
Its vast embankments aimed themselves

At absent bridges, cuttings ran
To seed among the dockleaves, and there too
Was always afternoon, a cold
And comforting evasion of the rules

With smut and cigarillos and your name,
Anne Broadwell, lavishly inscribed
In chalk on several hundred pipes
But rained away before you saw.

I sat inside the culvert's mouth
Past teatime, smoking, waiting for the snow
And reading *Penthouse*. I insist:
Et in Arcadia Ego.

Latinists

Trewartha, Gerald, Felix, Windy,
I see you ascending the stairs
From the Main Hall to heaven,
A place which I now understand
Is the school's upper floor, only bigger;
Ascending through clouds
In the era of pre-dustless chalk
To that rarefied zone
Where even *if* is absolute
As the organist stumbles
Once more through the last verse
Of *Lord Receive Us With Thy Blessing*,
You go with the rags of your gowns still about you,
Stacks of North and Hillard in your arms,
Making for your far-off rooms
To wipe the board and start again
With the verb for *I carry*,
The noun meaning *table*.
I go to every room at once
And I still cannot listen,
Remember or scan, and the table's
Still strapped to my back.
When you ask me again what the subject might be
In this sentence, I still cannot answer –
O'Brien, it's not the full stop –
And still make the foolish suggestion
That sirs, in a sense, there is none,
Phenomenologically speaking, that is.
When the stare you award me
Takes longer than Rome did
To flower and vanish, I notice
The bells are not working in heaven today.

AWOL

The fat-fingered leaves of the chestnuts
Have lost their particular ochre.
Lying in swathes on the grass
They're reaching the unnoticeable stage
At the near edge of winter
When detail and distance are smudged.
Mourners and gravediggers stand for a moment
In yew-framed remoteness, appalled
And in love with the very idea of themselves.
Smoke travels sideways across the estates
As if this must still be the Fifties
And I have absconded. Omniscient nuns
And mad parkies are waiting in huts
And expecting me hourly. But even at this point
I see we are not the whole story –
A fact which will be the true burden
Of what Sister Mary will tell me
With whispering fury whenever we meet.
Already I grasp how her keys and her rosary rattle,
How her black shoes click over the parquet
Between the main hall where I'm not
And the corridor's end where the milk-crates are stacked
By the hot-pipes and stinking already,
Where too I am not – not at school,
Not there with the wintering bulbs on the shelf
Or the poster of autumn
In which all the animals crowd to the roots
Of a single encompassing tree, and the vole
And the stoat and the badger are folded
As if in their separate drawers. Not there.
She will speak of my mother and father,
To whom I am lent, of my soul, of elaborate penance,

But part of the time she will look
At the street where the afternoon darkens,
The smoke going past at the rooftops,
The sky which has cleared to an arctic blue glamour
Behind which the stars have been steadily blazing.
Lorries and funerals pass at the junction.
The canon makes calls in the parlours
Of all his insoluble Irish, his boots
Going over the leaves with a sound like salt
As the temperature drops
And the sirens of factories bray,
Plain facts of the matter
Which do not respond, being absent themselves.

No One

No one, you must wait in all these rooms,
These overnight exhaustions of good humour,
In the stopped clock and the tone for *unobtainable*,
In cities we can never really see,
Where it is dark already and the windows opposite
Are this one multiplied as near
As makes no odds ad infinitum.

No one, you make salesmen of us all.
The hanging suits are hugged by loneliness.
The luggage has no other place to go.
The mirrors can never remember exactly
Who's who when we sit down before them
To write this in humorous terms
And invent the expenses and stare.

The rooms at our backs are the faintest idea
And you are the chill at the centre
That means we are where we belong,
Locked in, as if anything threatens
This privacy gripped like the photos
Of people we claim to have loved,
Whose faces, when we study them, are yours.

Valentine

The other life, the properly narrated one
You glimpse through flying carriages
Is there, on the opposite platform.
A girl with a shoulderbag, reading the paper.
Frame by frame you see her,
Not her face exactly or her clothes,
But how she's self-possessed, as though
She's never heard of the alternative,
Placing, you suppose, her toe against her heel
And balancing, as though alone.
Be silent, you think, to the oaf on the public address,
The school party, the earnest Americans.
Silence, you think, to the clock flipping over its cards
Like an unemployed gambler.
Either side the railway runs away
Through cuttings, other cities, bits of scrub, past standing pools
And brickworks, birchwoods, nightfall
When the strangers' faces watch themselves,
To oceans, deserts, icecaps,
All the life you will not stake a claim to now.
But while she's there it lives,
At Doncaster and Newcastle and York,
And all through-stations of romance,
There beside the footbridge,
Auburn, dark or sooty blonde,
In velvet, in a biker jacket or in decorator's overalls,
Unbothered, never late, on all the platforms
For a lifetime, practising her liberty
Without a name, a face, a destination.

Railway Songs

Trains go past. Their effigies do likewise,
Upstairs on the layout, all afternoon.
The world is private. This is the meaning of weather –
The icicle losing its grip at the roof's edge,
The white afternoons at the far end of summer –
Weather, and trains, with the world indoors,
Advancing its strangeness over the lino.

Squint through your specs, through the fog,
Through the downpour, the clear-eyed dawn of October,
At actual engines departing the city,
Intent on the serious north. No flock-grass
Or papier mâché, tunnel, viaduct
Or working prewar German water-mill
Can take you there, yet you believe
In the place where the points are iced over
And wolves have got into the signal-box,
Leaving their pawprints across the slick parquet
And windows steamed over with signalmen's terror.

Delight, as you crouch by the paraffin heater
And idly unravel your cable-stitch pullover.
Oh to be Scotland By Rail, a grey rock
In the shape of a tender, displayed
By a smoke-coloured sea; to have become
The merest fire-blanket in the corridor
When everything falls silent, when the smoke
Has borne itself away above the snowy cutting
With a tunnel at both ends, between
The lapse of conversation and the panic.

*

Rain is vanishing the hills.
All down the line the stations go missing —
Bridges, Markets, Highest Points and Heritage
Undone by rain, the coal-fired weather
Of almost-irreparable newsreel. Whole counties
Turn to smoking stacks of viaducts
From under which, by documentary miracle,
Engines by the dozen steam
In parallel straight at us.

*

Here inside this grey-green afternoon
Is where I've always lived. It stretches
From the War until they burn me like a sleeper.

I've stayed on at home. Our railings were stolen
For weapons, they told us, which left low walls
To run like blacked-out carriages

Around the parks and cemeteries.
I'm waiting today in the shelter
While a half-mad gardener explains

How corpses drive his floral clock,
Whose movement is based upon Kilmarnock station.
At the church after service are middle-aged ladies

Who dance through the trees to a small guitar.
But the children are looking at something quite different,
The tracks, perhaps, beyond the hedge,

And the phone in the vestry keeps ringing the once
For the vicar is also this small station's master
And Bradshaw is still in his heaven.

When the County Grounds are hailed on and empty
And the miserable old parties who snapped
In Leeds and Sheffield, Middlesbrough and Hull,
'We'll have that wireless off' are dead and stuffed,
The special lines remain between the cricket and their graves.

Likewise 'The masters who taught us are dead',
But we have hung on with our oddments of habit,
Pausing perhaps when the sun strikes the red and green glass
In the porch, or inclined to believe
That the groundsman was made an exception to death

And sits there grinning silently
At *Workers' Playtime* on the wireless in his hut,
With a goods train sliding past just out of earshot.

The Mallard comes steaming out of its frame
And the four-minute mile waits like Everest –
Cinder tracks everywhere, sodden and virtuous,

Coal-coloured sandshoes and wet, gritty legs,
While shunters go by, bringing rain to Hull Fair,
To the trains made of china, the trains full of goldfish,

The half-naked girl-in-a-tank-with-a-train,
The dripping back flap of the Ghost Train,
The driver's mate waving at no one.

A Provincial Station

The brutalized youth has returned
With the compasses, sketchbook, unhealthy ideas,
From his motherless home or the military school,
To stand on the clinker beside the low shed
At one end or the other of summer.
Grey, thundery weather, the sighing of reeds.

Three days ago he left
This very place, it seems –
Birchwood, marshes, village out of sight.
The train's lugubrious siren pulls away.
Here's Kostya!
Or whatever the hell he's called,
In his all-weather coat made of sacking,
Sitting in a coma in the trap,
With the old horse, Misha,
Dead for years, tormented by mosquitoes.

The Middle

That's him finished, halfway down the hall,
His good line gone, his afterlife unsure.
Then this one's written on the mirror
With her lipstick, *Fuck you Jim*. She sits
Imprisoned in the gesture, and her breath
Will neither clear nor wholly cloud the glass
In which we glimpse ourselves behind her, there
To sympathize or think of something else.
Useless at this point to rifle the drawers
Or go over and peer through the blinds:
The hat suspended from its chute of smoke
Is there, or not. It makes no difference.
This is the case for everything in sight –
The barbershop, the take-away, the steps
That climb to the cathedral where they met;
Or down the other way towards the bridge
Where the receding globes of milky light
Have met the dark's advancing rain halfway
And are reflected far below, in what
We shall imagine is the rising tide.
We must accept the sickle moon as well,
Quite openly reclining on its page
Of rotten weather, granting with its gaze
The general irony designed for nights
That will not be remembered when at last
The horsemen choose to come, delivering
Their fire and sword, supposing that's the case.

A Secret

There isn't much in this town to compare
With breaking into vestibules at night –
The scuffed brown panels, parquet floors,
The counter-bell you fix to make
A farting noise resembling a bluefly
Drowning in a thimble, right?
I choose the office, check the desk. The drawers
Are stuffed with ancient phone directories.
There's Lana Turner's photo on the wall,
In '49 about to shoot or sing.
She looks as if she knows what I'm about
But never tells. I sit there by the hour,
Smoking, saying, randomly, the names
Of Ma Bell's Fifties' clients, wondering
What they did to get themselves in print –
I speak of you, Marzial Unzurrunzaga,
Sadie VanDerBo and Henry Polk.
I watch the hatstand's shadow on the glass
In the continued absence of the hat
Which in another story, worn by someone else
Would glide like paranoia down the hall,
Its mind on intervention, meaning facts:
I watch the sweep-hand wiping out the night
As radar would the after-hours sea,
And this ends where it started – gloves on,
Honour satisfied, my kind of justice done
And no one wiser, least of all myself.
At dawn I take the service lift back down
To walk the not-unreasonable streets. Perhaps
You wonder where the money is, the sex,
The crazed abuse of power at the top,
The screaming statues plunging to the bed.
Not me. I live the Big Beguine
And pray no explanation makes it stop.

Le Voyage

after Baudelaire

The child in love with maps and lithographs
Finds everywhere a match for appetite;
But though it's infinite beneath the lamp,
As memory the world sails out of sight.

One morning we embark. The mind ablaze,
The heart blown up with rancour and disease,
We set out with the rhythm of the tide,
Infinitude adrift on finite seas.

Some do it to escape the hated State;
Some flee the horrors of indoors, and some –
Stargazers blinded by a woman's stare –
Outrun the lure of Circean perfume,

And rather than be beasts consign themselves
To space and light and skies of molten brass,
Where biting cold and heat that roasts them black
Will slowly mask the imprint of her kiss.

But the authentic travellers are those
Who, light as balloons, take off and never give
Consideration to the claims of fate
And, never asking why, demand to live.

Such men's desires map themselves in clouds.
They dream, the way a squaddie dreams a gun,
Of unknown pleasures, protean and vast,
Out where the writ of language cannot run.

Paysage

(a long way) after Baudelaire

To get these eclogues written I must sleep
Like an astrologer, beside the sky,
Among the belfries, hearing while I dream
The high wind bear their solemn songs away.
Chin in hand, in the remotest attic
Let me know the factories' song and blether,
Cowls and campaniles like steamer funnels,
Big skies which must also sleep forever.

The fog burns off: I see the birth of stars
Out in the blue as evening's lamps come on,
The coal-smoke glide like rivers into heaven,
The moon pour her intoxications down.
I'll dream on with my windows open wide
Until in winter's frozen monochrome
I close the shutters, lock myself away
And name the only world where I'm at home.

In the absence of horizons waits the garden:
Statues in the fountains weep and kiss,
The birds will name themselves at dawn and dusk.
Our life is nowhere much compared with this
Formality that does not need or think,
And is the whole of what can be expressed,
This graveyard on the blessed Isle of Ink
Where language learns to lay itself to rest.

Homework

That girl isn't doing her homework.
She sits in her room and looks out
At the place she grew up in.

It's neither one thing nor the other.
She looks at her parents, knee-deep
In the garden, pretending

They live somewhere else, in a dream
Of unceasing improvements.
It's summer, or nearly.

A southbound express hammers under the bridge
Past the field where the scrap-dealer's horse
Stands chained to a sleeper —

Gone in a moment
The long-shadowed field
Bitten down to the quick

With its ragged-arsed horse,
The hawthorns obscuring the buildings.
Then the next bridge and the long braking curve

To the city. The girl tilts her head
For a minute, listening
As the air re-seals itself.

'The summer trains run on all night,
Coming from northward, in blue never-darkness,
Past islands of fog, by the seashore,

'Rocking the guard with his crossword,
The drunks and the children sleeping at last
When the sound of the train is like silence.'

Biographer

Now it's time to pull yourself together.
So tip me a metaphorical wink,
There in that photograph's black-and-white weather,
Held between youth and the long dry wank
The book club wants to bind in pseudo-leather.
That's you done. I'm pouring us a drink.

Look where your imperfect tenses led.
Observe your weird insistence on the right
To live (*or else near offer*, you'd have said)
Ten thousand times the same provincial night
With third-string fucks across a narrow bed.
All here, dear heart. You shrink to fit my sights:

From birth to fluky first to shrivelled prick,
Plus cancer to confirm you're one of us.
But it's adultery that does the trick
(You *rode in style* although you *missed the bus*).
The punters need the poets to be sick:
It makes the absent gift less onerous.

Stiff with insights life could never give you,
I write what you could only wish you'd said.
Balls, of course, but who will quite believe you?
After all, I raised you from the dead.
I made you up, because I mean to live you.
Bet you wish you'd thought of me instead.

Something to Read on the Train

'the unknown unwanted life'
      RANDALL JARRELL

When the lights fail at a tunnel's mouth
There is a moment when the rain's
Projected on the page and then runs dry

Across the reader's hands – the reader
Who sees this as we do and wants
To find something behind it. The reader,

Middle-aged now and knowing in detail
What a disappointment looks like,
Glimpses the shape of a roof, a lit window,

A branch line the train never follows
Through those woods and consequences;
Marks the place, unwraps a stick of gum

(This train does not encourage smoking)
And for the umpteenth time enjoys
The drops the brakes send skating off the glass,

As a station takes shape
From an arc-light, a bench and the name
Of one place, not another. I've read this

So long I've begun to invent it.
Europe's real name is Insomnia,
Night after night going over these points

As if to be elsewhere sufficiently
Often or long could amount to belief.
Night-lit rooms beside the iron road

In other languages, I want you.
Priest with a thriller; cop with a pony book;
Bore, with your Railways of Fact;

You, yes, you, with your hand down your pants;
And the hopeless case, reading this poem: let's look.
Can you show me the map of the system, the clock

That speaks German and stands at dead centre?
Even its guardian is sneaking a read:
There's a girl in a house by the railway;

A reader at night, black rain, a compartment;
A man who can't sleep but who knows
He is dreaming and cannot wake up.

Cantona

One touch, then turn, then open the defence,
Then, gliding down your private corridor,
Arriving as the backs go screaming out,
You slide into slow motion as you score
Again, in the heroic present tense.
As Trevor says, that's what it's all about.

Like boxing and the blues, it's poor man's art.
It's where the millions possess a gift
As vital as it looks vicarious:
While Fergie chews and struts like Bonaparte
We see the pride of London getting stiffed,
And victory falls on the Republic, *us*.

But Eric, what about that Monsieur Hyde,
Your second half, who grows *Les Fleurs du Mal*
Who shows his studs, his fangs and his disdain,
Who gets sent off, then nearly sent inside
For thumping jobsworths at the *Mondiale*?
Leave thuggery to thugs and use your brain:

Now choose the spot before the ball arrives,
Now chest it, tee it, volley from the D.
Now Wimbledon, like extras, simply look,
And even Hansen feels he must agree:
This 'luxury' is why the game survives,
This poetry that steps outside the book.

Paradise

for Harry Novak

You say that you are poor but you are happy
In this city in the north. You say
The long ceramic tunnel underneath the railway
Where you wash in what drips down
Could be the lavatory of paradise.
It has the scope, the echo and the sense
That nothing changes, ever. Anyway,
A place to winter. Lying
In the workmen's trench among the cones
In the indigent glamour of dawn
When its blue O calls at either end,
You are shat on by dogs and arrested,
You say it's the real thing at last.
Your publisher works from a concrete emplacement
Attached to a school, now defunct,
For the training of criminals and/or
Security men. He likes a place with atmosphere.
He is your friend. He will wave,
Stepping over the trench, and will sometimes remark
That he read of your case in the papers.
You think he's becoming a god:
His compound has a special right to rain
And blinding grit, through which
You can manage a harrowing glimpse
Of the metro bridge crossing the river,
Symbolic of time, and the water itself
Far below, leaving town in a hurry. As ever
You think of yourself with your overcoat
Spread like a ray, going with it, face down.

All this and the doors have no handles.
There he is, shading his eyes
From the glare of the stockroom
In which your life's work has been waiting
For this, to be burned for insurance.
It's real, you insist, as you crouch
At the letterbox, hearing the daisy-wheel
Hammer out money for someone.
You've made your trench. Now lie in it.
I am the upshot, you shout at the bridges.
The bridges shout back in Chinese.
They have not understood. You're standing
Knee-deep in the prawn-scented Ouseburn,
Attempting once more to persuade
Your gaberdine to float. Or you are rustling
At the city farm. You sit on the metro,
A sheep on each arm, and await the inspectors.
You say, when I hear the word
Culture, I reach for my arse
With both hands. Then I kiss it goodbye.

On Not Being Paul Durcan

Let me be the first to admit it:
I am not Paul Durcan. Neither am I
Captain Bligh or Mandevil of the famous Travels
Or Prince or for that matter Debra Winger. But that is by the way.
Especially I am not Paul Durcan.
My life is more blandly confined
To the plane of the rational, to means and their ends,
Such as getting yer man to the mike
To deliver the business, ensuring the books
(*A Snail in My Prime: New and Selected Poems*)
Have arrived and the waterjug's placed
On the pure golden mean of the lectern
Or modest deal table, whichever's required
(A memo: examine the contract). An audience, too.
Let's not forget them,
The 'A' level students brought down
In a haze of Coles Notes off the Pennines in buses;
The poised aficionados of the art who come in late;
A scatter of lunatics haunting the fringes; and someone
Who thinks it's the Chilean evening. Hello there, Keith.
It is not my lot to expatiate grandly.
Yer man's the one gifted that way
With the left-handed head. My portion
Is booking his room at the Jackass Hotel near the station
In spite of the idiot trainee
Who answers the phone submarinely –
First language quite clearly not English
And possibly not of this planet. I do this
For love of the art of Paul Durcan.
Likewise I perform the grim divination
Of train-times as if they were true

In order that Durcan shall come to the mike
In the peak of condition and go through his paces,
That blend of exaltation and terror
For which he is everywhere famous
Except up on Tyneside, which takes it or leaves it,
Supposing it's not Basil Bunting that's on. But let's not
Get into aesthetics before they have opened the bar.
Give us yer suit, I have heard someone whisper
At dapper Glyn Maxwell. I hope
We shall have none of that when yer man
Steps up in his elegant corduroy leisure equipment . . .

Reading Stevens in the Bath

It is Newcastle at evening. It is far
From the furnished banks of the coaly Tyne
But close beside the hidden and infernal banks

Of the unutterable Ouseburn. Howay. It cries
Its native cry, this poisoned soup of prawns.
Howay. The evil river sings. The mind,

In Forest Hall, the haunted disbelieving suburb
Like a field of snowmen, the mind in Forest Hall
Lays by its knitting and considers

Going to the Fusilier. Howay. But in the upper room,
The room upstairs, the upstairs room,
The blear of glass and heat wherein

Not much is visible, a large pink man
Is reading Stevens in the bath. Howay. It is bath-time,
The time of the bath, the green-watered, where the mind

Lies unencumbered by the body as by time.
It is the bath as absolute, admitting
No conditional of green, the bath in which the bather

Lies considering. And the mind takes out
Its lightness to inspect, and finding nothing there
Begins to sing, embodying, emboldening its note.

It is the singing body in the bath, the mind.
Bookless Fruiterers, tell me if you can
What he may find to sing about, that man

Half-audible, and howling, as it were, the moon
That rests its gravity on weary Forest Hall,
That sends its tidal song by Tyne,

By Ouseburn, by the purifying plant
And ultimately here, to this balneum absolute,
Steam-punkah'd bath at the end of the mind, whose singer

Sings beyond the scope of tongues and sanity
Of neighbours, howling like a wolf among the snowmen
To the moon which does not listen:

'Say It's Only A Paper Moon' . . .
Howay. Howay. Howay!

Amours de Grimsby

When the sway of the exotic overwhelmed
My lyric impulse, I returned
At length to indigence and Grimsby.
On the quay where the fish-train set me down
And pulled away for Trebizond and Cleethorpes
No gift-box of herrings awaited me this time.
After the exhaustion of my early promise
In mannered elaboration of the same few
Arid tropes, I did not find in Grimsby
Girls in states of half-undress awaiting me
When they had got their shopping from the Co-op,
Had their hair done, phoned their sisters,
Read a magazine and thought I was the one.
I was *homo Grimsby*, brought to bed on spec.
When one bar in Grimsby turned into another –
Shelf of scratchings, half-averted clock,
The glassy roar when time was done
And steam rose from the massive sinks
In which the stars of Grimsby might have bathed –
I got my amicable end away
In Grimsby, or I sat on their settees,
My arms outstretched to mothers winding wool.
Therefore I live in Grimsby, cradled
In a fishwife's scarlet arms from dusk
To hobnailed dawn, my tongue awash
With anchovies and Grimsby's bitter Brown.
Mighty Humber's middle passage shrinks
To flooded footprints on a sandbar, each in turn
Inspected by a half-attentive moon. We sit
In smoke-rooms looking out. We know
That Grimsby is the midst of life, the long

Just-opened hour with its cellophane removed,
The modest editorial in which the world
Might change but does not, when the cellars
Empty back their waters, when the tide that comes
Discreetly to the doors enquires for old sake's sake
If this could be the night to sail away. From Grimsby?

R=U=B=R=I=C

It will not feature streetlamps, gable-ends
Or someone's fence thrown down by recent gales.
It will not tell us in a sidelong way
About your family's escape from Europe
In a *wagon-lit* disguised as pierrots, through forests
Thick with gamekeepers-turned-Nazis. It will not
Pine for Bukovina or for Rochdale.
It will not be Eurocentric, but in general
Atlases will leave it quite unmoved.
It will not satirize the times
Or praise a different period in terms
Which challenge our conception of the Good.
It will ignore the claims to eccentricity alleged
Among its fellow travellers on the Metro.
The library's oilclothed tables will not grant it
Access to black pools of divination.
It will not sing of ordinary life –
Of football, vinegar, domestic violence –
Or stake the claims of art by means
Of imagery drawn from books of reproductions
Where the hero in a black suit stands
Before a maze of ice, or – donning a monastic cowl –
Among the sullen precincts of a temple
Framed with cypresses, to which a black-sailed ship
Draws near. It will not be ironic.
It will not speak to you in person
In an upper room where twelve are gathered
At the taxpayer's expense to hear
An explanation of themselves before they go
For pizza and a row. You will not hear it
Hail you in the accents of broad comedy or Ras Ta Far I
As you sit and mind your business on the bus
Or in a padded cell. You cannot make it

Speak to your condition, nor to those
With a different sexual orientation,
Nor to those who neither know nor care to know
A poem from a cabbage or *Nintendo*.
Ask it not here, it won't be saying.
It will not glozingly insinuate itself
Through broadcast media. Sunday teatime's
Safe for washing up and dismal contemplation
Of the weather, which it also does not deal with.
It will not come between you and your lover
With a sudden intimation on the stairs
That all is lost, or place its hand imploringly
Upon your knee. It does not want to sleep with you,
Still less to drink its Vimto from your slipper;
Could not give a flying fuck for Nature
In its purest form or when as reconceived
At court it turns to pastoral; while God
Has never captured its attention fully –
Likewise the plains of Hell, the void or any
Combination of the three. It will not bear
The mark of Satan or the Library of Congress.
It will not write abuse in lipstick
On the mirror. Neither will it urinate
Upon the carpet having nicked the video.
It leaves the bathroom as we found it, like the world.
It would not slide the bad news from its folder,
Come to pray with you or hold your hand
As you confess a life of misdemeanours.
Nor will it permit you to interpret
Any of its absent gestures so
As to suggest an ur-, a sub-, a meta-text,
Having neither faith nor doubt
Nor any inclination worth a name, except
To know that it's what neither you nor I
Nor any of the pronouns lives to write,
Although we serve its sentence. Now begin.

Downriver

(2001)

Welcome, Major Poet!

We have sat here in too many poetry readings
Wearing the liberal rictus and cursing our folly,
Watching the lightbulbs die and the curtains rot
And the last flies departing for Scunthorpe.
Forgive us. We know all about you.
Autumn gives way to midwinter once more,
As states collapse, as hemlines rise, as we miss both,
And just as our teeth fall discreetly into our handkerchiefs,
Slowly the bones of our co-tormentees will emerge
Through their skins. QED and *hic jacent*.
Except we are seated bolt upright on customized
'Chairs' of the torturers' school. Here it comes,
Any century now, the dread declaration:
And next I shall read something longer. Please
Rip out our nails and accept your applause!
Stretch-limo back to the Ritz and ring home:
Bore the arse off your nearest and dearest instead,
Supposing they haven't divorced you already
Or selfishly put themselves under a train.
Please call them, at length and at public expense.
Send flunkies for cold Stolichnaya, an ox
Or an acre of coke and a thousand-quid hooker.
Why not make it three, in a chariot
Flown to your penthouse by eunuchs on leopards?
Whatever you like, only spare us the details of when
You were struck by your kinship with Dante and Virgil.
And don't feel obliged to remind us just now
What it was Robert Lowell appeared to be saying –
You'd read him the poem you mean to read us –
When the doors of the lift he was in and you weren't
Began closing. Just leave us the screams
You could hear as the vehicle descended: *Poor Cal.*
Up to then he'd been perfectly normal. Ah, well.

Acheron, Phlegethon, Styx

for Peter Reading

Now they're bricked over and leaking
Victorian adipose into the friable earth
In the heat of a seven-year drought,
They deliver that steady industrial suck-fart
(Like a Scots Pie machine making
Full use of the eyelids and sphincters of pigs)
At the foot of the drainshaft, down in the cack
With rubbers, rags and jaundiced *Telegraph*s
Rolled up in twos, sworn on by plumbers –
Themselves long pulled under –
For checking the flush. Furthermore
The crimson hiss of the exhausted brain,
Its library all clarted pages, corridors
Knee-deep in grease, the gridlocked blood
Attempting pinhole exits at the eyeballs.
Gore and shite, crap-nebulae
And greasy bubbles, steadily hurled
Downstream in a stench of finality. Cheers!

Nineties

I

Let's drift again in these vast solitudes,
The beer-and-tabs Sargasso of the shore,
Anachronistic legal waterholes
Down foggy chares alleged to have two ends –
We'll make a life's work of an evening out.

Let booths and gantries frame a ruined court
That grants our bores' and lone derangers' pleas
A hearing, though the verdict is the clock's –
Long boxes, six black horses, frosty plumes,
The diggers leaning on their spades to smoke.

Far overhead, a coal train grinds its way
Across the viaduct. A grimy clang
From the cathedral, echoed. Please call home.
Tonight's the nineteenth century *sans* crowds,
A boozers' heaven lit by blue dog-stars

Whose image in the empty river draws
Fanatics to the bridges for dispatch –
Spent gambling men we used to read about,
They seem to wear our faces as they plunge
In sequence from the parapets, as though

To cancel with a gesture thirty years
Drunk dry with infidelity and waste.
They print the water with their leader-dots . . .
Theirs was the truly historical work,
The ground on which we've been arraigned tonight –

Since we've outlived both usefulness and art —
A failure to imagine properly
Our place in the supporting cast, to move
From *rhubarb* to the boneyard in a blink . . .

As if there might be politics afoot,
The night the southside arsenal went up
The people thronged the quays like citizens.
Blood-lit in the inferno of the towns
They hailed their unimportant misery.
The river boiled red-black past walls of flame
And watermen like local Charons cried
Beneath the stairs for passing trade, their arms
Outspread like angels in the burning rain
Of lath and plaster, flesh and cobblestones
That blinded the cathedral weathercocks
And put the heat on whore and judge alike.

Or so the picture shows, that no one sees,
Crammed in beside a turning of the stairs:
Old Testament confusion, modern dress,
And on his non-existent crag, the bard
Who's too far gone to say he told them so.

II

Your hundred streets, your twenty names, all gone.
A stink of burning sofas in the rain,
Of pissed-on mattresses, and poverty's
Spilt milk, its tiny airless rooms designed
To illustrate the nature of subjection
To its subjects. They tell me politics
And history are done: here's grease
Extruded from the dripping tar-skinned walls
Of workingmen's hotels; the ropes of hair
Trapped in the sinks; the names perpetually denied
A hearing, waiting in the smoky halls
For their appointments with an age that bred
And killed and then forgot them – names that now
Forget themselves, the air's mere allegations,
Faces that the mirrors do not hold,
Lockers with no contents, neither razors
Nor the Bible nor an envelope of dimps
Preserved against the certainty of worse.
So Billy, Tommy, Jackie – did you live?
Could it be you that Benjamin's
Averted angel is ignoring now
As once again you leave your flooded graves
Like newsreel ghosts to greet the Kaiser's guns?

III

Blind walls and hidden roadways running down
To water. Black windows wedged with newsprint,
Morning after morning of the afterlife,
Anacoluthon of streets and bars.

The bar as survival, as figment,
Dog on the shelf and women to rights,
The Hole in the Corner where dead men meet,

The dead of emphysema
And of pneumoconiosis,

bickering

Beyond the grave like kids.

There is football, or football. Occasional boxing:
Jimmy Wilde and Woodcock, Billy Hardy
Brave as owt

and carefully done down,

A lesson you have to pretend you've forgotten.

Or else there was Hitler, that flag-waving cunt.
Should have been a referee. Should have been hung
By the balls and then shot at. The Jarmans want tellt.

*

Eternity's offside; a lockout.
It's stilted black coal-staithes becoming aesthetics.

It's the exacerbated calm,
The grey summer nights at the end of the world

Through which an old bloke walks his dog
Across that shitty stretch of no man's grass

Because it's his vocation,
Middle distant citizen of patience.

The Ideology

For John Hartley Williams

When the poem sneaks up on itself –
It wishes to be intimate
With history – it finds itself leaning
From a footbridge on the cutting,

Round at the back of the district
In part of the never-was Umpties
Where somebody probably dreamed of a cinema
Out on this far edge of town, that could show

Fort Apache for ever. And this is what's
Never been noticed or built on.
The clinkered slopes are foxed with autumn.
A lot to take in, even here. The desire

To pause, to repose, like a white-trash Horatian
Instructed in death as in what comes before it –
Descent through the fiery circles of drink
And finance, with a box from the Co-op to finish.

Instead, then, the poem imagines
The smell and the oil after coal-smoke
Here in the after-tea quiet
With nights drawing in for back-end,

And strangers' leaves arriving on the lawn
And people remarking on this
Before switching their fires on. Instead, then,
The gaze of the red lamp resembles

The rowan trees' troubling berries.
Site of pagan industry, the poem thinks —
Or Nature and Industry,
Weed coiling over the tracks,

Sliding the slates from the lineside hut
Until willowherb stands in the doorway,
Obsolete, proprietorial
And cap in hand. No woolly peach in view.

The sound that hangs behind the air
Could be wind off the hills or the one train a day
Hauling coal from the strip-mine.
Do you believe? believe truly? the poem enquires

In the soft, educational voice
That means, Not any more, not entirely.
From westward the white sky comes over on rollers
And up the hill on a far estate

A bus is masking one by one the lamps
As they harden from pink towards orange.
What cannot be said, the poem thinks,
Is the necessity in it, that means

A gang of girls is out in this.
Beneath a streetlamp by the pub
They stand with folded arms, comparing clothes,
Shouting as if they're expecting an echo.

The poem ages them. They go indoors.
They marry or not and bear children
And die, and are found in mid-shriek
In a different poem, still there in the cold

Wearing hardly a stitch, being happy
The way those who live with industrial parks and asbestos
Are happy, because if they weren't they would die,
On the need-to-know basis of beauty and truth.

At the Gate

This is the open gate to summer, beckoning
From the lane's end, at its back
The sound of distant water like applause
From re-grown woods, where sycamores
Have privatized the smoke-skinned chimneystacks.
Gate of summer. Summer of poverty,
Ignorance and Methodism, iron-willed
Pharaonic stone-walled engineering
Waged along vertical valley-sides. Summer
With the coiners hanged, with funeral lace,
With shoddy, mungo, bloody-bibbed
Consumptives carted to the pit.
Vernacular water is having
Its ignorant say, blathering perpetually
Through loopholes in the statute book
And sliding underneath death's door:
So now, as spring accelerates
Across the threshold into June,
Applause, and then a shock of shame
At all that's irremediably done.

The Eavesdroppers

There are no trains this afternoon.
Nothing is coming
From under the second-hand bathwater sky,
Through the zinc-tasting air,
Over the low hum of half-expectation
That hangs at knee-height where the tracks run away
Past frosty docks and groundsel
At the unadopted edges of allotments.
The clocks have shut down.
Deep in the roofing-felt shanties,
Sputtering quietly next to the kettles
The old gadgies' transistors explain
That the racing's abandoned
And this is our chance 'to enjoy once again
The remarkable day in 1957 when England' *click* –
No trains. But this end of the city
Is lending an ear – 'housewives and the unemployed',
The idle student eking out his blow,
The mortician's receptionist
Bent to her Angela Carter
(A slow day for death), and me doing this.
Never think nobody cares
For that thundery corridor
Painting its Forth into Scotland and back,
For the drizzly grind of the coal-train
Or even the Metro, that amateur transport,
Sparking and chattering every verse-end.
Where and for that matter who
Can we be without them and the world
They continually carry away,
To which, now it's silent, we find
We have spent our lives listening?

Last Orders at the Fusilier, Forest Hall

for Maureen and Eileen

Here's winter now – the first frost on the field,
Black stratocirrus, then a grid of stars
Pinned up behind the roofs. The freezing Bear
Extends a paw across the skies to greet
The North as we roll round: *so put it there*,
The Night Shift say, careerists of the bars.
We strive, we seek, we never bloody yield,
And Peter Beardsley grew up down the street.

So Stuart, Tommy, Micky, Dicky, Ron,
This is the life, with one eye on the clocks,
From boy to gadgie round the Fusilier!

That's ten to. That's another evening gone,
The bar staff crouched like sprinters in the blocks:
Now Letsby Avenue! Time on your beer!

Ravilious

Beneath the great white horse's one green eye,
The goods-train steams in blue-black miniature
Away from us, into the cross-hatched fields.
Perhaps this will be England finally
And not a further painful episode
In the discreet narration of a love
That when it learns its name will have to die.

*

Where are we now? Not on the O.S. sheet.
The wrong side of the glass, we stop to watch
The dapper engine cross a bridge by night
Beside a fingerpost with four ways back
To England, closed to us. We know the place.

*

The next time round, we take the train to see
The watchers down the line, preoccupied
With maps and catalogues, white horses, us.
They close their faces as we pass, to learn
More clearly where they stand and what it means.
At which we guess. All our excursions run
Not to our love but where we lived and died.

A Northern Assembly

So, then, let's strike a northern light
To blind those armies of the night
Who always place a southern spin
Around the state we're living in.

Remove the Westminster diktat?
Who wouldn't go along with that?
But can your North be North like mine?
Who gets to draw the borderline?

Who says where North begins and ends?
Are Makems and Smogmonsters friends?
Are Monkeyhangers on the run
Since Mandy's flit to Islington?

And what about the Boro? Soft:
I hear the clank of Chairman Croft.
And what about, you know, Gateshead,
Whose rusty Angel guards the shed

Where only thirty cared enough
To come and hear you do your stuff?
If folks don't think there's much at stake
For Pity Me and Bolam Lake,

And use their Saturdays to shop,
Not give big government the chop,
What chance of making Tory Blair
Firstly: listen, second: care?

– For in the mind of Chairman Tone
Democracy means Tone alone
Deciding what we all love best
While Warden Straw bangs up the rest.

New Labour likes to share its bed
With those who want the unions dead
And sends in Dr Cunningham
To make us love Monsanto spam –

Bizarre: one half school-dinner-hag,
The other Dracula in drag,
Living proof that food mutation
Raises you above your station.

Pols of this stripe don't rely
On principle to get them by:
If they cannot slag they bore.
Persistence: nine parts of the law.

When no one can be arsed to cast
A Eurovote, perhaps the last
Thing the electorate requires
Is mini-Quins and Browns and Byers

Crowding to the public trough:
The pols have pissed the people off
By playing at democracy
While flying to the moon for free.

So, world and politics on fire,
The poet chooses to retire
Where the pastoral is found,
In Tyneside's secret pleasure ground

Come North by North to Forest Hall,
Most South American of all
The suburbs where the pits were sunk.
Here giant snakes pursue the drunk

Administrators of the arts
In stolen Kular's shopping carts.
Here Spanish is the loving tongue,
Like music from the iron lung

Of pitmen sacked and pensioned off
To man the lunchtime bars and cough,
While on the news a sycophant
Extols the, well, the Siemens plant.

What is true North, what's bogus South?
Insert your money in your mouth
To prove your aim's as serious
As mere prosaic theory is:

A North that's not a party game
But can support a sovereign claim
Begins on Humberside and knows
How Andrew Marvell's metre goes —

Let North, from Humber's shore to Tweed
Exist in verse, if not yet deed,
And let a poem legislate
For this ideal imagined state,

The theoretical address
No king has managed to suppress.
Spirits of water, coal and stone –
Pick up the Muse's telephone

And let us hear your Northernness.
Affirm, affirm: the North says yes.
Let's say that we'll not now endure
The treatment suited to manure –

Let's aim to chuck a few lumps back.
Now then Cockneys, eat this cack.
From Cockermouth to Withernsea,
The North – the North is poetry.

It means that we can't tolerate
The dim, the daft, the second-rate –
In poetry or politics –
This is the North and not the sticks –

Still less expect the working class
To keep electing one more crass
Machine-head from the civic hall
To keep on taking home his ball.

So, bent old cooncillors, play dead
Or end up in the nick instead;
Prods and Masons, racists, Papes,
Wash your hands and wipe your tapes.

The latest crowd of suits won't do
To state what's beautiful and true:
If North is North and South is Wrong
The fact deserves a decent song,

Not subliterate conference papers
Scrawled by would-be history-shapers.
By all means rouse the Meadowell
But also learn to bloody spell.

But what the Northern sceptic fears
Is what mysteriously appears
In every meeting-place: the rump
Excreted from the parish pump,

A stale, unappetizing bunch –
The thick, the bought, the out to lunch,
Carnivores in eco-hats
Empire-builders, toadies, twats:

The shite that rises to the top
But couldn't run a corner shop
Somehow contrives to represent
Itself as fit for government . . .

You wear that visionary stare,
Believing that you're almost there.
You must have nothing else to do.
You must think we're as daft as you.

As Eliot said – you may recall –
No, that's not what we meant at all.
We want our representatives urbane,
Equipped with fully working brain.

Not furnished with opinions from
The P.M.'s spokesman's C.D.-rom.
In fact the North's not paradise.
Let's not indulge its favourite vice

– The sentimental one-eyed view
Of what's well known to me and you,
The 'natural nobility'
That whinges to be let in free

But can't be arsed to learn its trade
And sing whatever is well-made.
I'm told you shouldn't take the Mick
Because the North can't stand the stick –

To which the modern poet replies
That what she loves she'll satirize,
While those who cannot take a joke
Find reasons to be shooting folk:

Milosevic and Jean Le Pen
Began somewhere, as local men.

Baltica

for Laura Rota i Roca and Jens Fabrin

The pages of water are always revising themselves,
As if the truth is out there somewhere
In the blue contested space that giant ferries
Cross like diplomats, with huge discretion.

Land stops and begins with three dots . . .
Where we wait on a finger of concrete,
With buffers and warnings and grey wooden pilings
A vessel has lately bashed into.

This is the kind of a town
There must be where a ferry departs,
Somewhere the rails can run through,
Where no one lives and everybody comes from –

Bars, bad girls, a brand of Schnapps.
At six o'clock it closes down
And drinks itself to death,
Surfacing cross-eyed and swearing on bicycles.

Meanwhile a dredger is roaring away
To preserve the deep channel –
A frightening hungover military noise
Which has only volume to lend the debate

Over whether in fact we shall manage
To travel, or ought to go back where we started.
We sit on the bollards in sunshine, with crosswords
Like treasure-maps, dreaming our turn

To set out from one rock to the next.
Twenty feet down the green inshore Baltic
Sways gently, its spread hands commending
A breathable otherworld,

Names we cannot yet pronounce,
Glottal-stopped landfalls, ship-drinking gulfs
To be glugged with the brine
From a tin of sunk herring. Plenitude

Of copper coin, receipts and destinations!
Enviable archipelagians! Give us
A go on your rusty red coasters
Crammed with foot-passengers,

All staring ceremonially east.
Hold tight to your ruinous trawlers, raucous
With caterwaul Danish-and-Western.
For what could be simpler than loving the distance –

The numberless low-lying needlepoint islands
That narrow to barely believable farms,
The peaceable saltire, a stony beach
With firs and two swans, where a ferry sets out?

Riding on the City of New Orleans

From the Crescent City slowly
Over stormy Pontchartrain,
Through Louisiana dusk
And into Mississippi night,
To Tennessee and Illinois,
Which are impossible,
From rémoulade and sin towards
A klieg-lit German paradise,
The train goes, crying *Train, Train*.
We are travelling so slowly,
Two-four on the joints, two-four,
The journey could be proof, almost,
That home, or hope, or what you need
Are only now departing: run
And you could board it still
Beneath the cover of that cry.
That voice is returned from the walls
Of graves in the permanent lockdowns,
Over sweating antebellum lawns
Beneath the levee. Or it stirs
A snaredrum sat tight in its kit
On the stage of the Wild Kingdom Bar,
A concrete expression of popular will
Where music and murder take place
Every night of the long week of Sundays.
Train, the voice whispers:
Its breath clouds a saxophone's bell.
Train, down the tarpaper length
Of a shotgun slavehouse
Still upright beside the reactor. *Train*,
And the poor are once more reinvented,

Sleeping in the slowly rocking coach.
To name the states that lie
On either hand from sea to sea
Is neither here nor there, and to dismount
At the edge of a field, or a road, or a river
And watch the train depart, becoming
Swaying lights and then the dark
In which its very name recedes,
Could make a man forget his own
Or stay repeating it forever.

Indian Summer

these iron comforts, reasonable taboos
JOHN ASHBERY

Look at this frosty red rose leaning over
The milk on the step. Please take it. But leave me
Its fragrance, its ice in the mind, to remember you by.
The girlfriends of afternoon drinkers
(*O the criminal classes, their bottle-tanned lasses*)
Have locked up their halters and shorts –
Being practical girls, they have understood soon
What I struggle with late, getting grit in my eyes –
That the piss-palace garden is windy and dim
When the heat goes at four. It is over again.
Now the engineer turns up to service the heating
And says: *I see your bell's still bust*
From the Charon-cold depths of his anorak hood.
The dark house is a coffin of laws; early closing.
But if the clocks must forever go back
To the meantime of Pluto, leave me your voice,
Its rumour at the confluence of Portugal and Spain,
From whose entwining waters rises, like a shell
Within the echo in the ear, your own supreme Creole.
If I am doomed to winter on the Campo Mediocrita
Whose high plateau becomes the windy shore
Of an ocean with only one side, to wait
Where the howling sunshine does not warm me,
Let me speak your tongue, at least –
For yours is the music the panther laments in,
Retreating to Burradon, yours is the silvery
Script of the spider at midnight,
Your diary is scandal's pleasure-ground

From which a bare instant of cleavage or leg
Is all I shall have to sustain me. And yours
Are the text and the age I should like to be acting:
You lie on the bed of the lawn, painted gold,
With the base of your spine left naked to breathe,
And now I might seal the extravagant promise
To kiss you to life with your name, if for once
You could look at me – do it now – straight
In the eye, without smiling or shaking your head.

Kanji

for G.

Wish you were here, though I never arrived.
Here is a poem with no way in.
There are so many kanji. Each is a gate
Whose key waits on its other side.
The white-gloved taxi-driver keeps one
Safe indoors in the ignition of his linen-covered

Primly pornographic back-seat parlour,
While the bar hostess secretes hers
God knows where about her tiny person.
Professor N will show me his,
Which could, he says regretfully –
Here's where he stops quoting Shakespeare –

Be mine if I were not, ahem, *gaijin*.
I wonder when the poem might begin.
In restaurants where demons brandish choppers
Crabs the size of manhole covers
Gesture at its shape from holding tanks
As if like the Houdinis of the id

At any moment they'll be free to chase
Half-naked girls down streets of science fiction.
Even to be drunk's a foreign language here:
An empty space to fill in with the hands.
I meet you like a beggar at the airport.
Later, sealed for minutes in a lift,

I brush your dress. Is that your stocking-top,
A clue? I wonder what it might unlock,
Then whether, if I tried, your voice,
Familiar as my own, but infinitely sweeter,
Would suddenly be foreign with regret
And muffled by the closing of the door.

The Grammar School Ghost

Charlotte Square, Newcastle upon Tyne, 1860

The globe was spinning when I left the room,
But it was more than Geography I missed.
First I was impudent. Next I was dead.
You will wait in the corridor. You, boy –
Muddleheaded, dirty-minded, you, boy –

Wait and be struck by Victorian lightning
Aimed by God Almighty down the chimney
In a theorem of fire. QED.
And to this day I wait for Kingdom Come
Within this draughty whitewashed box,

While all the world rewrites itself, while ink
And chalk and sweat and cabbage are displaced
By ozone from the lights, and *Opium*
My secretary dabs between her breasts.
Behind the cloakroom mirror now, I blow

A kiss into her mouth, that lipstick rose
It seems to be her life's work to perfect.
My looks will never touch her, but I'm true,
Admiring the future from afar.
By night I try to love the elements:

Repaired, repaired, then broken yet again,
For years on end the skylight lets me read
The hand of stars that I've been dealt, or watch
The moon ascend behind its pane of ice,
The snow come falling through my empty head.

Cities

and still some down to go
  KEN SMITH

What are cities made of? Steam vents. Blue light. Murder.
Steps going down from the dark to the dark
Past yellow helmets aiming anxious lamps, past padded coats
Making sorrowing bearlike gestures of general
But hopelessly inarticulate love, past men
And their haircuts, their eyebeams, unspoken advice.
Everyone knows. Whoever it is must already be dead.
Eviscerated, eyeless, boiled – in a thousand conditions
They wait to be found and lamented, chained
Amid the perpetrator's stinking hoard of symbols:
Nail-clippings, fingerbones, rat hair, milk,
Scorched pages of an ancient book
That holds the key. But down you go
And the hours stretch, and the clocks in the offices
Stare at each other in rigid hysteria.
Your colleagues in the daylight world
Yawn with despair, an hour from sailboats and beer.
But you go on descending until you have left
The last outpost of order some far landing back
Before cast-iron stairs gave way to wood.
Isn't it tempting to dump the aluminium suitcase
And stop here, making a place of this nowhere?
The staircase folds back on itself
And the silent tunnel plunges further in
Under the last of the railbeds, the last bottled river,
Graveyard of oystermen, library of masons, latrine of the founders,
Stained-glass temple of carnivorous Morlocks,
Deadlight, corridor, cupboard, box.

Sit with your torch playing over the brickwork
Still hoarse with graffiti – *'looks like Aramaic'* – and listen
To the silence breathing *This is and this is and this is*,
Endlessly folding and reading itself,
A great book made of burlap and dust,
That is simply digesting the world –
Its drips and rustles, the screams from old cases,
Trains that were heading elsewhere
In a previous century. Soon
You will come to believe you have eaten this book,
That your gullet is lined like a tenement room with its print,
That your tongue has illustrations
And your breath must smell of pulp.
Isn't it tempting to answer, *Just give me the reason
And then we'll go up to the air* – it is dawn above ground
And the manholes stand open, steaming
For the resurrection, straight up in the blue
Where we seek reassurance – *go up there
And start to forget it all over again.*

Songs from the Drowned Book

I

In the beginning was all underwater,
The down-there-not-talked-about-time,
Deep North its drowned masonic book
And inaudible bubbles of speech,

Creation a diving-bell seeking its level
Down stone under stone, the slick passages
Fronded by greenery, flashlit by ore
And acetylene candles –

The blind fishes' luminous ballroom,
The pillars of coal, the salt adits, the lead oubliette of the core
And the doors upon doors, all lost
To the surface long since, with the language. Now
Is there anything there, underneath? Is there more?

II

See
I can remember when
All this was manuscript:

How
Down the green deep we tipped
Law-clerks schoolmen state and church

And with them kingliness,
The night we sank the crown
Off Holderness.

Adam delved
And Dives swam
And sank, swam
And sank:
So who was then the gentle man?
Ourselves, or them
Whose deaths we drank?

III

Name me a river.
I'll name you a king.
Then we shall drown him
And his God-given ring.
Drown him in Gaunless,
Drown him in Wear,
Drown him like Clarence,
Except we'll use beer.

Name me a river.
I'll name you a price.
River's not selling –
Take river's advice:
Dead if you cross me,
I'll not tell you twice.

My river's from heaven.
Your river's been sold,
And your salmon have died
Drinking silver and gold.

Your river's a sewer,
A black ditch, a grave,
And heaven won't lend you
The price of a shave.

IV *(Baucis and Philemon in Longbenton)*

– Hinny, mek wor a stotty cake,
Wor needs it for wor bait.
– Hadaway, pet, away and shite:
You'll have to fookin wait.
Or mek yer stotty cake yerself
If yer sae fookin smart.
– Aye, ah will, wor divvent need ye,
Ya miserable tart.

V *(From the Dive Bar of the Waterhouse)*

I was dreaming underwater
When you swam into my bed:
How like you this? The tail, I mean,
And my long hair, rich and red?
A naiad of the standing pools
Of England's locked back yard,
It is because of you, my dear,
That makars live so hard.

Sherry from Kular's (see beggars; see *choose)*
Red Biddy, Thunderbird, non-booze booze,
Hair oil, Harpic, shit in your shoes –
It's casual drinking, it's paying your dues.

What would you give to know my name
And speak it in your verse,
And if I tell you, will it be
A blessing or a curse?

You are not the first, my dear,
Nor will you be the last —
Thousands sit for my exam
But no one's ever passed.

Songs from the Black Path

I Beginning

Build me a city all builded with brick
And in that place endeavour
Builded with iron and mercury sweat
Cyanide pour bleu de Nîmes
The elementis, changed for ever

Culvert, tower and cannon mouth
Where war and science meet together
Commodiously dancing on
The head of heaven's pin
Where man presumes on God's despair,
Original as sin

And to this gated city let
The black path enter in
Cyanide pour bleu de Nîmes
Carbide, cadmium, arsenic, gold
And men to drive the engines through
The gates of Kingdom Come
And to this gated city let
The black path enter in

Build me a wall by a stormy sea,
Mile-deep in brick and blood
Where no man's voice is heard
A pit of dark where fire lives
Without a beast or bird
Let the sun come up a burning eye
And sink in fiery flood

Build me a city of iron and brick
Whose name shall be Endeavour
Gunpowder, cyanide, mercury sweat —
The elements dance together
And to this gated city let
The black path enter in
And to this gated city let
The black path enter in

II The Iron Hand

I once loved a boy with an iron hand.
He kissed me and he said:
Come for a walk on the old black path —
You can sit on my iron bed.

When I sat on his iron counterpane
He kneeled down before me and said:
Kathleen slip off your sensible shoes
And lie in my iron bed.

I'll bring you whisky and silver,
A bird in an iron cage.
I'll read you this poem and let you look
At the other side of the page.

It's true I loved my iron man
From the depths of his iron bed.
I loved him and my life ran out
And I was left for dead.

I learned how his poem continued
On the far side of the page —

The hero could never distinguish
Tenderness from rage,

And locked me in the iron bed
From dawn till dead of night,
Mending children's jerseys
While my coal-black hair turned white.

I gave him thirteen children
And ten were dead at birth –
Professor now you tell me how
To estimate my worth.

It's true I loved my iron man
From the depths of his iron bed.
I loved him and my life ran out
And I was left for dead.

III Lament

Lay the cold boys in the earth
At Mons and Hartlepool:
Prove to anyone who doubts
That blood and iron rule.

Let the river thickly speak
In tongues of silt and lead.
Teach us our impediment:
We cannot face the dead.

Run the waters furnace-red,
Afire all night long.
If we're to live then we've to make
An elemental song:

The object of the exercise
Is furnishing the world
With battleships, and thunderbolts
The gods would once have hurled.

How shall we know ourselves except
As sparks on blood-red streams,
Where fire-tongued our utterance
Incinerates our dreams?

Lay the cold boys in the earth
At Loos and Stockton town.
Still the blazing rivermouth
And shut the engines down.

Bells of lamentation preach
The law from every spire
To those whom nature could not teach
The language of its fire.

Lay the cold boys in the earth
At Passchendaele and Yarm.
Let the headstones hold them safe
From history and harm.

Twenty thousand men ablaze
Have found their lives outrun
As certainly as if you'd killed them
Singly with a gun.

When the tide is singing
At the steel doors of the bay,
Maybe you can catch its drift:
The world has gone away.

O when the tide is singing
At the steel doors of the bay,
Maybe you can catch its drift:
The world has gone away.

Songs from *Downriver*

I On a Blue Guitar (Lulu Banks)

Dreamed I sat on Daddy's knee
By the dirty riverside
He played his blue guitar
I sat and sang and couldn't tell you
If I lived or if I died

Daddy show me how it goes
The dance the devils do in hell
When you play your blue guitar
It seems you do it very well
Live or die I cannot tell

Dreamed my mammy told me once
Life's a prison, not a pleasure
Dreamed my mammy told me once
Good girls never spend their treasure
That was after the event
I thought my treasure wisely spent

II Horizontal (Bobby Smart)

I was never strong on navigation
I could hardly find my way around
I could never see the slightest difference
Between the China Sea and Puget Sound
But I kept my weather eye on the horizon
Certain that wherever I might stray

There's one test I could beat the other guys on
Where there's a broad involved I know my way

Oh, the adjective deriving from horizon
Goodness me
Would that be
Horizontal?
It may take years to reach you
But stay there on the beach
And you will see
If you remain
Horizontal
That neither hurricane, dead calm
Nor an octopus alarm
Nor the fearsome Hellespont'll
Keep me from the place I have to be
Whether what I really want'll
Happen, who can tell
But you'd look lovely horizontal to me

Some people praise the sextant and the compass
And other great devices of the deep
But standing there just marking off the headings
Is guaranteed to send me off to sleep
Of course my seamanship requires refining
But out there where the ocean meets the sky
I know that a young lady is reclining
Just waiting for when I come sailing by

Your mother keeps a rolling pin to warn off
Me and other monsters of the billows
But I recall my clothing was all torn off
When last we laid our heads upon her pillows
The likes of me sustain a great tradition,

We draw the straightest line across the sea
So help me by assuming the position
And opening your compasses for me

III Smoke Signals (Bobby Smart and Sailor Chorus)

Duke Ellington was very firm upon it
Don't smoke stuff unless there's writing on it
But speaking as a fiend whose mind is blown
I generally prefer to roll my own
It's frowned upon by moralists and vicars
The sort who can't get girls to drop their knickers
But I've found the way to win a girl's affection
Is by offering her the use of your . . . connection

Some like em small and some prefer em jumbo
And Doctor John dips his into his gumbo
A spliff made all the difference to Rimbaud
Verlaine took his with arms like this – akimbo –
Mandela liked a drag and so did Tambo
Folks smoke the stuff from Amazon to Humbo
It will endow the straightest whitest combo
With unsuspected talents for the mambo

So come into my lair and be enslaved
Below decks we're remarkably depraved
There's a snap of Rita Hayworth on the wall
And one of Lollobrigida
That could inflame a Frigidaire
In which she's hardly wearing clothes at all

It's a place of unimaginable sin
So convent girls are queuing to get in

And our revels are just itching to beguine
Leave your morals at the door
You won't need them any more
And be sure to tell your sisters where you've been

This is where we all go up in smoke
It's lovely gear – I scored it from a bloke
Who told me that it's Himalayan Black
The Yeti's very favourite type of tack
I couldn't give a knack
If it's pickled monkey-cack
As long as it can pack a proper wack

So sod the Queen and sod your hearts of oak
To sex and drugs I dedicate this toke
– And to music, but not country and not folk
Admit it, I'm a really handsome bloke
I'm Dracula without the opera cloak
And I'm prepared to offer you a poke
But first of all let's have another smoke

V Time on yer Beer Now (The Company)

It's time now let's have your beer
It's time in the Fall and the Golden Ball
Time you were out of here
Time in the Letsby Avenue now
Time in the Dying Gaul
On Scotswood Road and Percy Street
Let time go by the Wall
It's time, my dear, in the Do Feel Queer
There's no time left at all

Time after time in the Paradigm
Time in the Watch This Space
It means it's time when them bells chime
I'm sick of your fuckin face
Time in the Berkeley, time in the Hume
Time in the Leibniz too
Time in the Baruch Spinoza
And time in the Kants Like You

In Tunis Street, in Tunis Street
It's time in the Blue Manatee
It's time, it's time, it's time on your beer
In the White Man's Grave
In the Price of a Shave
In the Bugger off Back to the Sea

It's time in the Clock and the Dog Watch
It's time in the Graveyard Shift
It's time in the Manifesto
(Three times last night police were called
To an ideological rift)
Time in the Pay You Tuesday
Time in the Christ Now What
And time in the Well Then? and well past time
In the Honest I Forgot

The river-bell rings
When the tide roars back
Under the bridges, down in the cack –
Wallsend and Jarrow
The Old Straight and Narrow
Their hollow mouths howling
Time on your beer now. Go back to sea now.
The coppers'll come with a barrow.

O put on your pants and roll off the bed
There's a taxi at the door.
Stop off at the Tomb and the Hanged Man's Head
'Cos you won't be back no more
You're barred, you're barred, as Enid said
With her brush up the crack of your arse
You're barred from the Johns and the Bear and the Queens
But the Cathouse is different class

Leave the meter ticking over
The driver asleep in his cab
You never can tell just what you'll catch
When you drink with a lass in the Crab
Pissed in the Gents
And the Landlord's Bent
Spark out in the Night Was Young
Brayed in the Privates
Frenched in the Pope
Then you fell off the Bottom Rung
You measured the Coffin
You counted the Bricks
And awoke in the Iron Lung
Time on yer beer
Time on yer beer
Time on yer beer now PLEASE!

from Sports Pages

1. Proem

From ancient days until some time last week
Among the poet's tasks was prophecy.
It was assumed the language ought to speak
The truth about a world we've yet to see;
Then in return for offering this unique
And eerie service, poets got their fee:
And yet, what any poem has to say's
Bound up with all the vanished yesterdays.

Imagination lives on memory:
That's true of love and war and thus of sport:
The world we love's a world that used to be.
Its sprinting figures cannot now be caught
But break the flashlit tape perpetually,
Though all their life's a yellowing report.
Forgive me, then, if speaking of what's next,
I make the past a presence in my text.

For me it starts in 1956,
The Test against the Indians at Lords
As Roy runs in to bowl and Hutton flicks
A long hop to the crowded boundary-boards.
Or did he miss? Or hammer it for six?
But I don't care what *Wisden*'s truth records.
When I dream back, the point is not the facts
But life enlarged by these imagined acts.

Forgive, then, the large licence I assume:
What I know's not the truth but what I like.

The Matthews final found me in the womb
But still I went to Wembley on my bike.
When Zola Budd sent Decker to her doom
The gods had aimed their wishes down the pike.
This isn't just a question of my bias:
All members of my tribe are bloody liars.

2. The Origins of Sport from Remote Times

Listen now, how far back sports began,
With cavemen at the weekends throwing rocks.
To play, it seems, is natural to man
(On rainy days they sat comparing cocks)
And woman too: the Amazons of Thrace
Could score far more than *one hundred and eighty*.
Their arrows wipe the smirk off Bristow's face
And Jocky Wilson's. *Mugs away then, matey.*
The Greeks wrote rules to make sport orthodox;
Found purposes – to keep the *mens* quite *sana*,
To stop Achilles going off his box
When he found he could not be top banana.
It was the smart alternative to war,
Although the two were closely interlinked
As when at times they added up the score
And half the opposition were extinct.
If sport can blend the savage with the best
It illustrates a human paradox:
Meanwhile we're hoping for a classic Test
And, for our friends Australia, a pox.

3. The Olympics

I Efficient

As schoolkids know, the modern games began
In 1896 with Coubertin,
A count who thought sport must be amateur.
At this the Ancient Greeks would all demur:
O'Sullivans and Gunnells and Bulmerkas
Far out-earned the nymphs and vineyard workers;
Sponsored by the cities they were from
The Baileys and the Johnsons earned a bomb.
Their Linford had his lunchbox cast in gold
(Of which a million replicas were sold,
For though their names were never on the cup
It helped mere mortals keep their peckers up).
They'd tell you where to stick your laurel leaves.
All this the modern punter quite believes,
For human nature, magnetized to greed,
Is eager to disguise excess as need.
And since the winnings tended to be heavy
(Back before the Horse Race Betting Levy)
Then as now there was unsporting rancour:
Ancient Greeks yelled *Oi ref you're a wanker*
As loudly as the crew down Cold Blow Lane –
As wild, as leonine and as insane.
Surprisingly, the Spartans won the prize
For good behaviour, though this could be lies:
More likely, when they saw they could not win
They kicked the opposition's chariots in.
A Christian emperor banned it as a cult
Because his team could not get a result.

II Dignified

On grim estates at dawn, on college tracks,
In rings, in wheelchairs, velodromes and pools,
While we snore on towards our heart attacks,
They will outstrip the bullet and the fax,
They will rewrite the body and its rules.

Athletes who amazed Zeus and Apollo,
Rivalling their supernatural ease,
Must make do nowadays with us, who follow,
Breathless, on a billion TVs.
Should we believe it's us they aim to please?

The purpose stays essentially the same:
To do what's difficult because they can,
To sign in gold an ordinary name
Across the air from Georgia to Japan,
To change the world by mastering a game.

The rest of us, left waiting at the start,
Still celebrate, as those the gods adore
Today stake everybody's claims for more
By showing life itself becoming art,
Applauded by a planetary roar –

The gun, the clock, the lens, all testify
That those who win take liberties with time:
The sprinter's bow, the vaulter's farewell climb,
The swimmer who escapes her wake, deny
What all the gods insist on, that we die.

4. Football! Football! Football!

My sporting life (may I refer to me?)
Was never all it was supposed to be.
Mine was a case of talent unfulfilled.
I blame society, which blames my build.

From trap and pass and backheel in the yard
To deskbound middle age is something hard
For the Eusebio of '64
To grasp: you don't play football any more.

Your boots and kit are all gone into dust
And your electric pace a thing of rust.
Whatever knocks the football fates inflict
On Shearer now, your chance of being picked

If England reach the Mondiale in France
(Does Umbro really make that size of pants?)
Is smaller than the risk of being brained
By frozen urine falling from a plane,

And though you'll stop by any rainy park
To watch folks kick a ball until it's dark
You don't expect Dalglish will seek you out
To ask you what the game is all about.

But more fool him, you secretly suspect:
You've seen the lot, from Crewe to Anderlecht,
From Gornik to Stranraer to River Plate,
The Cosmos and Montrose and Grampus Eight,

The Accies, Bochum, Galatasaray,
Finbogdottir, Dukla Prague (away),

Botafogo, Bury, Reggiana . . .
Football! Football! Football! Work? *Mañana.*

Sponsored by IKEA and by Andrex,
Butch in sacks or mincing on in Spandex,
The great, the mediocre, the pathetic,
Real Madrid and Raggy-Arse Athletic –

Twelve quid a week or fifty grand an hour,
The game retains the undiminished power
To stop the clock, accelerate the blood
And sort the decent geezer from the crud.

From 5-3-2 to Kaiser Franz libero
Is there a team formation you don't know?
Experience! There is no substitute
For working out why Andy Cole can't shoot.

The fields of dream and nightmare where the great
Line up beside the donkeys to debate
Who gets the league, the cup, the bird, the chop
And whether Coventry deserve the drop

Are graveyards of a century's desire
To keep the youth that sets the world on fire –
Pele's '58, Diego's '86,
And Puskas hushing Wembley with his tricks . . .

And back, and back, to James and Meredith
And all the tricky Welsh who took the pith,
Until West Auckland marmalize Juventus –
World on world through which the game has sent us,

Until at last we stand in some back lane.
You're Cantona but I'll be Best again.

Who gives a toss what any of it means
While there are Platinis and Dixie Deans?

There life is always Saturday, from three
Till *Sports Report*, as it's supposed to be,
The terrace in its shroud of freezing breath,
Hot leg, crap ref, a soft goal at the death,

Fags and Bovril, bus home, bacon sandwich –
Paradise in anybody's language
Is listening for the fate of Stenhousemuir
(Robbed by Brechin 27–4).

5. Amerika

The subtleties are wasted on the Yanks.
They like their football players built like tanks.
And find it hard to understand that skill
May well produce a scoreline of nil–nil.

A journalist in Minneapolis
Enquired, 'Hey, what kind of crap is this?'
The Majors' baseball strike had cancelled out
What all his summer columns were about.

And he'd been sent to see Bulgaria's
Brilliant but nefarious
Stoichkov–Lechkov–Kostadinov team
Punch holes in half of football's so-called cream –

Although this fact had somehow passed him by.
It seemed to his uneducated eye
This game was kind of complicated, weird
And somehow even longer than he'd feared.

'This thing', he said, 'has possibilities.
But let me tell you how it really is.
America means *short attention span*,
So let me run some changes past you, man.'

We want a wider goal, a bigger ball.
We want real bricks in the defensive wall.
We want the pitch divided into four
Plus fifteen time-outs making room for more

Commercials. That, my friend, 's what we call sport.'
Poor sod, one more imagination bought
And rented out to commerce as a site
Where money = nation = right.

It seemed from watching the Atlanta Games
Americans alone possess their names;
That those who came to represent elsewhere
Might just as well not bother being there.

Of course this wasn't a deliberate act,
But it revealed a national want of tact.
America exists to be the best:
And second's nowhere; second's for the rest.

But I remembered, while the strike was on,
How this friend's friend and I had one day gone
To watch a minor league game in the sticks –
A bunch of has-beens taking on the hicks.

That summer's end between two railroad yards
Were men whose lives were faded baseball cards,
Who wound it up and from their far-gone youth
Unleashed in dreams the balls that baffled Ruth,

Or hammered one past Nolan Ryan's ears –
The kind of thing a failure stands and cheers:
When all you are's a mortgage and a job
You'd like to kick the crap from Tyrus Cobb

Or pass Ted Williams' average by a street.
This is your other life, the short and sweet: –
The afternoon when you're DiMaggio
And some girl wants to meet you, called Monroe . . .

All that was just a trick played by the light,
But since then, if I have a sleepless night
I listen for the sound of far-off trains
Like those that carried teams across the plains –

To me they sound like poems in the air
By those who write their epics then and there:
An hour's enough for immortality,
And if they had to they'd still play for free.

Noonday

The sultry back lane smells of fruit and shit
While everybody's binbags wait, stacked up
Like corpses in the ditch before Byzantium,
Late morning on the last day in the world.
The sun stands in the heavens. One by one
The binbags split asunder to disgorge
White regiments of maggots seething quietly.
At Rhodes, the Knights concealed the engineer
Who fashioned them the leather stethoscope
That diagnosed the sappers in the walls;
But gave the Sultan's nephew back to death –
And what is there in this to understand?

Great Suleyman, the one men call Magnificent,
Let it be night. Now let us hear the owl
Calling in the towers of Afrasiab,
The spider spin in ixarette around the Porte
The caravels go home to Venice burning
And in a velvet bag the severed head
Be brought for your inspection. No reply.
So later, from the noonday heat, we come
To beg the shade and silence of an hour
In Suleyman's branch library at Rhodes,
A cool white cage five paces cross, where nothing
Dares to live or rot without his word.

Lines on Mr Porter's Birthday

Nowadays
People are worried by art-historical poems,
Made angry by musico-literary-critical poems,
And pissed off by serpentine dream-driven poems
With Audenesque spoilers and Browningesque trim.
Some are driven to spasms of spittle-flecked rage
By poems with bits of Italian or German left in,
And made to feel
Anxious and sweaty and dim
By poems regarding the past and the future as if they were real.
Nowadays 'people' say,
Porter? Oh, Porter, we cannot be doing with him.
He's too hard. It's elitist. It's not of this age.
When readers are ignorant, cowed and ashamed,
Appearing on film as a stammering blur
Which (due to a forthcoming court case) regrettably cannot be named,
When popular culture comes on like the Stasi
And the last decent mag is away down the khazi,
When it's all up with us, and the sky has gone black
And the gods will not, repeat not, no, never be back,
When all the above preconditions occur
And about the whole compass stretch oceans of shite,
When the sun has just offered the moon the third light
You may fairly suppose his prognosis was right.
Yet here in the meantime the poems of Porter
Enliven the cortex and flush the aorta,
Make wine-of-aesthetics from Westminster water.
The world may be doomed but the bugger can write.

Postcards to the Rain God

For Peter Didsbury on his fiftieth birthday

1

Pluvius shelters under the hawthorn
At the end of Reservoir Lane
In an old gaberdine and a cricket cap,
Listening intently
For that handful-of-thrown-gravel sound.
The hills have all vanished. Excellent, excellent.

2

With echoes drowning
In far-below darkness and silver,
Wedged on the slippery ladder
In rags in the stinking brick shaft
With his newspaper turning to papier mâché,
He drinks the drips
That fall from the manhole cover.

3

She stands for a moment in the florist's window
When lightning and downpour
Have emptied the lunch-hour street
And the sky has gone purple.
She looks out through a bouquet of wet bloody roses
She holds in a kid-gloved hand, smiling
At her own perfume, feeling wet silk on her skin
And biting her rose-coloured underlip.

4

The house has been up for sale for months.
An old legal family down to its uppers,
Haunting the rotten, trapdoored passageways,
Drowned in the mirror
The brother, the sisters, doolally, then dead,
With an orange-tree bursting the greenhouse.
Sad, very sad, intones the locality, watching.
You can't see him but he's there:
The after-downpour smell of shit and dockleaves
From the blindside of the fence.

5

The narrow brick foot-tunnel under the railway
Smells of rain and bonfires
And something else that might be sex.
Some of the oldest leaves in Northumberland
Lie there for the diversion of the rambler.

6

The bank on the corner of our street
Wears its impractical lead-cladded helmet
In honour of archers
Who practised in fourteenth-century rain
With blistered string-fingers
And anvils of cloud overhead.

7

When you are in the swimming bath
And it rains on the glass roof so loudly
You can hear above the swimmers' cries,
It is pornography.

8

Damp gravels on the landscaped bombsites
Where a long-term experiment (long enough
To see the life cycle of the Packamac)
Studies the transformation of asbestos prefabs (1947)
Into adipose and cancer. Rain doesn't help.
But think of the concrete made utile!
The slab-roads laid down as for Shermans and Churchills
Along the old drainsites –
Miles of straight and dry white lines
Up which the rain advances
Between the sheds of the allotments,
Gauzily, roaring.

9

To take ship.
The White Ship (not that one)
Clearing the mouth of the Hull,
The rebel banner raised
At the arsenal. Rain like grape-shot
Scalding the canvas. Below decks
Prince and poet, drinking Bastard,
Bowed to his diary of rain.

10

The field is much bigger than when you arrived.
The old gas, the old rain
Have come up from the ground towards teatime.
A Craven 'A' drizzle to greet them.
The girls have gone indoors
An hour ago in their ill-advised late-summer
Cottons and heels. Like peasants
You carry the posts home.
Split boot and wet arse,
And a shite-coloured dog to go with you.

11

You sit in your shed in the rain.
In its peppercorn racket
You have a much better idea:
Marks on paper, made from the pluvial sexual
Ink of the Iris and Pearson Park pond-rain.
Messages unread, a century
From now: *Today a cloudburst settling*
Its anvil on the slates,
Then longer, softer rain — I cannot tell you how —
Is like piano-islands
In the pond. Ad
Maiorem Pluvii gloriam.

Synopsis

In the small, the final, town of X,
If you should feel about to leave
The Home Guard will remove your brains.

You'll hear them turning up
With ladders and a stirrup-pump
Beneath your windows, pissed and shushing.

Next day you'll feel as if there's water
Trapped in your ears and walk dazedly round,
Tilting your head like the Persons of Mad

Who litter the place in a surplus of Heritage,
Taking you back to its ancient foundation
By lepers and saints, 'by the one river twice'.

Passing the doctor in the market square
You see him nod approvingly,
Brandishing a bag of crabs you might suppose

Extracted from the pubic hair of corpses.
You're bidden to dinner that evening.
God's in his Heaven, so he cannot help.

In spring you'll wed the doctor's daughter,
An asexual vampire type of a girl
With coathanger bones and one enormous

Middle tooth, which in another life
You might suppose was joking. As things stand
Your nights will all be ecstasy instead.

You will give up your job as a poet
To work in her dress hire shop –
Ballgowns for Walpurgisnacht,

Glass slippers, ropes of hair;
And in your evenings as a potman mutter
Cryptic, hopeless warnings to the next

Poor sod whose train has left him here
As it left you, although you won't remember.
If you're lucky he might read you this.

Ex Historia Geordisma

a sorrowful conspectus

I. *from* The Go-As-You-Please Songbook

'Tha divvent sweat much for a fat lass, hinny'
ST CUTHBERT THE SPOT-WELDER

'Lyric poetry is not possible after Darlington'
MURDO (YOUR CHIEF STEWARD THIS MORNING)

The A66 in Cumbria was blocked for several hours today by early medieval warfare.

The reason for the collapse of Germany in 1945, said Geoffroi, fingering his Hornby coal-tender, was the diversion of so many troops to assist with the removal and transport from galleries and palaces, east or west, of gold, art treasures *et cetera*. Hence also the congestion of the railways. *Mint!*

The holly; the ash; the bale-fire; the birch; the stony scriptorium; the critics; the stotties; prayer-frost and repentance; bring back the birch, for the sons of birches. *I'm with you now*, said Biffa. *Canny.*

II. *from* The Poems of Mercedes Medioca

A Fruit

'Jesmondo! Mondo Jesmondo!'
         El Canto Jesmondo

Hand me that banana now.
The great big blue one on the shelf.

Behind the scrim
And the cinnabar yoni

And the hostas. Look,
Look. Are you blind? Over *there*.

Give me that blue banana now
That I may ease myself

And think of entire
Historical periods.

You do not – *hélas* –
You do not understand.

You, a mere man,
How can you grasp the banana,

You who do not like it up you,
Eh?

III. Seriously, Like

Winter again with the forces of Northern reaction,
Vanguard of the 'bitter' ampersand,
The marmoreal slash.
The Modernist incontinence!
Pale scolds with posh addresses,
Still more Socialist than you, like.
The little presses fold away like trousers,
Dead men's trousers with the hanged
Tongues sticking out. *For in my Father's house*
Are many trousers. All shall be
Donated to await the gratitude.
Let a filing cabinet be named for this
And launched at Monkwearmouth
At nightfall with torches.
The corpse of the erstwhile promoter
Delays in the mouth of the Tyne
That underlined remark that changes everything,
L'esprit d'escalier sousmarin.
Shall these bones live? – Not
If we can help it, Sonny. Not round here.

Poem for a Psychiatric Conference

'Thou thyself art the subject of my discourse.'
BURTON, preface to *The Anatomy of Melancholy*

'Melancholy is . . . the character of mortality.'
BURTON, 'The First Partition'

I

When Marsyas the satyr played and lost
Against the god Apollo on the pipes,
The god lacked magnanimity. He skinned
The howling creature to his bones and tripes,
There in the nightmare canvas by Lorraine
Arcadia is green, and deaf to pain.

II

You were staring, one teatime, into the sink
When the voice made its awful suggestion. It seems
You were really, or ought to be, somebody else
In a different house, with a different wife –
May I speak plainly? the voice enquired.
It glozed, like the serpent in Milton –
Turned out for *years* you'd been making it up:
The kitchen, for one thing, the tiles and the draining-board,
Drawing-pinned postcards and lists of to-do's,
Even the crap round the back of the freezer.
The evidence *after all spoke for itself.*
The view up the steps to the garden, for instance,
The lawn with its slow-worm, the ruinous glasshouse

Up at the top, where the hurricane left it half-standing.
The woman next door as she pinned out her washing.
The weathercock's golden irregular wink
In the breeze from the sea to its twin on the spire
A mile off. Besides, the grey Channel itself
Setting out for the end of the world
Was the wrong stretch of water beside the wrong town.
You stood with your hands in your pockets and waited.
Very well, then, the God in the details disclosed:
Bus-tickets, receipts, phone numbers of people
You shouldn't have met in the pub
At the wrong time of day, the wrong year
With the wrong block of sunlight to stand
In the doorway. Your tread on the stair-carpet:
Wrong. You skin between the freezing sheets
At dusk: an error. No matter the cause.
There is error, but not correspondingly cause.

III

The name of your case is *depression*
Although Doctor Birmingham favours
A failure of nerve. The files on the desk
In his office are fifty years old
And he, it seems, is just pretending
That he works here, sharing your gloom
And your startled gaze at the slice
Of bitter-green grass where a bottle
Keeps rolling about in the wind
At the top of the city, where everything –
Buildings, the streetmap, the people –
Has run out of steam and delivered the ground
To an evil Victorian madhouse

Complete with cupola and coalhole
Which may or may not have shut down,
Though the bus shelter waits at the gate.
The overcooked smell is like weeping,
The cries are like nursery food
And the liverish paint on the wailing walls
Is a blatant incitement to stop being good.
Call for Nurse Bromsgrove and Sir Stafford
Wolverhampton, call Rugeley the Porter.
There are vast misunderstandings
Lurking in the syntax by the stairs.
The worst of it is, there are rooms
Not far off, waiting and book-filled
For someone like you to arrive and possess them;
A hedge at the window, and lilacs, and past them
A street that can take a whole morning
To saunter downhill past the flint walls and ginnels
Adding up to harmless privacy. This perhaps
Is what some of the mad people contemplate,
Reading their hands on a bench in the park
In their ill-fitting clothes, as if someone must come
To explain and restore and say *Put that behind you*.

The Railway Sleeper

We are entering *L'Angleterre profonde*, which does not exist. We apologize for any delay and for the inconvenience history may have caused to your journey. On leaving the train please ensure you are completely possessed.

1

This was a siding or maybe even the entrance to a spur. Coal wagons rested here for weeks during winter strikes or in the overnight panic when the Luftwaffe breached the main inbound line. You could look it up. There are archives and historical maps.

Somewhere a ceramic map is mounted on a lost brick wall which is no longer understood to be part of a station. It has been part of a school, a bookshop, a restaurant, and now it is nothing especially and looks out on nothing. It is not part of its own map: the remembered smoke goes by on the other side of the hill, in the next valley, in different livery, its passengers eating different pies and drinking different brands of beer. A mad old bloke is seeking out such facts even as this sentence forms: what he needs next is an audience, this man you may become.

2

White sky of a summer evening. A green light waits at the entrance. No one up at Fat Control has bothered to switch it off. Meanwhile the roadbed vanishes slowly under willowherb, dock, the moraine of mud and grit sliding back into the cutting. The metaphysics of material culture.

3

The old come here to walk their dogs, the young to fuck each
other, the middle aged to fuck their dogs. It is a sex landscape,
the far edge of legitimacy, the last ditch where fences turn to paper,
boundaries waver and goats are secretly housed among the
hawthorn scrub. A site of penetration, excretion and
unrecognizable objects, or of objects inexplicably deformed, such
as a briefcase full of concrete. What a story that could tell! if its
mouth were not full of concrete. This is a branch of railway
land, cousin to the sunset pang as the lines divide at York, or the
much-abridged viaducts of Leeds, or the vast white elephant of
Liverpool Edge Hill – that sexual warehouse and carpark.

4

The train and its landscape, you must understand, is a sex. An
iron sex, an oil sex, a coal sex, weed-dripping-bottom-of-the-
sandstone-cutting sex, the red-raw backbroken sex of exhausted
navvies and their whores, and the choked sex of collapsed
embankments, earthworks of the 1840s. This is the sex of
modernity: lost to us now; the language and the gestures of blood,
iron, crusty upholstery, leather window-straps, and twelve-inch
toppers full of concrete.

5

The Omar Pound. The Elaine Jackson. The Cushie Butterfield.
The Grave Maurice. The Trial to His Family. The Bring Me
the Head of Dr Beeching. These are some possible names, possibly
archived by the aforementioned head-the-ball for the great steam
revival when we step back in tight formation, following the
railwaymen's silver band, down the cutting into the smoke of
the nineteenth century under light rifle fire from the tribesmen.
We are retching, lousy and spavined by rickets, but strangely
happy, listening later at the tunnel's mouth for oracles of rich
disaster.

6

I am lying in bed when the train goes by – on summer nights,
that blue sound, like remembering an unlived life. And another, and
another, audible here at the triangle's centre. Promises, promises.
The fulfilment of desire on the chilly evening sands of far-off
resorts where the fathers parade with their shirt collars flattened
on their lapels and the mothers say it's getting on Ted and you
suppose it is, though you're not Ted. You're you, just listening.
Cacophonous plumbing awaits you. The sexual creak. The fart
of unbuttoned self-regard. The sound of waves, of trains; the
silence of the blue night that frames them.

7

Nobody knows what desire is: a train brings you to the threshold
with a suitcase and your sister, with your preoccupied parents.
Desire is a street opening for the first time as you walk: gasholder,
graveyard, pie shop, cobbler's, church, the ribbed fishermen's
terraces climbing back into black and green woods. *Thalassa!*
Thalassa! Railways! Railways!

8

No one knows what desire is. It is here and not here. Running
down the steps to the beach as the tide pulls back under fog you
feel belated. A train is crossing the long bridge over the narrow
neck of the bay. The curtains of the great hotel are drawn, its
alpine gardens shrivelled with salt.

9

A man with rusty hands has strained for fifty years to shift the
points. In his back pocket waits a piece of paper with a word
written on it in dried-blood copperplate: *homoerotic*. Neither of
you would know what it meant. Around him the ashy fields of
sidings are afire after sunset. Yonder lies Ferrybridge, lies
Castleford. He bends like a reaper to his task. He serves the sea
by sweating there so far inland after the sea trains have gone.

10

A woman draws the curtains, turns from the window and leaves the room but comes back to peer out again at the line that runs at the end of the garden. It is a long evening in late summer, the heavy blueness hanging everywhere, and visible among the branches the one green eye.

11

It may be that I lie upstairs, unsleeping at this very moment, sent to bed at summer's end, in the last thick light, *A la Recherche* Volume One abandoned on the counterpane in favour of this English reverie, so intimate that England seems abroad. The smell of heat and rot beneath mown grass. A frog on the garden path. A creosoted shed settles minutely towards the ruin it will meet long after its owner's death. And round its head-high hand-carpentered shelves wait box upon box of locos, tenders, carriages and wagons; cardboard boxes, their angles and edges worn down to reveal the gingery weave of their stiff cardboard; boxes driven out to the end of the garden by a female disapproval that despises things for merely being things, or details, or imitations of serious objects.

12

Wrexham. Gentlemen. Do Not Cross the Line. Kein Trinkwasser.
Penalty Forty Shillings: By-laws of the Railway: these letters in
cast-iron relief, brick-red on range-black, stolen themselves along
with their supporting posts and borne away (but how? on a
crossbar? by barge up the silty, corpse-rich canals which are the
ghost-twin Abels to the Cain of rail?) to a backyard in Thirsk,
a growing collection of rail-realia in Coalville, a carpark in
Hinckley, a salt-rotted lean-to in Millom. Our barmy old party
is writing everything down, amanuensis to an abolished god with
wings of fire, a surveyor's telescope and a black top hat. Railway
flora: scorched dock and desiccated willowherb; crisp groundsel
for Billy the budgie.

13

In the tallest heaven, a frost of summer stars. Below, black
branches against blue air. The train is coming but I have to sleep.
The mouth of the sleeper silently opens. There is the faintest
breath like the suspicion of a train entering the far end of a long
tunnel, one of those Pennine epic glitter-black inner spaces,
consecrated to the drip of *Urmutterfurcht*. There is nothing to be
afraid of yet.

The Genre: A Travesty of Justice

For Jo Shapcott

'The Porter found the weapon and the glove,
But only our despair can find the creed.'
          DEMETRIOS CAPETANAKIS, 'Detective Story'

Chapter One

Do we live in small murderous towns
Where history has ended up?
Under their grubby insignia,
Summed up by mottoes
In greengrocer Latin? Do we reside
In the abolished Thridding? Have we always?

Were our towns constructed
From coal or manure, as kaufmanndorf
Or jakes, at a trivial confluence,
By deadly caprice (*oh let it be he-ere*)?
Divined in scripture? Destined
To defeat the understanding?

Are ours the homicidal sticks
In whose early spring evenings
Armies of policemen go down on their knees
In the scrub by the taken-up sidings?
Or do they peer from the edge of gravel pits
At frogmen who shake their slow heads,

Pointing like embarrassed Grendels
To a larder paved with torsos?
Do we answer these questions

Without taking legal instruction?
Can we not see how the trap is left
Open to claim us, the blatant device,

The traditional fit-up? Can we
Be what the atlas has in mind,
Twelve miles from a regional centre
With adequate links to the coast
And a history of gloving and needles
And animal products?

Is this the back of our station,
The clogging stink of the tannery yard,
And are these our gnats in suspension
Above the canal, and this our melancholy
Born of contiguity and quiet,
Whose poets are not very good?

Is this the poet? The immense
And anxious-making egg of his head?
His vast squirearchical torso?
His air of always being somewhere
Else in spirit as he turns
To hold your gaze a moment

And discard it? Is the poet
Here tending his irony, making a phrase
With the same offhand stylishness
Seen when he's chalking his cue
Or admiring the sheen of his waistcoat
In the smoke-filled mirror

In the afternoon hall, unfussily
Clearing the colours? And are those
His friends the police, who salute

With their pints, and not for the first time
Declare he's too clever by half?
Is this the poet? Well, is it?

Chapter Four

Clocks, clocks, what about clocks?
What about all those station clocks
Ticking away like tyranny prophesied
In waiting-rooms whose stolid old benches
Spend for ever trying not to fart
And the ghosts of governesses wait
To be apprised, abused, sent
Packing with never a penny? Tick.
Afternoons. Seasons. Epochs. Tick,
A railway age in Bradshaw's hell.
Cold spring sunshine. The random
Brambly lash of the March rain. Tick.
The immortal half-length clocks,
Complacent moustachioed minor gods
Of the up-line, the down-line,
The sinister spur to the quarry,
The girls' school, the old place
The army had out in the woods. Tick.
When you are dead the clocks will step out
On the platforms and wink at each other
Before you go by, with your throats cut,
One per compartment, blood smeared
On the strap of the window, the photo of Filey,
Your faces, your crusty good coats, the matching
Crimson carriage cloth. Stiletto heels of blood
Tick away down the corridors. These trains
Are special. Tick. Their schedule is secret,

Their platform remote from the roar
Of the great vaulted terminus. Tick. They are coming
To get you one dim afternoon
With a John Dickson Carr in your bag
And a packet of three, or a cake for your auntie.

Chapter Five

I am the one you've been looking for,
The singular first person
Here at the death.
                    The square-ended shout
Has gone up from the stand,
So the Duchess's Cup has raced
Into the records again
In a thunder of wall-eyed no-hopers
And foul-mouthed effeminate midgets in silk,
While round at the back of it all, in the sheds,
Among mowers and oildrums, down on my knees
In a doorway of sunlit Victorian dust,
I done it. I mean, I done *this* one.
I lie in my caravan, feeling it rock
On its bricks by the abattoir. Windy.
I'm scanning *Reveille* for creatures like me,
The bad apples of Lustgarten's eye,
From the class that has feeble excuses and onanists' tremors,
The work-shy, enthralled by America,
Reached by race-music picked up at the fair
With the clap and the ravenous
Oil-based charm that makes us at home
Among engines in pieces and under the skirts
Of your daughters. Our sort are barbers
And butchers gone bad

From a failure of deference.
I do hope you're writing this down
And ignoring my fraudulent idioms.
They look for a soldier. They fancy a Yank
Off the airbase. So let them.
Come rain on the roof, come wind,
I lie here and rock. I'm awful. I've sinned.

TO BE CONTINUED

From *Inferno*

(2006)

Canto III

The Entry to Hell

'Beyond me lies a city full of pain.
Beyond me you will meet eternal grief.
Beyond me lie the souls of all the lost.

It was justice moved my holy maker.
It was the power of God that shaped me so,
His wisdom and His great creating love.   6

Before me all that He created were
Eternal things. I am likewise eternal.
Enter now: abandon every hope.'

I read these words engraved in sombre shades
Across the lintel of Hell's gate, and said:
'This is a cruel sentence. Please explain.'   12

Virgil replied as one who understands:
'You must abandon all your terrors now.
Here every kind of cowardice must die.

Now, as I promised, we have reached the place
Where you will see those wretched souls who lost
The intellectual power to believe.'   18

And saying this he took me by the hand
And looked at me with kind encouragement,
Then led me down among the secret ways.

Immediately sighs and sobs and shrill laments
Resounded through the dark and starless air.
When first I heard them, I began to weep.   24

In that swart climate time itself had stopped.
Strange languages and terrifying words,
Low mutterings of pain and bursts of rage,

Shrill far-off cries and sounds of beating hands
Whipped up a whirling, never-ceasing mass,
As sea-tornadoes strip the bed of sand.   30

My head began to swim and I cried out:
'Master, tell me what this noise is! Tell me
Who these people are that feel such pain!'

The poet said: 'This is the miserable fate
Of wretched souls deserving neither
Praise nor blame but mere indifference.   36

Swept up with them we find that wicked gang,
Those angels who would side with neither God
Nor Lucifer, but stood apart and watched.

Since Heaven may not grow less beautiful,
God casts them down, but not to deepest Hell,
Because the damned would glory in them there.'   42

I asked, 'But, master, what can cause the grief
That makes these creatures weep so bitterly?'
'Let me explain it briefly,' Virgil said.

'These sinners know they have no hope of death.
Their blind existence is so far debased
That they must envy any other state.   48

The world will not allow their memory
To live. They are disdained by justice as
By mercy. Say no more, but look: and go.'

When I stared back, I saw a banner raised.
It swept so quickly on and flapped so hard
It seemed that it could never come to rest,   54

And flowing under it there came a crowd,
So long and vast that I could not believe
That death had ever claimed so many lives.

Among the mass were some I recognized –
And one stood out immediately. I knew
That this was Pilate who refused his word.   60

And then I grasped the crowd's identity:
These endless walkers were the dismal sect
Despised by God, and by God's enemies.

These wretches who had failed to live their lives
Went naked and were stung continually
By wasps and hornets which encircled them,   66

So that their faces ran with streams of blood
Which, mingling with their tears, dripped on their feet,
Where yellow maggots seethed among the pus.

Then next, when I looked further on, I saw
A host of shadows on a mighty river's bank,
At which I said, 'Dear master, may I know   72

Who these grim figures are, and by what law
They wait so anxiously to take their turn
To cross – for so it seems in this dim light?'

And he replied: 'All this will be made clear
When we arrive, for we shall have to pause
Beside the bitter river known as Acheron.'   78

Afraid that I had given him offence,
For some time then I did not meet his gaze.
Nor did I speak until we reached the bank.

Imagine, though, the sight that greeted me –
A boat hove into shore and at the helm
An ancient white-haired man roared out: 'Despair!   84

Lost souls, no heaven awaits you here!
I come to ship you to the further shore's
Eternity of darkness, fire and ice.

But you there, yes, you still appear to live:
Now step aside. Don't wait among the dead.'
Then, when he saw me hesitate, he called: 90

'You chart a different course. A different port
Must welcome you to land. The craft that comes
To carry you is lighter than my own.'

My guide called back: 'Now, Charon, calm yourself:
This matter has been settled by the will
That wills the world. That's all you need to know.'   96

Although his eyes were Catherine-wheels of flame,
When Virgil spoke, the pilot of the marsh
Fell silent. Then he set his white-haired jaw.

But all those weary, naked, waiting souls
Had overheard the ferryman's harsh words
And they grew paler still and ground their teeth.   102

They cursed the Name of God, their parents too,
The human race itself, the place, the time,
The seed they sprang from and their very birth –

And then in one great weeping crowd they came
To flood the shore damnation has reserved
For all those souls who lack the fear of God.   108

The demon Charon, with his eyes like coals,
Then summons each to take his place aboard
And clubs the laggards with his dripping oar:

As in the autumn leaf must follow leaf
Inexorably one by one until
The parent branch can see itself stripped bare,   114

So Adam's wicked offspring hurl themselves
Successively from shore into the boat,
Like hawks returning to the master's hand,

So they depart across the inky marsh.
Meanwhile, before the one crowd disembarks,
Another gathers, waiting in its turn.   120

'My son,' my courteous master then explained,
'All those who perish in God's holy wrath
Are gathered here, from end to end of earth.

When they arrive they long for Charon's boat.
It is God's justice drives these sinners on:
It turns their very fear into desire.   126

But only damned souls ever pass this way,
And so when Charon seeks to turn you back,
You understand the reason for his words.'

My guide fell silent. Then the darkened plain
Shook with such force that even to recall
My terror makes me sweat as I write this.   132

Out of that plain of tears a wind rose up
And with it came a blast of crimson light
That stunned my shaken senses utterly.

I fell, like someone sleep has overwhelmed.

Canto VIII

Crossing the Styx

Let me continue. Long before we neared
The foot of this great tower, my gaze was drawn
Towards its distant summit, on whose heights

Two tiny flames were placed; still further off,
So faintly that the eye could scarcely see,
Another blinked a message in return.   6

I asked my wise companion Virgil,
'What do they mean, these fires? And that response?
Who sends these signals out?' And he replied:

'What they are summoning is on its way
Already, out among that filthy swell.
Perhaps the marsh-fogs hide it from your eyes.'   12

No arrow left the bow or cut the air
As swiftly as the craft that came in sight
The very moment Virgil mentioned it,

And as it flew towards us I could see
Its single steersman, and could hear him yell:
'Yes, evil spirit! Yes, I have you now!'   18

'Phlegyas, Phlegyas!' my master called.
'You sail in vain. You'll have our company
No longer than it takes to cross this swamp.'

Like someone told of a deception who
Discovers that the victim is himself,
The boatman muttered, full of bitter wrath.   24

My master climbed aboard the little ship,
Then summoned me to follow: only then
Did Phlegyas' vessel seem to bear a load.

The moment that the pair of us embarked,
His ancient craft set sail, though now it rode
Much lower in the water than before.   30

Then, midway down that channel of the dead,
A figure thick with mud rose up and called:
'Who are you? You have come before your time.'

I said: 'We are not planning to remain.
But, underneath this foulness, who are you?'
And he replied: 'I am a man that weeps.'   36

'In weeping and in sorrow you must stay,
Polluted spirit, for your suit of filth
Does not prevent me recognizing you.'

He reached out with both hands towards the boat
But then my skilful master beat him off
And cried: 'Stay there with all the other curs!'   42

Virgil placed his arms around my neck
And kissed me and declared: 'O righteous soul,
Great blessings on the mother who bore you!

This man was arrogance personified.
Since memory records no good of him,
His shade must linger here consumed with rage –   48

While many others who are living now
And think themselves great kings shall stand like pigs
In their manure, remembered with contempt!'

'My Master,' I replied, 'now I should like
To see him marinated in this broth
Before we end our crossing of the lake.'   54

He said, 'Before the other side's in sight
You'll find your wishes satisfied. It is
Appropriate that your request be met.'

The sinner's fellow creatures tore him limb
From limb, a scene of such ferocity
I thank the Lord who let me see it all.   60

They roared: 'Get Filippo Argenti!' Then
The shade of that rage-maddened Florentine
Joined in and ripped his own flesh with his teeth.

We left him there. I say no more of him,
But from astern his howling followed us,
So that I turned and fixed my gaze ahead.   66

The master said, 'My son, we now approach
The city known to men as Dis, with all
Its sober citizens and men at arms.'

'I can already see its mosques,' I cried,
'Down there, within that valley, glowing red
As if new-forged and lifted from the flames.'   72

'Within the city,' Virgil said, 'there are
Eternal fires burning. That is why
They wear that rosy glow here in Deep Hell.'

We came at last along the dismal moats
By which the doleful city was entrenched,
And now I saw the walls were ironclad.   78

We seemed to circumnavigate the place
Before the ferryman came in to shore
And growled. 'Here is the landing. Disembark.'

A thousand angels flung from heaven stood
Above the gate and angrily cried out:
'Now who is this who dares – while he still lives –   84

To travel through the kingdom of the dead?'
And my wise master made a sign to them
To indicate that they should talk apart –

At this they said, controlling their disdain,
'Then come alone, but let the other leave,
The one who trespassed here so daringly.   90

Let him retrace his ill-considered steps.
Or let him try. And as for you who served
As escort on his journey here, you stay.'

Imagine, reader: I grew sick at heart.
When I heard these accursed words it seemed
That I should never find our world again.   96

'My faithful leader, seven times and more
You have restored my confidence and saved
My soul from every danger on the road,

Now let me not be lost like this,' I said.
'If further progress is forbidden us
Then let us quickly leave the way we came.'   102

The guide who after all had brought me there
Replied: 'There is no need to be afraid.
The One we serve will clear a path for us.

Wait here for me, and let your spirit rest,
And feed it with the comfort of good hope,
For I shall not abandon you in Hell.'   108

With this my gentle master walks away
And leaves me there, still troubled with my doubts,
As 'yes' and 'no' contend inside my mind.

I could not hear whatever he proposed,
But barely had they met before the whole
Vast crowd of demons scrambled back inside.   114

Our adversaries slammed the massive gates
Closed in the gentle poet's face, and then
He walked back slowly down the shore to me.

His eyes were downcast and his face had lost
Its boldness, and his words came in a sigh:
'Who bars my passage through the house of pain?'   120

He said to me: 'You must not be dismayed
By my frustration. I shall overcome
Whatever they contrive to keep us out.

This insolence of theirs is nothing new.
They tried before at a less secret gate,
Which ever since has stood without a lock: 126

You saw the dread inscription on that door.
Someone is now descending towards this deep
And passes unescorted through the zones:

He will admit us to the city soon.'

Canto XIII

The Wood of the Suicides

The centaur had not crossed the stream again
When we set out into a stretch of woods
In which there was no path to lead the way.

No green leaves grew here, only ashen husks
On pockmarked boughs that wound themselves in knots
Whose only fruit was poison-bearing thorn: 6

Not even those ungovernable beasts
Who roam between Cecina and Corneto
Favour undergrowth as rough as this –

For here is where the loathsome Harpies nest,
Who drove the Trojans from the Strophades
With dismal prophecies of doom in store.   12

They have broad wings and human necks and heads
And feathered, bloated bellies and they roost
Among the rotten trees to shriek laments.

'Before we venture further,' Virgil said,
'Remember, this is now the second ring,
Which lasts until we reach the dreadful sand: 18

Now study your surroundings carefully.
See for yourself what I shall not describe.
If I should try, you would insist I lied.'

Around me echoed wail on wail of grief,
Yet there was no one there to give it voice.
I stopped then, out of sheer bewilderment.   24

It seems my master thought that I believed
That all the voices calling in the wood
Belonged to people who were hidden there.

He told me then: 'What you must do is break
A little twig from any of these trees,
And then your train of thought will break off too.'   30

Therefore I raised my hand a little way
And snapped a twig of thorn off as he said.
The trunk cried out: 'Why must you injure me?

We too were men, but we are changed to wood.
I swear you'd lay a kinder hand on us
If we had been the crawling souls of snakes!'   36

And just as when one end of a green log's
Ablaze, the hissing sap and oxygen
Come bubbling from the other, so I watched

As from the broken branch ran mingled blood
And words. I threw the little twig aside
And stood immobile, horribly afraid.   42

'If Dante had been able to believe
The teaching of my poetry alone,
Then he would not have laid a hand on you.

But since your fate defies belief,' my master said,
'There was no choice except to cause you pain.
I know your suffering. It weighs on me.   48

But tell him who you were: to make some small
Amends, he may revive your fame on earth,
Since he will be permitted to return.'

The branch replied: 'Your gentle speech holds such
Allure that silence is beyond me: please
Forgive me if I speak a little while.   54

In life when I was keeper of the keys
To Frederick's heart, I turned them to unlock
Or seal again, with such soft subtlety

That I excluded almost everyone,
While my devotion to high office grew
So great I robbed myself of sleep and life.   60

The whore whose lustful gaze is always fixed
On Caesar's dwelling-place, the common death
And the immortal vice of courts, inflamed

The common mass of hearts to enmity –
And this ignited Caesar's wrath: so then
My world's bright honour charred to mourning black. 66

My spirit, feeding on its own disdain,
Believing death would free me from my shame,
Provoked me to a crime against myself:

But by this tree's new roots I swear to you
That never once did I betray my lord,
One man who does deserve the world's esteem.   72

If ever you regain the earth above
Give comfort to my memory, that suffers
Even now the blow that envy dealt.'

After a pause, my poet said to me,
'Now he is silent, do not miss the chance
To question him in detail – if you wish.'   78

'Ask him about the things I need to know,'
I said. 'I find myself incapable.
The simple weight of pity holds me back.'

'Incarcerated spirit,' Virgil said,
'So may this man do freely what you ask,
Explain, please, if you will, the means by which   84

The ruined soul is bound into these knots
And then, if possible, reveal to us
If any soul has ever freed itself.'

The branch responded with a hiss: the sound
Was then translated into human speech:
'The answer you are looking for is brief.   90

When the infuriated soul departs
The living flesh – if it uproots itself –
Then Minos hurls it down the seventh pit

Where it falls randomly into this wood –
Mere fortune will dictate its landing place –
Takes root and springs up like a grain of wheat   96

Into a shoot, and then a woody plant,
While Harpies, feeding on its leaves, provide
Both pain and means of giving pain a voice.

Like all the rest, we shall reclaim our flesh,
But we shall never dress in it again:
What we have stolen from ourselves is lost.   102

Then we shall drag our corpses here, to hang
In this despairing wood, each on the thorn
That grows now from the soul that murdered it.'

We listened most intently to the branch,
Believing that it still had more to add,
Until another sound distracted us.   108

Imagine times when first you hear the boars
And then the hunt itself approach your post –
You track the beasts by every branch they break:

So from our left there ran two naked men,
Both cut to ribbons, scrambling so fast
They snapped off every branch that blocked their way.   114

The one in front yelled: 'Hurry, death! Be quick!'
The other, slower runner cried: 'Your legs
Were not so nimble in the jousts at Toppo!'

And then, perhaps because his wind was gone,
This second, slower fugitive lay down
Inside a thorn-bush, seeking camouflage.   120

The wood behind them – in a moment – filled
With slim intent black dogs who'd been half-starved
Before their master let them off the leash.

They sank their teeth into the hidden man
And working as a team dismembered him,
Then dragged away the still-tormented limbs.   126

My master led me by the hand towards
The grieving bush. We heard its lamentations
Pouring vainly from its many wounds. 'O

Giacomo di Santo Andrea!' it cried out.
'What help was it to use me as a screen?
What has your guilty life to do with me?'   132

My master paused beside the bush and asked:
'Who were you in the world, that now you speak
So bloodily and from so many wounds?'

The thorn-bush then replied: 'O souls, you come
In time to see my very branches stripped
Of every leaf in shame and violence.   138

Please gather them and leave them at my foot.
The founding patron of my home was Mars,
Whom we replaced with John the Baptist: thus

The war-god grieves us, always, with his art.
And if some trace of him did not remain
Beside the Arno, those proud Florentines   144

Who built their city once again, upon
The ashes of Attila's rage, must then
Have found their civic labours all in vain.

And I? I made a gibbet of my house.'

Canto XVII

Geryon; the Usurers

'Now see the monster with the pointed tail,
Who soars above the mountains, smashing walls
And weaponry, infecting the whole world!'

Thus my master spoke to me, and meanwhile
Beckoned to the beast to come ashore
Out where the rocky pathway reached its end.   6

That foul embodiment of fraud swam in
And beached his head and chest along the bank
But left his scaly tail to hang in space.

His face was like an honourable man's,
Its skin the image of benevolence.
His trunk, though, was entirely serpentine,   12

His arms, from paw to oxter, thick with hair,
His breast and back and both his sides adorned
With painted galls and circlets. Neither Turk

Nor Tartar ever wove brocades with tones
And patterning and background depth like these;
Nor could Arachne match them at her loom.   18

Just as a boat will sometimes lie inshore,
Half beached and half afloat, just as among
The gluttonous Alemanni you find

The beaver sitting ready to wage war,
So this, the vilest of all beasts, lay there
Upon the rim of stone that bounds the sand,   24

While his great tail was quivering in the void
Or stabbing upwards with the poisoned fork
That arms it like a scorpion at its tip.

'We must continue now,' my leader said,
'A little further. Therefore let us walk
Towards that evil creature crouching there.'   30

Descending on the right-hand side, we took
Ten steps along the verge in order to avoid
The burning sand and ever-raining flames.

Then when we reached the beast, there came in sight
A little further on another group,
Who sat there on the black gulf's very edge.   36

And now my master said, 'In order that
You understand the nature of this ring
In full, approach these men and learn their plight.

But keep your conversation with them brief,
And in the meantime I will ask the beast
To lend his mighty shoulders to our task.'   42

And so I went alone, still further down
The far edge of the seventh circle, where
These wretched men were seated, wracked with grief

That seemed to burst out through their very eyes
As they attempted to defend themselves
Bare-handed from the flames and burning ground,   48

As dogs in summer lash out with their paws
Or nip themselves when maddened by the bite
Of fleas and horse-flies and mosquitoes.

When I looked on the faces of these men
On whom that grievous fire falls, I found
That there were none that I could recognize,   54

But from the neck of each there hung a pouch,
Uniquely coloured, with its own device,
And each man seemed to feast his eyes on this.

And when I moved among them, looking round,
A yellow purse displayed an azure sign
That bore a lion's form and countenance,   60

And going further on to look again
I came across a further purse, blood-red,
That bore the image of a snowy goose.

Then one of them, whose pure white wallet showed
A pregnant sow in azure, called to me:
'You there, what are you doing in this ditch?   66

Be on your way. And since you're still alive,
Hear this: my townsman Vitaliano's
Due here soon to sit on my left hand.

I am a Paduan, stuck with Florentines
Who deafen me with their incessant noise.
They cry: "Now let the sovereign knight appear   72

And bring the purse whose image is three goats!" '
Then with a grimace he stuck out his tongue,
Just like an ox that wants to lick its nose.

Afraid to anger Virgil, who had warned
That I should only stay a little while
With these exhausted souls, I took my leave.   78

I found my leader waiting there astride
The back of the fierce beast. He said to me:
'Have courage and be strong. From this point on

We shall descend by means of stairs like these.
Climb up in front – I wish to sit between
So that the monster's tail does you no harm.'   84

Then like a man with quartan when his fit
Draws near, so that his fingernails turn white,
And shade can make him shiver head to toe,

I trembled when I heard him speak these words,
But shame, which makes a servant brave when faced
With his good master, caught and steadied me.   90

I climbed those ugly shoulders and I meant
To say: 'Hold tight to me!' except the words
Remained unspoken on my frozen tongue,

But Virgil, who had often succoured me
In danger, when I mounted up took hold
With both his arms and settled me, and said,   96

'So, Geryon, it is time to move. Be sure
To make your circles wide; let your descent
Be slow: remember your unusual load.'

Just as a vessel setting out will leave
The quay stern-first, so Geryon drew back
And when he felt that he was in the clear   102

Reversed himself in space. Then, stretching out
His tail, he played it like a swimming eel
And with his paws he gathered in the air.

I do not think that there was greater fear
When Phaëthon let the horses' reins slip loose
So that the sky was scorched, as it remains,   108

Or when the wretched Icarus first felt
His limbs unfeathered by the melting wax
And heard his father cry: 'Wrong way! Wrong way!'

Than I felt then. On every side I found
There lay mere air, in which the only thing
That I could see was Geryon himself.   114

And on he swims and slowly, slowly, wheels,
And sinks, but I can tell this only from
The wind that rushes up into my face.

Beneath us on our right now I could hear
A whirlpool's fearful roaring, and at this
I leaned out from my seat and looked below,   120

And then my fear of the descent increased –
For I could see the flames and hear laments,
At which I trembled, holding tighter still

But saw now what I had not seen before,
The steady, wheeling course of the descent,
The evils which approached on every side.   126

Just as a falcon – long upon the wing
Without a sight of lure or bird, which makes
The falconer cry out, 'You're down at last!' –

Descends through many tired circuits, till
It meets the spot which it so swiftly left,
And perches there, disdainful, out of reach,   132

So Geryon bore us to the very foot
Of that great jagged cliff and set us down,
Then having shed his living burden

Vanished like an arrow from a bowstring.

Canto XXII

Escape

I have seen cavalry break camp before,
And mustering and mounting an assault,
And sometimes driven headlong in retreat.

I've seen light horsemen fly across your lands,
O Aretines, seen raiders forage there.
I have seen tournaments and jousts,   6

With trumpets blaring and the peal of bells,
And drums, and castle-signals day and night,
Both in our style and that of foreigners,

But never have I heard a horn like this
Employed by horsemen or the infantry,
Nor when a ship sets course by land or stars!   12

So now the ten fiends kept us company:
A lairy crew, but, as they say, to church
With saints and with the drunkards to the inn.

My mind was focused wholly on the pitch,
To see the pit in its variety
As well as those who burned within its depths.   18

As dolphins do, who with their arching backs
Give sailors warning that the time has come
When they must act to save their ships from wreck,

From time to time a sinner showed his back
In order to relieve his agony,
Then instantly submerged it once again.   24

Just as along the margin of a ditch
Frogs lie, their noses barely visible,
Their feet and heavy bodies still concealed,

The sinners lay on every side – except,
When Barbariccia approached, they all
Withdrew beneath the boiling pitch again.   30

I saw – my heart still shudders at the thought –
One sinner hesitate, just as one frog
Hangs back when his companion has jumped,

And Graffiacane, who was near at hand,
First hooked him by his tarry locks, then hauled
His victim like an otter high aloft.   36

By now I knew who all the devils were –
I paid attention when the band was picked
And listened when they spoke each other's names.

Here the accursed crew cried out as one:
'Now, Rubicante, get stuck into him!
Let's see him with his skin completely flayed!'   42

I said: 'Now, Master, find out if you can –
What is the name of this unlucky wretch
Whose enemies now have him in their grasp.'

So Virgil then approached the man and asked
His origins. The sufferer replied:
'My birthplace was the kingdom of Navarre.   48

My mother set me on to serve a lord:
My father was a ne'er-do-well who wrecked
Himself as well as all that he possessed.

In good King Thibaut's household I grew up
And then went on to practise barratry.
Now in this heat I pay the reckoning.'   54

Then Ciriatto, from whose mouth a tusk
Stuck out on either side, just like a boar's,
Gave him a taste of how these blades could rip.

The mouse was at the mercy of the cats,
But Barbariccia caught him in his arms
And said: 'Stand back. I'll spear him on my fork,'   60

Then turned towards my master and remarked:
'Just ask away, if he can tell you more
Before he is dismembered by the crew.'

Virgil went on: 'Down there beneath the pitch,
Of all the other sinners, do you know
Of any who were born in Latium?'   66

The man replied, 'Just now I left behind
Someone from thereabouts: had I remained
I'd have no fear of grappling iron or hook.'

Then Libicocco cried: 'Enough of this!'
And with the grapple seized his arm, so that
In tearing it he ripped a muscle out.   72

When Draghignazzo made as if
To hook the sinner's legs, the captain turned
And gave the lot of them a dirty look.

And when the demons quieted themselves,
My master asked the victim straight away –
The man was gazing at his injury –   78

'Who was the friend from whom you said you made
That ill-advised departure, when you came
Ashore?' The wretch said, 'Fra Gomita

Of Gallura, fraud-in-chief, who once had
All his master's enemies in his hands,
And by his treatment of them earned their praise.   84

As he himself has said, he took their gold
And in exchange ensured their smooth release;
He was the barrator of barrators.

Don Michael Zanche of Logodoro
Is his boon companion here: they talk
Unendingly about Sardinia.   90

But see that other one who grinds his teeth —
I'd tell you more, except that I'm afraid
That any moment now he'll scratch my scurf!'

Then that great Marshal, Barbariccia,
Seeing Farfarello move to strike, roared,
'Back in line there now, you wicked bird!'   96

The frightened soul went on: 'If you would see
Or hear from Tuscans or from Lombards, then
I can arrange to show you some of them.

But have the Malebranche stand further off,
So those who come will not fear their revenge,
Then sitting here like this I will contrive   102

That on my whistle seven will appear —
The whistle being our accustomed sign
When anyone escapes the burning pitch.'

On hearing this Cagnazzo raised his snout
And said: 'Now hear the cunning stratagem
This one's devised to get back in the glue!'   108

To which the damned soul, rich in trickery,
Replied: 'How cunning I must be to bring
Worse pains on my companions below!'

Now Alichino could contain himself
No longer, and despite the others said:
'Just jump for it. I won't come after you,   114

But hover just above the pitch. We'll leave
The bank and hide behind the ridge. Let's see
If you can manage to evade us all.'

Now reader, here's a novel sport. As one,
The party looked towards the farther bank —
Cagnazzo was the keenest of the lot.   120

The Navarese chose his moment well.
He braced his feet against the ground, then sprang
And instantly escaped the leader's grip.

Each felt a pang of guilt, especially
The one whose fault it was, who started up
And cried: 'Well now, you're caught!' But saying this   126

Availed him little for his wings could not
Outstrip the fleeing soul: as one submerged,
The other turned his breast aside in flight,

Much as the wild duck suddenly descends,
Faced with the angry hawk's approach; much as
The hawk ascends, defeated and enraged.   132

Now Calcabrina, raging at this trick,
Went flying in pursuit, in case the prey
Would still escape, which meant there'd be a scrap,

And when the barrator had disappeared,
He turned his talons on his fellow imp
And grappled with him there above the ditch,   138

But his opponent was a full-grown hawk
And matched him in the struggle, so that both
Fell in the middle of the boiling pond.

And though the heat at once untangled them,
Their wings were so befouled with glue that now
They had no means of getting out again.   144

Barbariccia, grieving like the rest,
Made four of them fly to the further bank,
Each with his fork; and quickly on their marks

From both sides they stretched out their grappling hooks
Towards their slimy comrades, who were both
By now cooked through inside their crusts – and so   150

We left them there, still utterly embroiled.

Canto XXV

Snakes and Metamorphoses

And when his speech was done, the thief flung up
His hands and made the fig sign with them both
And cried: 'Now take these, God! They're aimed at you!'

And from this moment serpents were my friends,
For one then coiled itself around his neck
As if to say, 'Now you shall speak no more.'   6

Another wound itself about his arms,
Then wrote itself into a knot in front,
So that he could not even flex an inch.

Pistoia, ah, Pistoia, when will you
Decree that you be burnt to ash and gone,
Since you outdo your seed in devilry?   12

In all the inky rings of Hell I saw
No one – not him who fell before the wall
At Thebes – as proud before his God as this.

He fled and spoke no more. And then I saw
A centaur full of rage come bellowing:
'Where is he now? Where is this bitter soul?'   18

I do not think Maremma with its swamps
Can hold as many snakes as coiled between
His rump and where the human form begins.

Along his shoulders and his neck there lay
A dragon, with its wings outstretched, whose breath
Incinerates whoever it may meet.   24

My master told me: 'This is Cacus, who
Has often filled entire lakes of blood
In caves that lie beneath Mount Aventine.

He is not with his brothers on their road
Because he undertook the cunning theft
Of that great herd that used to graze near him –   30

On which account his evil met its end
Beneath the club of Hercules: though dealt
A hundred blows, this beast felt barely ten.'

While Virgil talked, the centaur passed us by
And next, unseen by us until they spoke,
Three spirits then approached us from below   36

And cried: 'Who are you?' Hearing this, we ceased
To talk between ourselves and gave these three
Our full attention, although none of them

Was known to me. But then, as frequently
Occurs by accident, one of the group
Referred to someone else by name and said,   42

'Where can Cianfa be?' And hearing this,
I put a finger on my lips to show
My leader he should listen carefully.

If, reader, you are slow now to believe
What I shall tell, no wonder, because I
Who saw it scarcely credit it myself.   48

There as I watched, a serpent with six feet
Sprang up in front of one of them and then
Attached itself to every part of him.

It grasped the belly with its middle feet
And with its forefeet took his arms, then pierced
One cheek and then the other with its teeth.   54

It spread its hind feet on his thighs, then slid
Its tail between his legs, extending it
Until it met his buttocks from behind.

A creeper is not fastened to a tree
More closely than this dreadful creature bound
Its swarming limbs among the victim's own,   60

And then as if they both were heated wax
They first adhered to one another, then
Their colours mixed and neither was itself –

As darkness moves across a page before
The flame itself begins and though the page
Is not yet black the white begins to die.   66

The other two looked on and both cried out:
'My, my, Agnello! What a change is here!
Already you are neither two nor one!'

By now the two heads were becoming fused,
And we could see two shapes within one face
Where both identities were lost. Two arms   72

Emerged where four had been, the thighs became
The legs, the belly joined the trunk and all
Were limbs no man had ever seen before.

The features of the pair were quite erased
And the perverse imago that remained
Was both and neither, and moved slowly off.   78

Just as a lizard flitting hedge to hedge
Beneath the dog days' awful scourge will seem
A lightning-flash across the dusty road,

A tiny flamy snake, the black and white
Of peppercorns, appeared and seemed to aim
Straight at the bellies of the other two,   84

Then pinned one in the navel, which is where
We first receive our nourishment, and then
Fell down before the victim and stretched out.

The bitten spirit gazed upon the snake
And did not speak, but merely yawned, as if
A sleep or else a fever held him bound.   90

He eyed the snake, who eyed him in return.
The smoke that both gave out – he from his wound,
The serpent from its mouth – began to blend.

Let Lucan now be silent where he tells
Of poor Sabellus and Nasidius
And let him wait to hear this tale emerge.   96

Let Ovid's tongue be still where he would speak
Of Cadmus and of Arethusa: for
If he makes one a fountain, one a snake,

I do not envy him, since he did not
Transpose two forms when they met face to face
So that their very natures were exchanged.   102

They answered one another in this way:
The serpent split its tail into a fork;
His victim drew his feet together; legs

And thighs joined up so seamlessly that soon
It was no longer possible to see
The point at which the two of them had met.   108

The serpent's cloven tail assumed the shape
The man had lost, and correspondingly
Its skin grew softer while the man's grew scales.

I saw his arms draw back into the oxters, while
The serpent's two short feet were lengthening
To match the diminution of its twin.   114

And then its hind legs, twined together, grew
To form the penis, while the wretched man
Acquired two legs extending from the groin.

Now while the smoke was masking each of them
With different colours, growing hair on one
To strip it from the spirit, so the snake   120

Rose upright while his other half fell down,
And neither turned aside the evil gaze
Beneath which both their faces were transformed.

The one who stood grew narrow at the brow
And from the surplus matter made two ears
To frame the cheeks it now possessed, and then   126

With what remained of the excess it shaped
A nose to sit upon the face, as well
As thickening the lips to human size.

The one who lies, meanwhile, sticks out his snout
And then withdraws his ears into his head,
Just as a snail retracts its horns; and next   132

The human's tongue, which previously was whole
And fit for speech, divides itself, just as
The snake's is healed. And here the smoking stops.

And now the soul that has become a beast
Flees hissing down the valley, and the snake,
Grown capable of speech, spits after it,   138

And turning his new shoulders, tells the third:
'I want to see Buoso run like me
Along this very path, on all six feet.'

In this way I observed the freight borne by
The seventh pocket change, then change again;
Let novelty excuse my feeble pen.   144

And though by now my sight had grown confused,
My spirit weakened, nonetheless the souls
Who fled were not so furtive that I missed

Puccio Sciancato, who alone
Escaped the transformation; and the third
Of them was Francesco Cavalcanti,   150

Because of whom, Gaville, you still weep.

Canto XXVI

Ulysses

Rejoice, O Florence, that you are so great
You beat your wings on land and sea; that now
Your name is recognized in Hell itself!

Among the thieves there I discovered five
Who were your citizens: this brings me shame
And hardly adds more honour to your state.   6

But if, as dawn draws near, our dreams are true,
Then shortly you will feel what Prato craves
For you, as many others do. Suppose

This had already been, it could not come
Too soon. Would that it had – because it must –
For it will weigh on me the more in age.   12

We left that place, returning by the stairs
The jutting rocks had made for our descent.
My leader climbed again and pulled me up,

And following the solitary way
Among the spurs and rubble of the ridge
We needed hands as well as feet to move.   18

I sorrowed then, and sorrow now to turn
My mind once more to what I saw. I curb
My talent more than I could wish, for fear

It runs where virtue does not lead; so if
A kindly star or – better still – if grace
Makes me that gift, I shall not grudge myself.   24

As when the peasant rests upon the hill
And looking down along the valley where
Perhaps he tills the earth and gathers grapes —

At that time when the light-giver conceals
His face the least — he sees the fireflies
Collect before they yield the ground again   30

To the mosquito, so below, as soon
As I had reached a vantage point I saw
The eighth ditch glowing with as many flames.

And just as he who was avenged by bears
Once saw Elijah's chariot depart,
Drawn up to heaven by its horses, yet   36

Could follow nothing with his eyes except
The flame itself in its ascent, that seemed
A tiny cloud — so likewise every flame

Is moving down the gullet of the ditch,
And none of them reveals its theft, though each
Is spiriting a wicked soul away.   42

I stood now on the bridge, where I leaned out
So far to see, had I not seized a rock
I would have fallen in without a push.

My leader, seeing me so intent, remarked:
'Inside the fire, spirits are confined:
Each chooses fire as his winding-sheet.'   48

'My master,' I replied, 'what you have said
Makes me more certain, though I thought before
It must be so, and have a question now:

Who is inside that flame whose top divides,
So that it seems it rises from the pyre
Where Eteocles and his brother burned?'   54

'Ulysses and Diomedes are both
Tormented there: both go to punishment
As once they went to wrath. Within their flame

They still bemoan the ambush of the horse
That made the gate through which the ancestors
Of noble Rome escaped; within their flame   60

They still lament the art by which the dead
Deidamia still mourns Achilles; there
They pay for stealing the Palladium.'

'If they can speak within those flames,' I said,
'I pray you, master, and I pray again
That one prayer represent a thousand, please   66

Do not insist that we be on our way
Before the horned flame reaches us: you see
The fierce attraction it exerts on me.'

'Your prayer deserves much praise,' he said,
'And therefore I accept it, but be sure
That you restrain your tongue and let me speak,   72

For I have understood what you desire.
Perhaps since these two souls were Greeks, they might
Regard a stranger's language with contempt.'

We waited. When the flame had reached the place
And time my leader thought most suitable,
I heard him speaking to its prisoners thus: 78

'O you who form a pair within one flame,
If I gained merit with you while I lived,
If I earned much or little gratitude

For those great lines I wrote when in the world,
Then do not go, but let one of you speak
Of where he went, when lost, to meet his death.'   84

At this the ancient fire's taller half
Began to murmur, shuddering as though
It cowered from the scourging of the wind.

Then flickering its tip this way and that
As if it were a tongue that spoke, the flame
Threw out a voice, which said: 'When I escaped   90

From Circe, who had held me there a year
Near Gaeta – which great Aeneas named –
Then neither my affection for my son,

Nor reverence for my aged father, nor
The debt of love I owed Penelope,
Which should at last have sealed her happiness,   96

Could quench the longing that I bore: to gain
Experience of the world, and of the kinds
Of human vice and virtue it contained.

But I set out upon the open deep
With one small vessel only and those few
Old crewmen who had not deserted me.   102

I saw the shores to north and south as far
As Spain, Morocco and Sardinia
And other isles that sea encompasses.

My company and I were old and slow
When finally we reached that narrow strait
Where Hercules had set his markers up   108

In order that no man should pass beyond.
To starboard I had left Seville; to port
Ceuta had already slipped behind.

"My brothers," I said then, "we reach the west
Despite a hundred thousand dangers. Now
Let us not deny ourselves experience –   114

In this, the last watch that remains to us
To know – of going on, beyond the sun,
Into the world in which no human lives.

Reflect upon your origins: such men
Were never born to live their lives as brutes,
But go in search of virtue and the truth."   120

And with this little speech I made my crew
So ardent for the voyage now at hand,
I did not have the power to hold them back.

We turned our stern towards the morning then,
And gaining always on the larboard side
We made our oars the wings of that wild flight.   126

The night now saw the southern pole and stars.
Meanwhile, the skies of home had sunk so low
They never broke the surface of the deep.

Five times we saw the moon rekindling,
Five times we'd seen it quenched since we embarked
Upon our crossing of that sea, and then   132

Before us there appeared a mountain, dark
And distant, which it seemed to me must be
The highest I had ever seen. At this

We all rejoiced, but soon our joy was turned
To grief, for out of this new land there rose
A whirlwind which then struck us at the bow.   138

Three times it whirled us in a waterspout
And on the fourth it raised the stern aloft
And plunged the prow beneath the waves, as pleased

Another, till the sea closed over us.'

Canto XXXIII

Ugolino

The sinner looked up from the brutal meal
He made upon the mutilated head
And wiped his mouth upon its hair, then spoke.

'You ask me to renew a desperate grief,
The very thought of which must wring my heart
Before I even speak a word of it.   6

But if my words are seeds whose fruit shall be
A traitor's infamy – I eat his brain –
Then you shall see me speak and weep at once.

I do not know your name. I cannot tell
By what means you have made your way down here,
But truly you sound Florentine to me.   12

I am Count Ugolino, and this man
Is the Archbishop Ruggieri. Now
I'll tell you why I love my neighbour so.

His evil plot, my trust in him, the way
That I was captured and then put to death –
All this requires no rehearsal here,   18

But what you cannot yet have understood –
How cruel my death was – I will now explain.
Then you decide if he has done me wrong.

The tiny window in that room for hawks,
Since known as Hunger, on account of me,
And where men are imprisoned even now,   24

Had shown me several moons already when
I dreamed that evil dream in which I saw
The veil that hides the future rent apart,

Where Ruggieri figured as a lord
Who hunted wolf and cubs into those hills
That block the view from Pisa to the coast.   30

His hounds were lean and eager and well trained.
Gualandi and Sismondi and Lanfranchi
Rode as beaters in the van, and very soon

The father and the sons began to flag:
So then I saw the chasing pack begin
To rip the quarry's flesh with their sharp fangs.   36

When I awoke before the dawn I heard
My children, who were there with me, cry out
Though still asleep, and ask for bread. You must

Be cruel indeed if now you do not grieve
To think of what my heart foretold. And if
You do not weep, when would you ever weep?   42

My sons awoke just as the hour came round
When normally our food was brought to us,
And each grew anxious, thinking of his dream.

I heard them downstairs nailing up the door
To that grim tower, and without a word
I looked into the faces of my sons.   48

I did not weep, for I was turned to stone.
They wept. My little Anselm said to me,
"Now, Father, what is wrong? You look so strange."

I did not weep at that. I did not speak
At all that day nor through the following night,
Nor till the sun next shone upon the world.   54

Then when the faintest ray shed light inside
Our dreadful cell, I saw in each boy's face
The look he saw in mine, at which I bit

Both hands in agony. The four of them,
Supposing I did this from hunger, rose
And said to me, 'Now, Father, it will cause   60

Less pain to us if you should eat from us.
Since it was you who clothed us all in this
Our wretched flesh, now strip it from our bones.'

I calmed myself to spare them further grief.
Then all that day and next we held our tongues.
Hard earth! Oh, why did you not open then?   66

The fourth day came and Gaddo flung himself
Outstretched before my feet and cried out, "Father,
Why do you not help me?" There he died.

And plain as you see me, I saw the rest
Fall one by one, between the fifth day
And the sixth. And then, already blind,   72

I lay, embracing each of them in turn.
For two days after they were dead, I called
To them, till fasting did what grief could not.'

He spoke, and then he turned his eyes askance,
Then clenched the wretched skull between his teeth,
And like a dog, gnawed fiercely on the bone.   78

Ah Pisa! Since your neighbours hesitate
To punish you, you bring down shame upon
That lovely land whose tongue says *Si* for *Yes*.

May Capraia and Gorgona come ashore
And throw a dam across the Arno's mouth
So every soul within your walls is drowned!   84

For though Count Ugolino earned the blame
When he betrayed your fortresses, his sons
Did not deserve the torture you applied.

Just like the two my story names above,
Uguccione and Brigata's youth
Proclaimed their innocence, you modern Thebes.   90

We moved on further now. Though here the frost
Still wrapped the sinners roughly in its cloak,
The faces of this tribe were all upturned.

It is because they weep they cannot weep;
For grief, which finds no exit at the eyes
Flows inwards to increase their agony,   96

Because at first the tears produce a knot,
And like a visor made of crystal, fill
The socket at the eyebrows like a cup.

Although, as happens with a callus, all
Sensation had departed from my face
In that extremity of cold, it seemed   102

That now I felt a wind arise, and so
I asked, 'My master, say who moves the air,
For is not every breeze extinguished here?'

And he replied: 'Soon you will reach the place
Where sight of what rains down this arctic blast
Will make the answer to your question clear.'   108

One of the wretches in that freezing crust
Called out to us, 'O souls so cruel
That yours must be the final station, break

These hard veils from my face, so that I may
Relieve a little of the misery
That clogs my heart before the ice grows back.'   114

'If you would have my help, reveal your name,'
I said, 'and if I do not aid you then,
May I go down to where the ice begins.'

'My name is Fra Alberigo,' he said.
'The evil host who called, "Bring in the fruit."
And here they give me dates for all my figs.'   120

I said, 'So are you dead already, then?'
And he replied, 'I have no knowledge of
My body's state up in the living world.

The privilege of Ptolomea is
That souls will often fall into this place
Before they are sent on by Atropos.   126

Now so that you will help more willingly
To scrape the glassy teardrops from my face,
Know this: the moment any soul betrays

As I betrayed, a devil takes the flesh
And will retain control of it, and when
The body's time on earth is at an end,   132

The soul falls down into this reservoir.
The body of the shade that winters here
Behind me is perhaps at large on earth.

Since you have just arrived, you surely know.
His name is Branca D'Oria: the years
Are many since he was confined like this.'   138

'I think you are deceiving me,' I said,
'For Branca D'Oria is still alive.
He eats and drinks and sleeps and wears his clothes.'

'Michael Zanche had not yet arrived
There in the purse of Malebranche amid
The boiling pitch,' he said, 'when this one left   144

A devil in his place. The same is true
Of one of his near relatives, who worked
Together in that treachery with him.

But now reach out your hand: unlock my eyes.'
And then I did not open that one's eyes:
To give offence to him was courtesy.   150

O Genovese! You strangers to good works,
Men bloated with corruption of all kinds,
Why have you not been driven from the earth?

For with the blackest soul Romagna bore
I have found one of you whose soul is bathed
Here in Cocytus for his crimes, and yet   156

In body still appears alive on earth!

From *The Drowned Book*
(2007)

Dedication

It took you forty years to reach this empty room.
Repaint the walls in arctic white.
Construct the desk. Draw up the spartan chair.
Then please repeat the question if you must.

The Apprehension

'Oh reason not the need'
      King Lear

'a protester was arrested under the act for "staring at a building".'
    GEORGE MONBIOT, the *Guardian*, October 4th 2005

I apologize: I have by heart the names of clouds
For no good reason, and the waterways of Europe
Run three wet dimensions through my sleep,
And I confess my gaze has drifted on
To light on your discreet glass eye –
'The smallest Gothic window in the world' –
Above this still canal where Fascists walk
Their little dogs before they go to pray
For the deliverance of Flanders from the French.

Supreme Commissioner, your world of crime
Extends from Vistula to Finisterre
And in your tower at Bruges-la-Morte
You're early at your desk to know it all.
The relict of theology and lists,
How like a god you occupy the pause
Between intent and act, the subject and its sign,
How comprehensive the disdain to which
Compassion has migrated now.

But my concerns are accidental, Commissaire:
The double wooden gate where CINEMA
Is painted in that lettering first found
Between the wars: the bowed brick wall above,
About to yawn and split and fetch

The whole place down in one slow blink –
But not this evening. Now the lamps
Beside the Théâtre Grand sustain Magritte's
Miraculous and sourceless dusk-aubade,

Now blonde girls zip with flying skirts
Across the cobblestones on iron bicycles:
Rooms wait for them, and voices on the stairs, and sleep,
Where I imagine rain is merely falling too.
See: they let slip their pillow-books, whose names
I must invent, as if it mattered, sir,
The way it does to you, whose only energy
Is fear, that will forbid the world
Its momentary love and happenstance.

Water-Gardens

Water looked up through the lawn
Like a half-buried mirror
Left out by the people before.

There were faces in there
We had seen in the hallways
Of octogenarian specialists,

Mortality-vendors consulted
On bronchial matters
In rot-smelling Boulevard mansions.

We stood on their lino
And breathed, and below us
The dark, peopled water

Was leaning and listening.
There on the steps of the cellar,
Black-clad Victorians

Were feeding the river with souls.
They left us their things,
Reefs of blue ware

In the elder-clumps,
Tins full of rust in the shed,
And on the bookshelves

English poets, all gone damp
With good intentions, never read.
Their miles of flooded graves

Were traffic jams of stone
Where patient amphibian angels
Rode them under, slowly.

The voices came back
From sinks and gratings,
The treasure seekers

Gone downstairs, while all the time
In King Death's rainy garden
We were playing out.

River-doors

River-doors are not sea-doors. They open
Through mirrors and library shelves,
Through glasshouse sweat and damp attic walls.

They are the isomers of boredom.
Fleeing through a river-door the adult world's critique
You will hear the foul yawn of low tide caught

Au naturel in its khaki-tripe skin
Between the dented ironclad revetments
Of Drypool and Scott Street:

Barges, drowned dogs, drowned tramps, all are
Subdued to its element, worked
Into the khaki, with ropes and old staithes,

Estuarine polyps and leathery excrescences
No one has thought of a name for.
So much for childhood. Later you sit

From the long afternoon to the full moon's evening,
Blowing your dole on the landlord's voice:
At high tide, he says, in that intimate gurgling tone,

The river revisits his cellar,
Caressing the chains of the exciseman's ghost
Where he swings between this world and water's; but no,

It is never convenient to go down and see for yourself
How the river might stand at the foot of the steps.
The problem's the safety. The wife. It's the council,

He says, giving off the warm odour of bullshit.
However, you seem to be drinking the river in mild
And be eating its fruits from the pickled-egg jar

And as the product of refreshment hear
The river-door quietly open downstairs
Under the weight of the waters.

Eating the Salmon of Knowledge from Tins

The open drains began a long way off
As chalky freshets coming off the Wolds

– But by the time the city had its way
The water, if you glimpsed it, looked as thick
As jelly from a tin of Sunday ham.
A brick would shake it slowly
While the shawl of sputum-algae
Gathered up its threads again
And went on rotting from within.

– But it was water so we fished.
The drains are buried now – bulldozered down
To thin black seams that when it's wet
Climb up to drown the ground again

– But in the drought of 1959
They were polio rivers, street-long
Inch-deep stinks with one black fish,
The Witch Doctor we chased for weeks
From street to street with nets and jars.
At six p.m., TV, the facts in black and white,
Sick districts where the numbers
Epidemically rose – not ours

– But not far, a dozen streets downstream.
I think we took it in. We washed our hands
Then hurried back into the evening
To lean from the bridges
And study the lawns of green cress
With the salty heat still coming

Back off the water to madden the gnats.
Those treacly sewers bred no Grendels,
No fishers of children, no Bradys-in-waiting.

— But what was it made us a little afraid
In those huge summer dusks
Where the sun and the moon
Stood on opposite sides of the heavens
And clocks stopped at curfew?
They must have been down in the shade
On that wrong-angled sycamored bend
Where at the road the water slid
For thirty feet between the culvert's jaws,
And came out in a different light.

— But in those days the murderers
Came from elsewhere. We could read
Their bad names in the bits of *The People*
That rustled in dusty hedge-bottoms.
Diana Dors was guilty by association.
Crime, sex, the smell that wasn't fish.
Then we went back to fishing, staring down
Into the viscid stink as it got dark.

By Ferry

The ferry, *The Waverley*, churns on the sandbar.
In New Holland harbour the jellyfish
Hang in the murk at the jetty
Like plastic rain-hoods –
A race of drowned aunties
Come back to chastise us
For something we don't know we've done yet.

Sea Area Humber: poor visibility.
The jaws of the estuary? Infernal the gloom.
And Lincolnshire beneath the rain?
A plate of cabbage
Laid down at the door of sulking Cleethorpes.
For the sea had gone away
Round that great corner of the map,
Leaving us wormcasts and Biblical distance
With skeleton crews
Dancing hornpipes on islands of birdshit.

Drains

Sites of municipal vaticination,
Vents for the stench of the underworld.
In dreams we are digested there
And 'in that Catholic belly curled'.

There we are sunk for Barbaricchio's crew
To heft upon their tuning-forks.
We dream too much. We talk too much.
The future of the market lies in corks.

Re-edify me, drains. Give me again
The under-city's grand designs.
Let me explore your slimy malls,
Your long drops and your flooded mines.

Some say the drains are heaven's guts,
Out progress intestinal.
Wherever peristalsis leads
The outcome will be final.

A Coffin-Boat

In Memory of Barry MacSweeney

Today you must go for a walk in the dark. Go in
Where the stream by the graveyard falls
Into the tunnel and hurries off hoarse with graffiti.
You will be hauling a brass-handled narrowboat,
Mounted with twin candelabra, containing
A poet who managed to drink himself dead,
With heroic commitment, at fifty-one.
Packed up with books and manuscripts and scotch,
In his box from the Co-op, a birthright of sorts.

Get used to the visible stink. It will cling
In a tissue of soot to your hair. Get used
To the silence that stares and says nothing,
A graveyard of clocks with the time on the tips
Of their verdigris'd tongues. You should neither
Look back nor examine your luminous gaze
In the water. This place (the word is used loosely)
Gives off an air of religion decayed
To aesthetics and worse. At least one of everything
Finds its way here to this copyright Hell.
Item, jar of cloudy eyes; item, carved
From bone, a grove of hatstands; item,
Detachment of ambient gargoyles with knouts;
Miscellaneous slick coils of excrement
And rag. And down the dripping galleries
Cartoons of howling inmates hang for sale
Between the stacks of disused literature,
Including some of his – and curiosity
May set him knocking on the lid for one more read,

But don't you stop: down here's the speechless
History of everything and nothing,
Poetry's contagious opposite. Go on
To the imaginary light.

                             Much later, far up,
Cries of gulls; a weedy birdlimed gate
That opens on the Ouseburn's curdled trench. Go on.
A mile upstream the tide turns back
Round weedy knobs of brick and stone
And clags of grot that wind themselves on mooring-rings.
Here is the rubbled anonymous slipway, left
Among black warehouses designed to look
Resigned and stoic in the hands of lawyers.
They are waiting out the era of unwork
When all the clocks run sideways
And the workers are walking the roads daylong
(From famine road to Scotswood's but a step)
Or imbibing the milk of amnesia. This place
Will be nothing, was nothing, is never, its tenses
Sold off one by one until at last the present stands
Alone like a hole in the air. But still
This is history, this silence and disuse,
This non-afternoon, and it must also serve
Biography – to whit, your man's, for here he goes
Out through the space left for comments made
Over the coffin. You and I, my friend,
And all the rest have who found their way here
Down Jesmond Dene and under Byker Bridge –
We must give an account of our presence.
We shall have to find words for the matter. So, then:
We've come on account of inadequate answers
To phone calls at midnight, to phone calls
Ignored and left ringing. We've witnessed

Italianate umbrage in bar-rooms, read
The poems of recovery and relapse and wondered
What in God's name could be done, and as we did so
Heard the rumour and the death confirmed.
We remember his anger and hurt – and our pity,
That futile and dutiful feeling that hasn't a map
But relies on itself to continue, that shrivelled
When met with the fact of his rage like a bucket of lava
Flung over the listener. Rage. It was tireless
And homeless, and though it walked out on the body
It could not be quenched by affection
Or drink: even now, at the death and beyond, oh yes
It must carry on dragging its grievances into the dark,
For the want of a nail, of a home, of a matchbox,
A drum of pink paraffin, anything fiery enough
To let the man rest by the waters of Tyne.

The River in Prose

I

Down to that area of retired water, among gridlocked stone
docks barely the size of football pitches, fed by the tides
through broken lock-gates which the mud is digesting. The
word 'inshore' — jaunty river-coppers hooking what turns out to
be only a sack from the wake of the ferry. Jaunty Humber pilots
squawking over the radio: bad weather in the mouth of the
estuary, miles away.

Identify, please, the point, not officially recorded, at which a
barge ceases to be simply unvisited and at rest and becomes
derelict; becomes an interior the water goes over at leisure,
something condemned by the fact it can never be water.
Does somebody look at a kitchen clock in a nearby street and
give in to indifference, lassitude, despair, economics? Is there
any element of deliberation, or is the barge's history simply
exhausted, something effaced with the illusion of speed
produced by inattention?

II

Say: *here is a dream of extinction.* Say: *it carried coals from Selby,
bashing through the swell like a Merrimack boat, part perhaps of
Zachariah Pearson's dream of blockade-running empire, of the
manutenency of slavery undertaken, from the city whose MP was the
abolitionist Wilberforce, whose house of exhibited shackles is a mere
five hundred yards away. The reformer stood at the end of his garden,
thirty years before the War Between the States, inwardly calling on the
Creator for assistance and looking down into the Hull, while round the*

corner the barge or its ancestor was going out to work in the cause of money. Water lies between the plank floor of the cabin and the hull, sieving the stinking ballast twice daily. The tide comes in through the broken lock-gate, investing every rotten inch of a vessel so 'much decayed' *as no longer to merit a name.* You come here in 1959, in perfect ignorance.

III

The rivermen. Rivermen's pubs, where the river is penned in the cellars. Somebody bit off the head of the landlord's parrot.

IV

Is this the Russian consulate? *No, this is the Club Lithuania, Dogger Street Branch. Are you a member?* No, but I've sailed through pancake ice on a Baltic ferry while Wagnerian bridge-pillars loomed past in the fog and been very afraid. Will that do? *You have to get signed in. You have to sit there on that sofa with that girl while she ignores you. Here at the Club Lithuania we specialize in continuous disappointment. We never close. Just sit there for the present. Eat your sild.*

Upstream, the riverbank and its hinterland are an annexe of Belgian Symbolism: low, grey-green, belated, formally a place but in fact an end to places, formally a flood-plain but in fact somewhere geography has finished dealing with. *No Fishing*, says a sign by the side of a dyke. Cannibals in skiffs come rowing smoothly down at dusk, with a barely a drip in the grey waters of the right-angled network –

The Mere

Its poplars and willows and sludge. Its gnat-clouds.
Smell of cooling animal at dusk. Grey-greenness.
Soup-suspension. Its having been
Here all along. It is nowhere, serves nothing, lives
On your behalf when you are absent.
Now they want to drain it. Now anticipate
The day when you will have to set this place
Apart, with sticks and stones.
Not for the mere the glum fate of
A run-of-the-mill Sussex valley.

Nor any great claims. No leverage sought
Beneath the aesthetics of crims from the deadlands
Whose task is to *make good* a landscape,
To drain it and extract the name
It never had. It's just
That you have to save something –
A fence-post, the shape of a firebreast
Nailed high on a wall by your ignorant gaze:
They will add up to love in a hand of decades.
Grounds for affray, are they not? So too the mere.

– Life is a word you can sometimes remember
And might never use, but that's
Nobody's business. Cracked heads and burnt hands,
On behalf of the mere. Soup by the brazier.
Standing pool, *body of water*, formerly
Arm of the sea, now chiefly *poet.* and *dial.*,
Anonymous, here with us now
In the order of things – this is what
You will find you have chosen,
If choice is the word, to defend.

The River Road

Come for a walk down the river road,
For though you're all a long time dead
The waters part to let us pass

The way we'd go on summer nights
In the times we were children
And thought we were lovers.

The river road led to the end of it all —
Stones and pale water, the lightship's bell
And distance we never looked into.

A long time gone
And the river road with it.
No margin to keep us in mind.

For afterlife, only beginning, beginning,
Wide, dark waters that grow in the telling,
Where the river road carries us now.

Three Lighthouses

for Ellen Phethean

When their history's over,
The rivermouth offers these lighthouses
Sheltered employment: watch, reflect

And let the square white towers
Take the light laid on at dusk and dawn
By Scottish colourists –

White that is blue,
That is nothing at all,
That is water and air,

And that says, although never
In so many words,
That the world we have lived in

Is real, and therefore does not lie
Beyond the dream of touching,
But places its light in our hands.

This evening the ferry will carry us
Home with the workers off shift,
An old couple, a mother and child,

And whatever our dead friends
Would say if they stood
In the bow alongside us, remember,

To take in the sight, coming back
On the gathering waters that slide
To the mouth of the Tyne, where the world

Is beginning and ending:
Three lighthouses wearing the weather,
In each of them a table laid

With rosemary and rue,
So that the dead may sit at peace
And watch with us tonight.

Grey Bayou

When I return to Grey Bayou, the mud-kingdom
Fed by dykes and chalky run-off
I would like my fire-ship to nose ashore

Beside the sheds near Little Switzerland
In memory of lust among the quarry-pits
A thousand years ago, before the bridge.

It is roads now, clover-leafs, pillars,
And only the bayou remains of that world,
Its reed-beds caged against the shifting channels,

Though the eternal flame to industry still burns,
Tiny like a funerary torch, far off
Downriver on the southern side, among the palms.

I would like a flotilla of tar-coloured barges
To happen past then, inbound for Goole,
The odd crewman furtively smoking and staring,

As though an ancient prophecy is vindicated now
When the fools who denied it are dead or in jail.
For this is the place, the rivermen know,

In which nothing need happen especially.
A boat burning out on the flats
Belongs with one more fording on horseback,

The first cries of love in the elder-grove,
Dark mild and cigarettes, the Mississippian
Expanses of the unknown Grey Bayou,

Its grey-brown tides, its skies
That dwarf the bridge and with their vast
Indifference honour and invoke the gods.

The Lost War

The saved were all ingratitude,
The lost would not lie down:
Reborn, their sacred rage renewed,
They razed the fallen town

And in the graveyard made their stand
Just east of heaven's gate.
We are the same. It is all one
Whom we exterminate.

Timor Mortis

Into the pit go all Estates,
All princes, pimps and potentates,
The fiend next door, the BBC –
The living and those yet to be,
Eminem, Ms Ruby Wax,
And Robert Johnson's vanished tracks,
Donald Rumsfeld, Richard Perle,
Madonna and the Duke of Earl,
Occam's razor, Charlie Chan,
Lord Lucan and the bogey man,
Mister Tony, Conrad Black,
The orchestra from *Crackerjack*,
The Andrews Sisters, Clausewitz,
That wasname who gets on your tits,
Captain Nemo, Guildenstern
And suchlike planks booked in to burn,
De Tocqueville and Thomas Hobbes,
Ascetics, charvers, Rent-a-Gobs,
Boadicea, Brian Clough –
The world itself is not enough
To satisfy the hungry void,
Though 'housewives and the unemployed'
Slip down with Marx and Jackie O.
Last sitting, everything must go –
Indifference and appetite,
The dimwit armies of the night,
Dispensers of banal advice,
Kate Moss and Condoleezza Rice,
Machine Gun Kelly, Iron Mike,
The Beemer and the butcher's bike,
Wallace Stevens, you and me,

The Devil and the deep blue sea,
The wonks who work the cutting edge,
Immanuel Kant and Percy Sledge,
With Peter Pan, the Golden Horde,
All travellers not yet on board
Plus those who think it don't apply,
Who witter, witter, 'I'm, like, *why*?'
Join Zeno, Zog and Baudelaire
As conscripts of *le grand nowhere* –
Some on ice and some on fire,
Some with slow piano wire,
Screaming, weeping, brave as fuck
And absolutely out of luck.
My friends, Lord Death is cruel but fair:
He loves it when there's nothing there,
No Baghdad and no Superbowl,
No *langue* and likewise no *parole*,
No Gulf Stream and no polar ice,
No evidence of Paradise.
His only mood's imperative.
He knows us all and where we live.
He sees no reason to record
The names of those whose bones are stored
In his extensive cellarage:
They are unwritten, like this page.
Come now, and board his empty ark –
What need of poems in the dark?

Sheol

It was different then, oh you cannot imagine
For one thing the war when these three generations
Were crushed into bone-dust one teatime.
These were lost at sea and this one trapped
On the floor of a lock till his eyes burst out.
To say nothing of murder, by shovel and arsenic,
By random malevolence snatching them up
At the roadside to boil them away, beyond
Sex, beyond names and belief. Or this child
From a cupboard, whom nobody killed, not exactly.

A Little Place They Know

To say that the sessions are long is to call
The Crusades 'an affray'. To say that you don't
Understand what the hell's going on
Is like finding Babel 'a little confusing'.
Here in the old world the clocks can run
Backwards or sideways at random, and when,
On the brink of despair, your turn is called –
By then you hardly recognize your name.

How suddenly empty the chamber becomes,
How discreet the Mercedes that spirit
Their regretful delegations homeward.
Now the clocks look at you pointedly. Quick!
You read to seven dead Bulgarians
And then they read to you, and afterwards
They take you to a little place they know
In a hole in the wall of the graveyard.

You wake now. The plates have been cleared. Your hosts,
Obedient to curfew, have departed.
The moon waits, and down at the end of the street
In its washed-out blue engineer's jacket
The sea too is tidelessly waiting, so
All you can hear where the waves ought to break
Is the fizz of butt-ends in the water
Drowning faint renditions of 'Volare'.

Yes, you tell yourself, let's go – *Thalassa,*
Thalassa, you know my true name – the stars
Awake when you and I take ship. But this
Is the shore that comes back through the mist
And the name of your death for this evening
Is Constantin Harbour, 1916,
Museum and slaughterhouse, beautiful hole
In the wall of the graveyard. Do step aboard.

Symposium at Port Louis

Drifting ashore on a salt-cracked book-box,
Buoyed up with Byron and Shakespeare,
Once again we ship Coles Notes
To Newcastle. No home these days
For obsolete litterateurs,
Only temporary anchorage
Deep in the southern hemisphere.
Safe for now in the cyclone's eye,
With scribbled notes on a borrowed page
And winging it like Hannay,
It seems our task is to discover whether
Concordia et Progressio can
Ever be more than contraries
Yoked by violence together.
– Someone would know, as your man
Remarked. We have come a long way
To sit in this elegant council chamber
Emblazoned with creole
Chevaux-de-mer; to hear
A grave centenarian entrepreneur
Set down his ledger and appeal
To his gods, to whit: Carlyle
And Chesterton and Masefield's 'Cargoes'.
Here the rolling English drunkard
Looks in secret at his watch and longs
For a sober world of prose,
Where objects are allowed
To be themselves, and stern embargoes
Seal the ports of commerce and of dreams
To grand abstraction and the soul alike:
Let Jesuit and Mameluke
Politely anchor in the roads

Till Mrs Hawoldar decides
To fire the sunset gun and bring
Proceedings to a close.
        The names of former mayors
Are allegorical in spades:
Monsieur Charon, Messrs Forget,
Tranquille and Martial. Their shades
Are words alone and yet persist
To haunt the carnival,
To make this page a sheet of foam
Dissolving as it slides
Across the reef, till danger meets
The sea-change into pleasure, when the mind
For all its radical intent gives in
To ocean light and Phoenix beer,
Reef-walking fishermen at dawn
Who glide and strut like Sega's
Dancing girls in skirts of flouncing surf –
And in the steady winter sunshine
Distances so wholly theoretical
That fear and ecstasy are one.
Yet on the *menu touristique*
There are items never mentioned:
Race and class and money
And the iron status quo,
Concerning which guests do not speak:
Out of this place, tradition states,
Desire not to go. Meanwhile
Like peasants in Van Gogh,
Cane-cutters with their cutlasses
Relax at noon beside the road
And over dinner at Grand Baie
Among the careless trove of pearls
And smirks and scallop-sconces
The Chinese minister confers

His poems on three hundred Hindu guests,
As Muslim families in fear secrete
Kalashnikovs between the joists
And Creole says what people mean,
Not what they ought, and all day long
The smell comes up the cracks
In concrete-covered gutters –
Rum and Phoenix, poverty
And wasted time, because
The afterlives of colonies
Are everywhere the same.
Inland at Cascade Chamarel
The rainbow will explode
And Ganesh, god of memory,
Will accommodate it all,
Gazing calmly inwards
Underneath the waterfall.

    This stormy chamber in its garden is
A southern cell where Prospero
Might set to right the grievances
Of this extended family –
But this time let the magus drown his book
Before he bids us all adieu.
Let poison run back up the leaf,
The will resume its innocence, and all
Before they go join hands downstage
To take the sea's applause and look
Once more at how the waves come in
As ever, faithful to the shore
And yet asleep
As soundly as the drowned men in the deeps
Beyond the coral shelf,
To whom the upper world
Is sealed, as firmly
As the mind of God himself.

Proposal For a Monument to the Third International

In Memory of Keith Morris

'All that is solid melts into air'

SOLO
I was dreaming in a station of the Metro.
The railbeds were freezing rivers of blood
With bergs of fat, where millions knelt
To eat and drink,

CHORUS
                and it was good.

SOLO
What are they singing,

CHORUS
                   the crowd

SOLO
That is never the same from moment to moment,

CHORUS
The crowd

SOLO
        whose faces vanish
And re-form, who have no names,

CHORUS

The crowd with its mouthful of blood,
The crowd

SOLO

            In which the million you and I are lost
Like information buried in an archive?
What is that song?

CHORUS

We are buried alive.
We are not what was meant.
Let history finish.
Let stones become stars. Let the stars speak.

SOLO

Let those inside the walls of adamantine
Ice-cream reply in a deafening whisper
As ice writes its name in the river again.
History, history, what are our names?

Little sister, tell me, can you see
Hosts of steam-angels, racing away
Down the blue Moskva at wavetop height
To confer their industrial blessings
On fur and glass, on felt and skin
And the old man who wearily enters
The forest of coats at the end of the day
To come back with ours? Likewise the babushka
Sweeping dead steam from the underpass
Is blessed and when the state withers will stand
With her brothers and sisters
On the wintry glacis by the Kremlin wall
By the site of executions.

CHORUS

The city runs like science fiction backwards.
Putin in his sheet-steel chariot
Is brandishing a grail of blood and vlaast
On a stem of twisted dragon-tails.

SOLO

I rode to the twenty-ninth floor
Of the Hotel Ukraina, then climbed the last steps
To the last locked room
Where a camera obscura portrayed the night city
As Stalin might dream it himself
From one of the seven dark stars he cast
So high that the heavens themselves
Were extinguished.

I turned to descend and there by the door
Was a wizened old man, sitting smoking.
A red fire-bucket was full of his ash.
He wore two watches and between his eyes
A bullet hole.
He looked indifferently through me.
Brothers, this is all I can recall.

CHORUS

The Tambov wolf shall be your comrade now.
This is your station now.
Press to the doors.

SOLO

Let us walk over the bridge
By the pool where the steam-angels
Spend their retirement.
Let us walk over the snow
In the field of dead statues.

We shall hand in our coats
To the dear old dead couple
Who add our black coats to the forest of coats
In the province of coats
And the bear Mikhail Semyonov
Presides in the court of the coats this day.

Shall we go in
And look at the art?

CHORUS
Up here is the modest proposal
A tower
A furnace
A children's amusement
Babel
And the key to all economies
When Eiffel took a potion he made this

SOLO
What is it made of?

CHORUS
Of matchwood and wire
Brown paper and misunderstanding.
This is no longer historical.
Art
And no longer historical,
Art
And can never remember the time.

SOLO
What shall we hope for?

CHORUS
To come here and see.
To have your curious half hour.
To go back through the crowd,

SOLO
To take our coats from the forest of coats
And tip the babushka
And walk to the Metro
And stand in the crowd between trains
When the blood is not running.

CHORUS
To know
We are buried alive,
To know
We are not what was meant.
Let history finish.
Let stones become stars
And let the stars speak.

Valedictory

Those living and those yet to be
Are all her immortality:
The subjects of the world she made
Still speak her language, still afraid
      To change it.
She saw her people as they were:
Don't-Cares who can't be made to care:
These sentimental hypocrites
Let her, their true-blue Clausewitz
      Arrange it.

Let poverty without parole
Replace the right to draw the dole.
Let coppers pulling triple time
Turn opposition into crime
      At Orgreave.
Let the *General Belgrano*,
Sunk to save our sheep, our guano,
Mark the freezing south Atlantic
As the empire's last romantic
      War grave.

Let children learn no history
These days, but only how to be
As economically astute
As all the dealers snorting toot
      For dinner,
Desperate to anticipate
Like destiny the nation state's
Ineluctable decline
To client status: *I me mine*,
      The winner.

Branch libraries and playing fields
Deliver rather slower yields
Than asset-stripping mountebanks
Can rake in flogging dope and tanks:
          Great Britain!
Strange: no one nowadays admits
To voting in the gang of shits
Who staffed her army of the night:
Our history, it seems, is quite
          Rewritten.

When it comes to telling lies
The change is hard to recognize.
What can't be hidden can be burned.
She must be gratified: we've learned
          Her lesson.
Now when some sanctimonious ape
Says, *No, there never was a tape,*
A bribe, a private meeting with
Et cetera, where are you, Smith
          And Wesson?

Let the histories receive
This lady, who did not believe
In treating with the TUC,
In guff about 'society',
          In turning.
Bid farewell to one who knew
Precisely what the world should do
In every case, without remorse,
And let her lie, unless of course
          She's burning:

– For though we are prohibited
From speaking evil of the dead
Might her conspicuous contempt
For weakness render her exempt
                From pity?
Tempted though we are, we must
Be merciful as well as just.
Let ignorance be iron-willed:
The task is always to rebuild
                Our city.

Fantasia on a Theme of James Wright

There are miners still
In the underground rivers
Of West Moor and Palmersville.

There are guttering cap-lamps bound up in the roots
Where the coal is beginning again.
They are sinking slowly further

In between the shiftless seams,
To black pools in the bed of the world.
In their long home the miners are labouring still –

Gargling dust, going down in good order,
Their black-braided banners aloft,
Into flooding and firedamp, there to inherit

Once more the tiny corridors of the immense estate
They line with prints of Hedley's *Coming Home.*
We hardly hear of them.

There are the faint reports of spent economies,
Explosions in the ocean floor,
The thud of iron doors sealed once for all

On prayers and lamentation,
On pragmatism and the long noyade
Of a class which dreamed itself

Immortalized by want if nothing else.
The singing of the dead inside the earth
Is like the friction of great stones, or like the rush

Of water into newly opened darkness. My brothers,
The living will never persuade them
That matters are otherwise, history done.

The Thing

The ring of fire in Act Three should actually
Evoke the SS chapel at Schloss Wewelsberg,
i.e. not Johnny Cash. The 'problem with Mephisto'

Is not in fact a problem with Mephisto, but with you,
'My friend', and while I'm not at all inflexible
Or precious where the script's concerned, the 'difference

It will make' if Mephisto is played as though
From Hartlepool is that you will be dead.
Apart from that I think we're up to speed.

Thom Gunn

We set out to explore the poison root,
To etch the brain with new cartography,
The harbour-glitter and the wine-dark sea.
The only rule was endless latitude.
Let the unready falter and retire —
We loved and feared your eager solitude,
The city as a man-made absolute,
A sunset grid of immanent desire.

Let those of us who longed to board but failed
Salute you *in absentia*, Captain Gunn,
Now attitude and argosy have sailed
Beyond the west. You had no other course
But mustering your whole 'hot, wasteful' force
To beach in the annihilating sun.

Serious Chairs

Upright, blue-cushioned, with curved wooden arms,
Waiting like habitués of vivas and auditions,
The serious chairs are never all taken –
Always there is someone missing, caught
In a delayed appointment, lost to us
In the stony glare of long summer streets,
Behind whose darkened windows other rooms like this
With their unbreathing patience hold
Their half-audiences, too, beneath the grave
Half-decent portraits of the wise and their mustachios
Reposing in the chairs of other days. Shall we begin?
All knowledge is a tragedy. Already we digress.

Far better to be nobody at all than serve
The secret cult of one's own personality,
As no one would deny, yet even here
In the serious chairs – or is it here especially? –
The friction of the self against these others
And the facts can seem intolerable, almost,
Because some radical injustice means
You may at last be absolutely wrong.
So the girl in the high-collared blouse sits
Knitting and worrying, and the man behind her
Struggles with the lifelong rage that makes
His Ernest Bevin spectacles expand alarmingly,

And lurking one row back in restless immobility
The ancient independent scholar knows
What no one else has grasped – that angels
Are not so terrible in fact, or not to him,
Who has taken the trouble to make their acquaintance.

Yet in this setting he is too considerate
To tell us that if he so chose he could
Address us now, complacently, in tongues of flame –
For he means to outlive us, to sit here alone
On that blue cushion, that serious chair,
With knowledge like a skull inside a box,
And wait for no one, patiently, like this.

Three Facetious Poems

Sung Dynasty

My lover tells me that when autumn comes
He will fashion me a boat of cherry blossom:
There's no way I'm getting in that.

Why The Lady

She represents the rose and universal hope;
The fiery core; herself before the court
Of man's conceit – exonerated, free;
The hidden bud for which the dead will rise;
The ruby on the salt bed of the sea;
A kiss. That's why the lady is a trope.

Of Rural Life

Pigs. Chickens. Incest. Murder. Boredom. Pigs.

Lost Song of the Apparatus

The curved platform of Cullen Station, 1963.
The house on the right, beyond the station building,
Was a typical L-plan stationmaster's home.

67 '*With elaborate art Virgil gives his language*
Here the appearance of careless ease.'
Portessie/ Buckie/ Aultmore*

*known as Forgie

Ladysbridge Asylum – Near Banff.
Many will remember the call
'Change for Fochabers Town.'

At the platform to the left of the station building.
70. *namque...*] '*for the well-known martial note of*
Harsh-sounding brass urges on the laggards.'

Hopeman 14 September 1931
72 *fractos...*] Cf. the well-known line of Ennius,
At tuba terribili sonitu tarantara dixit.

Burghead (first) 10th October 1892
Greens of Drainie November 1859
Coleburn* – *known as Coleburn Platform

Until April 1967/ 'A badly sited station
Some distance from the village.'
Kildrummie Platform/ Taucher's Platform/

Towiemore Station, August 1966.
It was still open at the time –
The carriage body served as a waiting room!

Drummuir Curling Pond Platform –
Date unknown. There was
130 *rarum in dumis*] *'here and there amid the bushes'*

A branch line to the harbour
On the east side of this building but
It ceased to be used in the 1880s.

410. *'and melting into insubstantial*
water will be gone.' 393. *trahantur*]
expresses the sequence or connection

Of events, and suggests the thread of destiny.
394. *quippe...*] *'for surely such is the will of Neptune'.*
Both *'quippe'* and *'visum est'* are stately.

Six Railway Poems for Birtley Aris

1. Inheritance

In this compartment you discover
The poems of De La Mare,
Left open at 'The Railway Junction',

The late-nineteenth-century rhetoric
Turning from art into history now
As you snuff up the gutter:

From here through tunnelled gloom
the track divides. These days
The grim-faced keeper with his gun

Patrols the madhouse walls,
The drooling curate's shut within,
And the bow-legged bridegroom,

Seduced and abandoned –
He must be you, confined for good
To this thin medium,

To coal-smoke, oil-sweat, gusty corridors
That thunder onto viaducts
Flung across gulfs of industrial fog,

Then into howling tunnel-mouths
As if each darkness were the last of all.
What use are your gifts now,

Your cage-bird and kind word,
Your old-world fidelity,
Infinite patience?

2. Cherchez la Femme

Trains cry in the night across fields
And bombed sidings – nearer, further,
Promises blowing their smoke in your eyes.
By now you would give anything.
And still she does not come.
'. . . all things that thou wouldst praise
Beauty took from those who loved them
In other days.'

Beauty's a practical girl.
She can bathe in a bare two inches
Then, dodging the bombers, slip out
To the ball in a gown made of blackout.
Cherchez la femme.
She leaves the Bible in its drawer,
A pair of stockings on the shower-rail,
But nothing with her signature.

Now seek her in the stations of the capital,
Where all the girls impersonate that look,
Peremptory, amused, with always
Somewhere else to be.
Her handmaids serve a brutal faith.
Look in their eyes, night after night
Beneath the clock, and see: it is not
She who is invisible.

3. Yellow Happiness

The painting over the luggage rack –
Its yellow happiness, that blinded bay
Whose figures are dissolving in the waves.

Clearly life's not possible.
Let there be art, of a kind. Let Rimbaud
Go to ground in yellow Scarborough

In the bowels of the Grand Hotel
Among plongeurs and chambermaids.
He's there, he's in the frame –

As you are, *cherie*, you who stole
My happiness to wear that yellow dress
You threw aside to run into the sea.

One day the sea train will mean what it says,
Ploughing into the waves like a special effect
At the birth of a submarine Yorkshire,

And out of the wreck you will rise
On an open gold compact,
Quite naked except for the powder-puff

Stylishly saving your modesty.
Those not yet dead will acclaim you
Sea-Gipsy, calling your creatures below.

4. Bridge

It would be sacrilege to put a word
Into that open mouth, that waits
And does not wait, while nothing comes.

And how you envy it the right to be
A sketch of smoke and ash at dusk,
An England hoisted to the light again

To send its breath of bone and earth
Into the unborn world – this sunlit
Arch of dust, this faith without believers,

And its language no one speaks. It has
No time for us, for matters of the heart,
But looks down alleys lined with birch and sycamore
Towards uncomprehending distances,
Unblinkingly in both directions, always.

5. Reasonable Men

They are reasonable men,
The railway guard and the doctor's assistant,
Filling the compartment door
With reasonable arguments
For getting off next stop and going back
Until you feel the benefit.
The train is crawling diplomatically
Across the levels, vamping
On a chord of steam. A river
Swims up close like an encouragement.
The fishermen look up and look away.
Willow, poplar, aspen, locks, a pub
And there behind the early haze the whole
Implied immensity of England.
You will never find it now. You can recall
A scarecrow in a streaming silver field,
The doorman of Anglian distances
Not to be entered this side of paradise.
You sought the place on large-scale maps
But here you are. The train is entering
A wood of silver birch. It's intimate –
A hundred acres of discreet attentiveness.

If they were nurses now, these trees
Would fold their hands together and look down.
You've missed what the conductor said.
He looks at you across his kind moustache
As if you must see reason shortly.
Would that it were so. But having been
Important to the world by being young
You understand that your decline, if not
Explained, is somehow warranted: why else
Would you be sitting looking out
And catching in the window the concern
Of those to whom you might be anyone
Or nobody at all – a gadgie on the lam
From the electrodes? They may say
The Midnight Special does not run,
That no one is redeemed by going North.
You know they must be wrong: how else
Could this embarrassing unhappiness,
This history of oddments – not this station,
One quite like it – justify itself at all?

6. Here You Are

This is the room that reminds you
Of the room you saw in childhood,
That you recognized and feared.

The bare boards and the iron bed,
Blue jug and faded hunting print.
And the view: back yard and bicycle,

A shrinking disc of snow
Upon a thawing water-barrel; steam
Escaping kitchens you must never enter.

And the sound: of shunting,
Like a game of iron patience
Played across the map of Europe.

Everything and nothing is waiting
There with the indifference of time.
You could be anyone at all.

It was none of your business
But nonetheless your turn would come
To wave at no one and depart.

So this was home. You turned away
Into the world again. The facts have waited
Patiently, a lifetime. Here you are.

Railway Hotel

In Memory of Ken Smith

Why this hotel, and this town and this province of X
On this night in the Year of the Turnip? Why
This name and this face in the passport? Well?

Out there the foggy road still curves away
Across the railway tracks. Young birches in the sidings.
Sounds of shunting, off in the rusty damp.

The suitcase. Full of books? It could as easily
Be drill-bits, lenses, chocolate.
You must be travelling in something. *Time,*

You say, flicking the locks to inspect
The interior. Something that glows? You give
Nothing away. It goes under the bed again.

Down at the end of the hall is a wolf in a case,
Howling at the moon in 1910, illuminated
By the beer sign in the street. Perhaps

It went like this: you stopped for dinner here
To view the curiosities, and this
Was one of them. You never know.

At her high desk the red-haired proprietress
Sits in a draught with the radio doing a polka
To death, and once again she's gotten

Lipstick on her teeth. And nothing happens
For a hundred years but fog and shunting,
Lipstick and polkas, the half-lives

Of objects marooned by imagined
Utility. So, are we going, or what?

Grimshaw

November – Copper beeches bare – The gates
Shut fast against the poor – Disconsolate
Illumination shed by gasoliers –
Damp garden walls and hidden escritoires.

The northern master Grimshaw understood
Belatedness: the passing of an age
That does not pass. In mourning clothes, the road
Bends out of sight to meet its widowed world.

Indoors now, lamplit hands turn over cards
Or patiently inscribe a page that might
Beguile the moral thirst of half-mad girls
Before whom winter opens like a grave.

The night has barely started on the clock.
We see no one. No letters come but yours.
Write soon. Around the globe's great curve,
Ship me your opiates of ink, my love.

Rose

You sit there watching August burn away
The waxy, crumpled pages of the rose

You love too much but cannot keep, or wake
With any word you whisper in its ear:

And neither will its hundred burning tongues
Call out to you, not once, not ever, now.

Blue Night

Blue night. Enormous Arctic air. Orion's belt.
A geostationary satellite.
The birds all sheltering or flown.

The world is North, and turns its North Face
Pitilessly everywhere,
As deep as Neptune, local as the moon.

First came the fall and then the metaphor
No other island, then. No gift of grace.
For this alone is 'seriously there'.

Therefore. Therefore. Do not be weak.
They have no time for pity or belief,
The heavens, in their triumph of technique.

Transport

after Stefan George

This is the air of another planet.
Friends' faces, that greeted me lately,
Are gone in the dark.

The forest paths I loved
Are fading now —

                and you,
My beloved, bright ghost, even you
Who gave me all my pain, even you
Are eclipsed in this radiant night,

For the quarrels and uproar are over
And something beyond me
Commands me to awe:
                  so the self
Burns, in the sound of no sound
And the ash offers praise
To abandon its voice
To a voice beyond hearing.

Dawn. Beyond the mountains rise
The sun and emptiness, the far
Blue gulf I am to cross if I believe,
A sea of burning ice —

Where I shall be one tongue of flame
Among the holy flame, a single note
Within the holy voice.

Abendmusik

This evening, Rilke at the harmonium
Plays sour chords of widowed expectation
Pedalled to infinity. Let it be now.
Everyone is here, discreetly,
Observing the stars through gaps in the curtains,
Down sightlines disrupted by bombazined women,
By shakos on piano-lids, by music-stands
And silver horns coffined in cases. Everyone.
An angel is promised; is promised.
The smell is the river in summer, the green earth
Laid bare to the heavens. An angel.
Heartless world, you alone persist.
You send us out into uttermost space
And exemplary silence. You promise an angel
To meet us, here in this room – let it be now –
In the stars, in the dusk-heavy pier-glass
Containing the river, those alders,
That perfect perfunctory curve of farewell
Whose only end is to contain our lives
Like Rilke's unresolving chords. Let it be now.
After so long an evening,
Star-blinded, deaf to the river,
Forgetting the names of our dead,
How can the Gräfin, the poet, the servant, the statesman,
That girl in the corner no longer attending,
Believe that the one we're awaiting,
Caught up in the curve of the river, the music,
The light of the stars from whose fires
We answer solitude with solitude, is here
Among us now and that its name is patience?

The Hand

A repeated procedure for Dupuytren's Contracture may
unavoidably result in stiffness and some loss of sensation.

My good right hand, farewell to you.
I must begin to take my leave,
And will depart through your extremity.
I cannot hold a friend's hand now,
Nor form a fist, nor open in a wave.
They say the only remedies
For what ails me are ailments too:
They had to kill the hand they fought to save.
Lie still and let me look at you.
You seem unmoved: I am the one undone,
And so let go of you, my hand.
Although you still extend on my behalf,
Now that my grasp of you is gone,
Nothing remains to comprehend.
Therefore I watch you endlessly
For your resemblance to the real,
And see the same smashed knuckle,
The scarring and the same club thumb,
The inability to feel
Made flesh, but unequipped for rage or love:
And yet you ache, as if with cold,
As armour might, remembering
Its heartlessness, its iron fist
Imprisoned in its iron glove.

After Rilke: To Hölderlin

In Memory of Michael Donaghy

We may not stay, not even with the most familiar things.
No sooner is the image comprehended than the mind
Accelerates into the waiting emptiness: and therefore
Only in eternity shall we encounter lakes.
Falling is all we must hope for, falling
From the known into the guessed-at, falling further.

For you the hero, for you who forswore it, life
In its entirety was the insistent image;
And when you gave that life a name
The line would seal itself like destiny. Though even
In your gentlest word a death was resident,
The god who walked ahead would lead you out and over.

Wandering spirit, none wandered further.
The others are proud to keep house in small poems,
To linger in narrow comparisons. Professionals. You alone
Pull like the moon: see now, below it grows light, it grows dark,
Your landscape, the sacred and startled night-landscape
That you comprehend in your leaving. No one
Renounced this more nobly and no one
Restored it so nearly intact, or asked for less.
So too, in the years you stopped counting, you played
With an infinite joy, as though joy were not shut inside us,
But lay in the grass of this earth, without ownership, left by
                                    celestial children.
What the best desire you built without desire,
Brick on brick: and there it stood. And when it fell
It could not discompose you.

How can we, after this timeless example,
Mistrust life still, when we could learn
To sense from all that's passing now
The planet's inclination to the earth, the world to come?

Praise of a Rainy Country

In Memory of Julia Darling

The popular song that first season, remember,
Was *Rhythm of the Rain* by The Cascades.
In tower blocks on dripping summer evenings
The impossible girlfriends stood at their sinks
In slips and curlers, rinsing out their blouses
While it pleaded – *Listen* – from the radio.
They mouthed the words and drew the curtains shyly.
It rained on the examination halls
And on parades and wedding photographs,
On funerals and literary episodes, on rich and idle hours
When we required no occupation but the noise
As rain, like imperial clockwork, ran down in the streets
Or thundered intermittently in vast
Defenestrated Steinways haunted by Debussy.
Rain fell in the hair of all those girls. It fell
In silver columns on the stroke of midnight,
Fell during the rows and the football results
Or while we were sleeping or eating or bathing
Or watching the telephone. Fell in the sea,
In the desert where no rain had fallen for years,
And fell behind the waterfall and on this book
Left out overnight in the garden
To flower illegibly. If there was a dry place
It waited for rain. If there was a damp one
It lay in a state of arousal. And we, my friends,
Were the innumerable heirs to this republic.
– Ours was just a period in the history of rain,
One called by some *The Inundation*
And by others *L'Après-Moi*, since we were young.

The rain is all digression, touching
Everything and nothing, as peremptory
As the Creation, emptying itself
Afresh into this iron river, pooling
In the hand I offer you, and still it seems
Behind the roar and hush there is a chord
We know but never hear, that rain awakes,
And leaves suspended, as between
Acceptance and desire, that calls to us
And, for no reason, speaks on our behalf.

Blizzard

The snow will bring the world indoors, the fall
That saves the Gulf Stream and the Greenland Shelf.
White abolitionist of maps and calendars,
Its Lenten rigour pillowed like a sin, it means
To be the only season, falling always on itself.
To put an end to all analogy, pure cold
That proves what it need never say,
It calls us home again, beneath a drift
In which the figure and the ground collapse –
No more redundancy, no more perhaps.

Look at these attic windowsills, look in the grate –
White after white against the off-white sheets,
The wafers of a pitiless communion
That turns a wood to Mother Russia and the night
To afterlife and then to a snowblind street.
With cataracts and snow-tipped breasts
The mermaids in their brazen lingerie
Wait bravely at the fountain in the square.
Green girls, they think it is their destiny
To offer the ideal to empty air.

Forgive me that I did not understand
That you were actual, not merely art,
That your fidelity was courage, that I failed
To honour you, to recognize your pain,
To grasp that snow once fallen will not fall again.
Now it grows clear: the world is not a place
But an occasion, first of sin and then the wish
That such self-knowledge may be gratified,
While snow continues falling, till we learn
There will be neither punishment nor grace.

Arcadia

I came back to municipal Arcadia
To walk among its foggy linden-groves
And count the line of benches slick with frost
That leads to the black waters of the lake.
There was the landing stage. The garbage scow
Knocked at the shore. The Brylcreemed ferryman
Looked up once from his *Sporting Life* to nod
With the supreme complacency of those
Whose work is waiting patiently forever.
Subtle servitor of Parks and Gardens,
Peerless in the stratagems of absence, Hail!
I wrote the sicknote up for both of us
And then he rowed me out to see the sights.

        Was this the destination then, this icy pool
Too shallow for a child, no use at all
To these three pale-skinned nymphs who climbed out now
In navy-blue school costumes and a cloud?
I watched them with a futile tenderness.
The dark, the fair, the fiery, their minds
Had every right to be elsewhere, in fits
That there should be a world, and that it must
Somehow make room for men as well.
They paused a moment, falling silent now,
And looked and did not see, then moved away
Into the dark, still towelling their hair.

        The steersman dozed. Snow fell out of the night.
I watched the glasshouse slowly taking shape.
Inside that icy tropic, where the mad,
The unemployed and the irresolute

Could serve their time among the frozen birds,
I saw the young myself still sitting there –
A book of verse, a glass of wine, and thee,
But I could see you'd lost your mind, my dear.
Or who was this bag-lady in the hat?
Why must I pity those I could not help?
I would have saved her if I could, but all
Such declarations show a want of taste,
For poetry deals only in the facts: fact was
That my poor friend was mad and thirty years
Beyond my reach, her terror and her need
Unknown to me, and though she took my arm
For comfort she was sitting with a ghost.

       I woke the ferryman. – *Go on. Where next?*
– *There is no next*, he said. *This is the place.*
We slid beneath the footbridge and emerged
Beside an island thick with snowy laurels,
Where he beached. – *Get out and walk from here.*
I entered that enormous miniature
And as in childhood forced my way among
The hypertrophied bushes and the drifts,
Until at what I knew must be the island's heart
I found myself once more beside the lake,
Where he was waiting patiently, as though
We'd never met, and roused himself to push
The iron coffin out from shore again.

From *November*
(2011)

Fireweed

Look away just for a moment.
Then look back and see

How the fireweed's taking the strain.
This song's in praise of strong neglect

In the railway towns, in the silence
After the age of the train.

Jeudi Prochain

The Muse, your ex, Miss Jeudi Prochain,
Keeps all your pleading letters but reads none.
One day in someone else's mail you find
A postcard from the nineteenth century —
A train, some smoky poplars, sheds —
But she's already gone to spend the winter
Nursing Rilke in a Schloss. The gods themselves
Don't have her private number. You once did.

The markets crash and war breaks out.
Meanwhile the state is withering away,
Not that you'd notice, while she rides a tank
Bedecked with roses through the ruined capitals.
She understands why even thieves and murderers
Have their appeal — or so they care to think,
For whether they will hang, or go to ground
In Paraguay, is all the same to Miss Prochain.

You should not speak to her of history or taste,
Though she defines them both. No apparatus
Nails her to the scholar's inky sheets
But in her lightest moment she's more serious
Than Auerbach and Sophocles combined.
You never know, and yet you thought you did,
And here's your punishment, this hell of time
Unbroken by amnesia or lies.

She lets herself be photographed
In Hitler's bath — as though she'd even be
American, when truthfully, for Jeudi, terms
Like 'international' and 'cosmopolitan'

Are too parochial to suit the girl
Who in one instant shyly bleeds a pig
Beside a sunlit window in Provence
And next is all severity in furs.

When Lenin's train obligingly chugs in
Beside a snowbound halt near Riga,
Miss Prochain will prefer to board her own
Discreet express for Lhasa, there to watch
M. le Comte de St-Germain expire:
And yet this very evening, look, she leans upon
An attic windowsill in Paris and removes
A shred of dark tobacco from her lip,

And then Miss Jeudi sings, inaudibly,
To rainy slates where angel-chaperones of cloud
Have paused to smile on her, at an address
That you can see from here but never reach,
And where, as you alone will understand,
From now until the crack of doom
(Which naturally will not affect her plans)
Miss Prochain is unable to reply.

The Citizens

We change the river's name to make it ours.
We wall the city off and call it fate.
We husband our estate of ash,
For what we have we hold, and this
Is what is meant by history.
We have no love for one another, only uses
We can make of the defeated.
– And meanwhile you have disappeared
Like smoke across a frozen field.

What language? You had no language.
Stirring bone soup with a bone, we sip
From the cup of the skull. This is culture.
All we want to do is live forever,
To which end we make you bow down to our gods
In the midday square's Apollonian light
Before we ship you to the furnaces
And sow you in the fields like salt.

We fear that the fields of blue air at the world's end
Will be the only court we face.
We fear that when we reach the gate alone
There will be neither words nor deeds
To answer with. Therefore, we say, let us
Speak not of murder but of sacrifice,
And out of sacrifice make duty,
And out of duty love,
Whose name, in our language, means death.

Sunk Island

She stares down the dead straight mile, at a walk,
While I stand by the lych-gate to let her
Arrive at this slow-motion replay of England.
Can I help you? asks the lady on the horse.
And I don't say: too late, unless your powers include
Self-abolition. *Me? I'm waiting.* I don't say:
Leave me be to read your graves, to stand and think,
To hear the water taking back the frozen fields.

It's not my place to tell you what I mean.
Perhaps I've come to use the weather up
And look too closely at your groves of oak and ash.
But we both know the fact I'm waiting here
Is cousin to a crime. We hold each other's gaze.
Who for? her bladed helmet asks. Her horse has turned
To steaming stone. I think I hear the sea far off,
Like evidence that each of us might call.

And why? – For the flood to accelerate over this ground,
For your helmet to circle and sink like a moral,
For a rag-and-bone man with his cargo of trash
To come rowing past slowly, his mind given over
To practical matters, the pearls of your eyes
Unforgiven and sold at Thieves' Market
For sixpence and never once thought of again.
You must be cold out here, she says. I think I must.

Salisbury Street

Correct. You can't go back. But then we saw the gate,
Or where the gate had stood, and it was nothing much
To step on to the asphalt lawn, to try to find
The rise of the old terrace, or the vanished fountain's
Vanished pool, the stumps that had been walnut trees,
Then slide down mounds of landfill to the orchard.

It was easy, standing in the wreck. The ragged elder-clumps
Had driven out the rest, except the cherry tree,
And that was sick with creepers. She was curious
To reach the very end, but I could see from there
The Bramley by the wall was gone, and in its place
A shed had fallen on itself and left a chair to wait.

The earth was pitted, friable, confused
With plastic sheeting, concrete, poisoned grass and rugs,
The inability to concentrate or care. Suppose
There'd been mosaics: someone would have made a point
Of shitting on them, when they'd burnt the books.
But it was nothing personal. Who were we, anyway?

These woods had held their own blue light, serene interiors
For autumn days like this, but now they stank –
Stale milk and burning mattresses. Smoke hung like ignorance.
You might have thought the place had always been like that,
A ruined grove of raw tin tongues, a sacred site
For drunks' amnesia and suicide. You can't go back.

Josie

I remember the girl leaning down from the sunlight
To greet me. I could have been anyone. She could not:
She was Josie, remember, and smiling – she knew me already –
Auburn gate-girl to the garden-world,
To the lilacs and pears, the first summer
Seen perfectly once, then never again. And she left.
The garden – the garden, of course, has gone under the stone
And I cannot complain, a half-century gone
Like the cherry tree weeping its resin,
The dry grass, the slab of white marble
The butcher propped up in the back yard to sit on –
Things of the world that the world has no need of,
No more than of Josie or me or that morning.
Still a child as I see now, she leaned down
To smile as she reached out her brown hands to greet me
As though this were how these matters must be
And would be forever amen. She was saying goodbye.
And I cannot complain. What is under the stone
Must belong there, and no voice returns,
Not mine and not hers, though I'm speaking her name.

Vérité: Great Junction Street

One weekday afternoon when we are dead,
We will be readmitted here for free –
Phantoms of sweat and smoke and ash,
Yet honoured patrons – to a special
Double feature that eventually
Begins with *Pearl and Dean: Complete*.
Back then we never saw the point
Of blotchy tedium and jaundiced lights,
And did not wish to live in nineteen fifty-eight
Among stiff perms and brilliantine and breath.
We had ideas, or we had hopes,
Beyond our meagre competence.
We could not see that what the adverts meant
Was us, the grubby herd among the stalls.
The sprauncing morons and fat girls
Who lusted for a Hillman Minx were those
We'd marry: these must be the photos –
See us grimacing with happiness
While two dogs copulate discreetly
Underneath a well-placed knacker's van.
Be silent, please. Watch closely. Now
Bite down, once more, my fellow citizens, into
The silver foil in which your choc-ice comes,
For when it meets your fillings that is all
The ecstasy eternity will grant –
No tongues, no hands up skirts, no chance.
And next, as if this were not quite enough,
Sit back to relish *Look at Life:*
The North Norwegian Lamprey Trade.
Somehow we must have missed it first time round.

After the painting Great Junction Street *by Jock McFadyen*

[418]

Cahiers du Cinema

As though between performances, the 'varnished waves' of seats are gone,
Their dreaming space abolished with those darkened afternoons
Spent sunk in sticky ginger plush, revising *The Belles of St Trinian's*
Or *The Three Hundred Spartans*, with David Farrar (Xerxes)
Sulking on his golden catafalque, his voice of cold command
Not only underused but dubbed for overseas. The end.
In Purgatory, that crawling corridor where we are only ever
Halfway up the queue, there will be questions asked, of course.
Herr Oberst, I can only tell you what I know: Karl Malden
And his hooter sniffed out Robert Shaw and all his Tigers
Camouflaged beneath the snows of the Ardennes. A dirty war,
When even Bronco Layne's a Nazi in disguise. Does any of this count
When the space closes into itself, the shadows go back in the box
And the box into nothing? In place of memory, 'dark nostalgia'. Bah.

A poster in a newly opened shop professes to preserve
A thing you never thought you'd need to own. You must re-learn
The dreaming gaze that formerly you aimed with gluttonous
                                                    indifference
At anything and everything that now you cannot prove was once
The past, in all its posthumous authority, plus free mistakes.
Begin with August's dusty cumulus at five o'clock, when you
And all the other creeps and criminals emerged unwillingly
Into the orange glare of actuality, to find the city charged once more
With an intolerable tedium whose grammar could not house
Your guilty joys. Oh, Natalie, *en deshabille*, detained by grim hussars
While climbing from a bosky pool in far Bohemia, somewhere
The glinting Tony Curtis, even, might not rescue you!
On one hand there were things the lard-faced devotee might have
                                                    absorbed

Officially (the 'facts'), and then there was the world, e.g.

This dark-eyed goddess, warm as breath, remote as a Czarina.
Forget the school of life: post-cinematic sadness taught me all I know,
For instance that a man may have to choose between a woman
And a train, and even though she's Jeanne Moreau, who makes
The glummest scullery an everywhere, the outcome's black and white,
And off limps Burt to keep his date with the *chemin de fer*,
To take revenge for Dufy and for France, for Papa Boule (Michel Simon)
Shot out of hand by Wolfgang Preiss quite early on behind the
                                                    engine shed.
'If we are to live, then let us live,' Kirk Douglas might have screamed,
Anachronistically, but he preferred to dance along the oars.
We all know men like that, oppressively ebullient, but which of us
Knows Janet Leigh, so strangely underdressed for her excursion
On the longship? And who else dare wave her past but Poitier and
                                                    Widmark,
Delighted by distraction from their own marine catastrophe?

Farewell, supreme foyer where it was always afternoon!
Arriving in the middle I could always leave when I came in,
Collapsing time into the image of an arrow shower
Curving out of sight, as in *The Charge at Feather River* –
Modernism, yes, but this was Hull: no 3D specs for us.
There in the silence between features, perching on a crumbling ledge
Above the gulfs and Thrones and Dominations of the grim Criterion
I wondered at the vast occluded system of the secondary stars,
Calhoun and Madison, Mahoney, Chandler, Aldo Ray and Gordon
                                                                Mitchel
Rough riders–Tarzan–beefcake–stuntmen and in Mitchell's case
Achilles, grieving, very slowly, at the pyre of Patroclus, when all at on
The credits rolled, the lights came up and here was that unnatural act,
An end without a settlement of blood. The gods themselves
Were tired, like the furniture of heaven. Outside the streets were dark.

– Dark as Edgar Wallace in his Albany of death. On every floor
A crew was grimly working to supply the second feature,
Like Catholics persisting in the forms when faith was gone
To frame an image of an underfunded English Purgatory
Complete with acts and fatal outcomes but with nobody to care.
– And yet one afternoon you wake to find yourself in Finland
Kissing Françoise Dorléac in her tiny knitted dress, and as she feels
To find the space between your vertebrae and with the other hand
Extracts a hatpin from the mattress, it is clear that you will
Live forever. It is snowing. As the Gulf of Riga drinks down
General Midwinter's army, then locks itself with ice once more,
Then, English, Colonel Stok observes, *you have no choice except to live
Forever.* It is snowing. Kiss her. It is snowing. Kiss the girl
And soon you will no longer know the blizzard from the screen.

– O Muse of Cinema, who taught us waking sleep, who warned
And guided with your sudden torch, and served us food
Intended for the undecaying teeth of gods, I think I saw you once
In mortal form, far down the long red corridor, with one hand cupped
Beneath your elbow as the other raised a cigarette, while you stared up
Into the smoke as though just then you longed to be like one of us,
To give back your omniscience and lounge at prayer with all
The other ladies at the matinee, with drunks and desperate old men
And games-evading schoolboys, all of those who shared a faint
And yet abiding sense that what was shown might prove to be
A trailer for the life to come, when all the Forms from slapstick
Through to evil via Rin Tin Tin and Vera Ellen would at last
Unmask themselves, and with our watching brief fulfilled
We'd make our way in silence through the exits into perfect
                                                    nonexistence.

But all this has been stolen – all the light, these dustmotes in the beam,
The self-forgetfulness and boredom and desire, headache, toothache,
Arse-ache, blessed privacy, these visions in the isolation tank
Of borrowed afternoons that for some unknown reason never found
Their way back into rightful ownership by idiots and bores. Till now.
Now is the victory for common sense, and those of us who spent our youth
In thrall to the delirious excrescences of self-consuming Kapital
Will have to find another means by which to cross the shadow-line
That separates Hilts from Switzerland, and Gina Lollobrigida from almost
All her clothes. We watchers in the cave are cast out once for all
Into that fearful teatime light where everything is being filmed
And narrative has given way entirely to its critics, who must read
A thousand screens at once for damning evidence of dreams.
We will confess to everything except the present tense.

White Enamel Jug

The Ardennes

There used to be a white enamel jug,
Its rim precise in Prussian blue —
Likewise the handle with its female curve
Through which a forage cap might fit: the jug
The maid's deserter drank from, slowly,
Boots off, his feet on the kitchen table,
Raising the thing like a trophy over his head
And licking his white cat-moustache,
While she kept waiting, trying not to laugh
At what a crime it was, behind him
In the doorway, naked, with her hand stretched out.
Midnight was all the time there was.
The stars froze, branches creaked, the cream
Sank in the jug, and so they took their happiness
For there and then and not for memory:
As, in his way, the Major also did
When he had sent his manservant to bed
And poured black coffee from this jug,
Then sat to write the letter home,
But paused, as though to read his palms
Within the circle of the lantern, while the jug
Attended, patiently, a kind of company
The night the war was lost, before
He rose and at the window watched the dark
Until at dawn the forest turned to flame.

Sleep

Like youth, this language has forgotten you.
Lost on the tip of its tongue, you could wait
A long time to be missed. Get up and read:
A poem, the Bible, a *roman policier*, *Hello!*
Or the blank white back of the bathroom door.
Some never lose the ear of sleep. They switch
Like diplomats descending aircraft steps
Into the lingua franca with a yawn,
But – you know who you are – you're too ashamed
At your incompetence to even share
A mason's grip: you lie there making do,
Until the clock itself nods off at last,
While every failure brings you its account
For signing, every sin its sweat, each gaffe
Its slo-mo loop for fresh analysis.
You sleepless masses, whither politics?
Your *Marseillaise* must be *Lillibulero*,
Daybreak more Dunkirk than Alamein.
At last, the drivel of unfree association
Trails you through the endless day, where you must
Imitate the living to the letter, dying
For a pod to come for you like all the rest
To snatch your sleeping body for rebirth,
However brutal the regime might prove.
You would run howling down the alleyways
In packs, to trap the rotten elements –
Your former self included, naturally –
And tear them limb from limb,
From pitiless necessity do anything
So long as you need never wake again.

Europeans

Now we are in Europe let us take
To selling mushrooms by the roadside,
Broad-brimmed platefuls and uniform buttons
Plucked before dawn in the forest of birch,
The dank delicious one-legged flesh
Climbing from grave-pits as big and as deep
As the forests themselves, for it does not
Take long to establish the custom, not long
To forget the beginning, to hold up
A bucket or basket of mushrooms
And talk about always and offer a shrug
That proves our knowledge and our ignorance
Identical, proverbial, entirely
Beyond the scope of history or law,
And since we have always been here
On our fold-away chairs near the crossroads,
Hunched in black overcoats, pale as our produce,
Seeking and selling the flesh of the earth
By the handful and kilo in brown paper bags,
We cannot be other than real.

Elegy

Just round a corner of the afternoon,
Your novel there beside you on the bed,
Your spectacles to mark your place, the sea
Just so before the tide falls back,
Your face will still be stern with sleep

As though the sea itself must satisfy
A final test before the long detention ends
And you can let the backwash take you out.
The tall green waves have waited in the bay
Since first you saw the water as a child,
Your hand inside your father's hand, your dark eyes
Promising you heartbreak even then.
Get on with it, I hear you say. *We've got no choice.*

We left the nursing home your tired chair.
They stole the sweets and flowers anyway
And bagged your clothes like rubbish in the hall.
Here in the flat your boxed-up books and ornaments
Forget themselves, as you did at the end.
The post still comes. The state that failed to keep the faith
Pursues you for its money back. *There's nothing worse,*
You used to say, *than scratting after coppers.*
Tell that to the clerks who'd rob your grave,
Who have no reason to remember how
You taught the children of the poor for forty years
Because it was the decent thing to do.

It seems that history does not exist:
We must have dreamed the world you've vanished from.
This elegy's a metaphysical excuse,

A sick-note meant to keep you back
A little longer, though you have no need to hear
What I must say, because your life was yours,
Mysterious and prized, a yard, a universe away.

But let me do it honour and repay your gift of words.
I think of how you stared into the bonfire
As we stood feeding it with leaves
In the November fog of 1959,
You in your old green coat, me watching you
As you gazed in upon
Another life, a riverside address
And several rooms to call your own,
Where you could read and think, and watch
The barges slip their moorings on the tide,
Or sketch the willows on the further shore,
Then in the evening stroll through Hammersmith
To dances at the Palais. *Life enough,*
You might have said. *An elegant sufficiency.*
There was a book you always meant to write.

You turned aside and lit a cigarette.
The dark was in the orchard now, scarf-soaking fog
Among the fallen fruit. The house was far away,
One window lit, and soon we must go back
For the interrogation to begin,
The violence and sorrow of the facts
As my mad father sometimes dreamed they were
And made the little room no place at all
Until the fit was past and terrible remorse
Took hold, and this was all the life we had.

To make the best of things. Not to give up.
To be the counsellor of others when
Their husbands died or beat them. To go on.

I see you reading, unimpressed, relentless,
Gollancz crime, green Penguins, too exhausted
For the literature you loved, but holding on.
There was a book you always meant to write
In London, where you always meant to live.
I'd rather stand, but thank you all the same, she said,
A woman on the bus to Hammersmith, to whom
I tried to give my seat, a woman of your age,
Your war, your work. We shared the view
Of willowed levels, water and the northern shore
You would have made your landing-place.
We haven't come this far to give up now.

The Lost Book

Here's where the far-gone Irish came to die
And having died got up to disappear
Into the space they wore into the air:
Smoke-room, bookies, God knows where –
They were a crowd who favoured solitude.
They came 'pro tem' and stayed, and stayed,
Bed-sitting room remittance-men
Whose files authority had usefully mislaid.
Dug out of 'kiln-baked' tombs, the gas left on,
This Tendency the calendar forgot
Kept suitcases of ancient paperwork
That could have grassed them up but didn't talk.
Poor demi-felons, dead of what? – of afternoons,
Whose rag and bone the council boxed and burned:
And you were of their party, were you not?

I owe you this. I watched you and I learned.
You lived provisionally, 'the man with no home team'.
Reliant on the Masonry of drink, you made
A modest and convincing entryist of crowds
Who only ever knew your Christian name,
Your trebles at Uttoxeter, perhaps
Your politics, on no account your game.
You seemed composed entirely of words.
'Tell no man – still less a woman – who you are.'
Who cares, now that the principals are dead
As the impossible morality

Whose prohibitions brought your lie to life
And in the end would send you off your head?
I care, for I was made to care.

You told a priest but couldn't tell your wife.
You were the author and the patient too,
And in another life another house
Imprisoned others and the clock had stopped.

You knew – and all you did was know –
That there was an appointment to be kept.
That was your art – to frame your punishment –
An endlessly extended sentence,
Solitary confinement in plain sight,
Nothing you could put down on the page,
Nothing you could ever simply name
But manifest in jealousy and rage
And episodes of heartbroken repentance.
There was nothing that could ever put it right.

'Yourself's a secret thing – take care of it,
But if it comes to handy grips you take no shit.'
Yours was a way of waiting, though you knew
That really there was nothing down for you
But vestibules and corridors and days
In which to seek permission to be old.
Kardomah Lampedusa, minus book,
Deported from successive realms of gold –
Longpavement and the Bronx and Hammersmith –
Or so you said, and who was I to ask?
Then when at last I came to take a look,

When you had sat it out as far as death,
Inside the case, behind the broken lock,
There were no secrets waiting underneath,
Just fragments of a poem you'd recite,
And scraps of stories you'd begun and re-begun,

In which the names alone would change, as though
You had forgotten who they were.

I found no history in this, no hidden world
Before I came – I'd heard your stuff bashed out
Through years of chainsmoked afternoons
And read it when you asked me to. I liked
The one where in the fog the sergeant found
His constable nailed up across a five bar gate,
But feared and did not understand the priest
In his deserted parish (fog again)
Who found his name had changed to Lucifer.
He lost his way and then he lost his mind
And that was that, with nowhere left to go,
Hell being where and who and what he was,
A state with neither origin nor end.

'The duty is to entertain,' you said, 'or else
To seek to make no sense at all.' And then
When you had filled the room with ash and smoke
There would be racing or the news, a second
Scouring of the *Telegraph*, a third, and no
Persuading you that you should persevere.
You were already old. Was that the plan?
To climb into the box and disappear
In smoke above the crematorium
And leave your furious pursuers unappeased
And shorn of purpose, standing in the snow
Beside the hearse, in mourning for themselves?

I studied you before the lid was sealed
And, as my mother had requested, placed
Rosemary for remembrance in your hands.
The deep, unhappy brow, the cloud-white hair

Combed back — oh, you were otherwise engaged.
In settling debts, or simply free to dream?
You wouldn't care to comment 'at this stage'.
Was there another world, where you belonged,
Or one more corridor where you still sit, rereading
With the patience of a lifetime
Last week's paper, hoping it might yield
To scrutiny and show the outcome changed?

Novembrists

This must be where I came in, gaberdined
Against the fog but part of it, to take the dark air,
Strolling on the glistening concrete of a tenfoot
When walking at night would be legal,
Which puts us somewhere in the nineteen fifties,
Entering the vast and ramifying silence
Issued by these garages and sheds that no one
Would think to repair or improve on. I admit
This is a version of the public good
Unthinkable to those not largely dead –
Those to whom a place is only somewhere on the way
To the apotheosis of transactions,
Those who fear the name Novembrists
And cannot see the point of it and in the end
Will probably decide they must forbid it,
Those who think that sentences like this
Should always finish with the number
Of a helpline, not more walking in the dark.
Here as we take the foggy night we hunger for it still,
And for the shoals of yellow leaves that come to rest
Beside a fallen fence where we can watch
The rabbi in his kitchen drinking tea alone.
Or Winifred Ratcliffe, teacher of pianoforte,
Staring back into a future from which she
Like us has vanished. She will make no sign:
We are Novembrists, are we not?
Reactionary elements combining in the dark
To undermine the decent light of trade
With futile knowledge of the spirit's appetite
For somewhere in between this world
And its discarded shadows. O Novembrists!

At the year's death, walking to no purpose
But to walk, among the rutted leaves
And dripping hawthorns, in behind
The sleeping yards and flooded lawns
And air-raid shelters piled with mattresses and comics,
Now I see it is my parents that I walk beside,
Her headscarf and his muted cigarette,
The desultory familiar talk, whose virtue
Lies in its routine, because it so
Resembles happiness we do not ask
For more, but only wish the night could be
Extended for an hour or a minute, though we know
The rules and limitations of November's paradise
And would not think to break them now
When not a bomb has fallen on the city
In a decade, and there is more or less
Enough to eat, and there are books at home.
I see the crime of this is modesty. I see
We should not universalise
A simple preference for foggy lanes
And intermittent lamp-posts, should not fall
Into the habit of the law, whose works
Are everywhere about us: and yet
Novembrists do not care to be
Entirely reasonable now. Come, then,
Fog and drizzle, frost and cigarettes
And dank austerity and blessed peace!
We merely wish the times, the state,
The market and the world and all
Their miserable implications could be brought
To silence for a moment by attending
Not to our unquantifiable delights
But closely to some business of their own.

Counting the Rain

Check the gas and hide the back door key.
Lock up. Make sure you have, and then
Go out and count the rain, and this time
Do it properly. You won't be home again.

The Plain Truth of the Matter

There are two tribes this world can boast –
The Marmite-lovers and the damned.
Fact is, though, everybody's toast,
Whatever breakfast they've got planned.

It's not for us to turn away
The sort who shun the dark-brown jar,
But sure as sure come Judgement Day
The Lord will know who His folk are.

First Time Around

You could make me believe with your fine tongue
That the sun rose in the west

I watch you cross the park out of the light,
At evening, for the sun falls in the East

To meet a pool of fire in the drain
Three streets away. It's me you're looking for.

The nuns at the French Convent disapprove.
Now Madam, where's your hat? Too short, the skirt.

Your life is not yet touched by mine —
The sun won't burn, the moon won't mask

And we must rule this kingdom as we wish —
These propped-up house-ends, bombsites,

Terraced lairs beneath the goods embankment.
Quickly, kiss me. Lie here. Learn to be imperious.

Sunday in a Station of the Metro

The pillars in the ruined church of steam
Reach up to rusty curlicues, whose branching forms
Once forged a second nature out of industry,
A forest where the wolves and Ridinghoods
Could figure both as cast and audience:
Victorian erotica on fire, with services
In both directions every twenty minutes.
Now through this sticky wood of suicides
Come morons and their monster dogs
To do their stint of shouting for tonight.

I fold my paper, turn it in my hands
Like a petitioner, and wait, and stare
Into the tunnel whose black throat
Is always on the brink of the oracular.
Brick-bowelled city, we would have a sign!
Should we applaud and go, or should we kneel
Inside the squares of light thrown down
Through broken sections of the roof?
How to appease or even wake the deity
From brick and iron and this evening-afternoon?

Is time still on the ration? More and more
I am inclined to do what everything
At once proposes and forbids. You, sir,
Dark-lantern man slipped out of time,
You with your skinny Eileen in your wake,
Take off your broken topper, shoot your dog
And look at me, as I break every
By-law known to God or man, walk slowly
To the platform's end, step down and then am seen
To vanish in the tunnel's mouth. As if.

Marine Siding

The final rusty flourish of the mountain ash
As it docks in a shower of sparks

At the scrapyard where railways and oceans
Merge at nowhere's entrepôt –

My friend, this is the famous happiness,
An alloy of the daylight world!

Closed

No cigarettes tonight. No tea. The spoon
Swings on a chain from the counter's edge.
Every cup and saucer's full of ash.
The buffet is pretending to be closed.
Inside it, under glass, a sandwich waits for you.
Stay here too long and it may speak your name.
The revels are but lately ended, bab.
You thought you understood austerity –
But fuck your sympathy and go without.
The white-tiled Gents is like a ruined temple.
Now it takes the democratic piss,
And would you care for a discreet disease?
What day it is. What time it is. What sea-coast
And what realm is this. The roof
Upheld by iron trunks, the arches uttering
New arches, further demarcations of
The darkness in the ramifying dark. The chance
That this might be the secondary place, that home
Lies just across the footbridge, through an arch,
Along a platform looking up and down
The ordinary night – and *there*, a steamy door,
Change counted out in halfpennies, received
With patience and a joke that no one but
The waitress and her pink-necked soldier hear.
You had to be there, you suppose. You never were.
It's in the way you tell 'em, in the fact
You know so well what you could never find.

The Island

Our island is full of detectives,
Believers in crime whose churches are stations.
See, they urge the engines on to justice
Down the slow branches of Sunday.
Abolished county towns
And ports deserted by the sea
And government establishments
On islands of their own on little lakes in woodland –
Bring them the gospel, detectives! By rail!

Who killed the White Horse?
The Long Man? Who severed his member?
Who did for the greenhouse? Who thrashed
The recalcitrant carpet to death
With a length of malacca?
Who commanded the hideous
Stockbroker villas be flung up like sets
For the Bad British Movie, redeemed
To a certain extent by the actors?

Perhaps we shall never be told –
For these are perfect murders, every one,
Yet our tireless detectives persist,
For example: the Jesuit literary critic,
His cursing-equipment concealed
In a modest valise; or the subaltern
Suddenly shell-shocked to forty,
Flinching in the ceaseless rain of limbs;
And the straight-talking lesbian polymath,
Clamped like a vice to the slightest evasion –

All have their says, taking turns
By the library fire on Sunday,
Or, weather permitting, outside on the lawn
As the fountains play over the pond
Where the dead in their green rooms look up
With expressions of genuine interest
As if this were something they might like
To read about properly later.

Where else could they possibly live,
Those who speak in that language
And gather in galleries, mourning themselves
In the work of Ravilious?
They are in the other country,
The place you might reach if you found
The right door and went in
To be treated as if you belonged
And heard yourself talk like a native
To summon a grey English beauty
From short afternoons, to be sure
How to live and believe
In the dark, near a railway.

Railway Lands

Over these moss-padded sleepers
The nineteenth century runs out of steam.
One rail vanishes, then both are imprints,
And next silver birches advance
Up the road from the other direction.
Yet people think this place has finished with itself:
An end to hawthorn, bindweed, brambles' practicality,
The accidental forest after work.
But here a level-crossing gate
Dividing nowhere off from nowhere else
Is losing its colour and pith in the rain
To the task of reversion, this sweet degradation,
Its O of red warning weathered into art
Among these labyrinthine galleries.
How shall we live, if not in this green anarchy?

If they take this there will be nowhere left,
No one to visit the turntable pit
For the fireweed rearing from oil-sweat,
To peer into the Marmite pools
For railway fish, no one to lie at dusk
Beneath cow parsley when it tilts
Its dishes to interrogate the moon,
No one to see the place become
Itself now that the meaning's gone.
It is as if we never lived, my love,
And never lay here afterwards
Where language takes its rest.
Where are you now?
Whose is this face I see
Inside the rusty water, just about to speak?

Infernal

It strikes you: you are here. It's quite a sight —
The pitchblack blazing lake of Hell by night
(The postcards stole their ancient joke from Hull).
And all alone, although it must be full.
There must have been a mixup on the quays —
You told them but the staff weren't listening.
Teabreak's over, lads — back on your knees.
All hail the chief. Prepare to kiss the ring.

Bruges-la-Morte

Suppose you lived in Bruges-la-Morte: this brown murk would be blue
Whistlerian the crepuscule, canals as thick as glue.

There to usurp the half-life led by M. Rodenbach,
Complete with thousand-metre stare and wispy ginger 'tache,

Your mission would be seeking out the Quartier Perdu –
A graveyard in a graveyard in the wake of Waterloo.

The beer would turn to incense. Demons would attack.
You'd escape from the asylum. They would come and fetch you back.

You'd be an ultra-Catholic and worship Satan too,
Then form the object of a cult whose devotee was you.

With the national question looming you'd anticipate Degrelle,
But survive beneath the floorboards as a dark traditional smell,

A victim of the plot against the beautiful and true:
Next time, you'd say, *next time we'll know exactly who to screw.*

The verses you composed would neither edify nor please
And slowly you'd succumb to an unspecified disease –

The doctors would allege it was *nostalgie de la boue*
But they'd be sick themselves and there'd be nothing they could do –

The fruit of pork and chocolate and aesthetic overdose,
Designed to prove that in the end all flesh is adipose.

Mud gave us Maeterlinck and Rops and (almost) you-know-who,
But rest assured that nobody would ever hear of you.

As you stared up through the sewage, black swans would stare back down:
If you could speak you would declare that it's your kind of town –

O Bruges-la-Morte! The sea itself has offered its adieux.
Whistlerian the crepuscule. Canals as thick as glue.
The streets are safe. No danger here of stumbling on The New.

The Drunken Boat

after Rimbaud

The vast indifferent river carried me, and in a while
The cries of sailors faded with the whoops of Seminoles
Who'd caught my crew and nailed them Roman-style
In decorative rows on totem poles.

Weighed down with Flanders wheat and English cotton,
I was of course untroubled by their fate.
Their cries were gone and they were soon forgotten,
And as the waters quickened I took flight.

Last winter in the furious beating of the seas,
While growing deafer than an infant's brain,
I ran! And the unmoored peninsulas
Were all seduced by chaos, so they won't be home again.

When I awoke at sea I had the blessing of the tempest.
Lighter than a cork I set off dancing on the surge,
The ever-rolling graveyard where the drowned may never rest.
Some put their faith in harbour lights: I never felt the urge.

The green sea found its way inside my hull of Swedish pine.
It was sweeter than the oozing flesh of windfalls to a boy,
And as it swabbed the decks of stains from puke and sour wine,
It also swept the rudder and the anchor-chain away.

Since when I have been bathing in the Poem of the Sea,
Infused with galaxies, lactating, drinking down
Green-azure, watching now and then, like flotsam drifting by,
A long-dead sailor turn in sleep and dream that he will drown.

Out here before your eyes the blue will drain out of the sea
When slow delirious rhythms working underneath
The glow of dawn, too strong for drink or poetry,
Ferment red love, more bitter on the lips than death!

I have seen waterspouts, seen lightning murdering the sky,
Seen undertows and currents and the evening's crepuscule,
Seen dawn's exalted race of doves set free to fly
And I have sometimes seen what men imagine to be real.

I have seen the low sun smeared with mystic horrors,
Projecting vast illusions on a screen of purple-grey;
Meanwhile the shutters of the waves, a Sophoclean chorus,
Beat and beat into the distance but will never get away.

I have dreamed the green night blinded by the snows,
Dreamed a kiss that rises slowly to meet the ocean's eyes
While sperm and ichor circulate on currents no one knows,
And dreamed the phosphor singing blue and yellow as the
                                        sun begins to rise.

For months on end I've followed where the swells
Stormed at the reefs like herds of maddened cattle in a pen,
Never dreaming that the Virgins' shining feet could quell
So suddenly the uproar of the ocean.

I have collided, I would have you know, with fabulous bayous
Where panthers go disguised in human skins,
Inseparable from flower-heads, while arching watergaws
Extend their underwater reins for anything with fins.

I have watched the fermentation of immeasurable mires
Where a complete Leviathan lay trapped among the rushes,
Seen water fall like stone upon flat calm from clear blue air
And distances sucked down into abysses!

And glaciers, silver sun and pearly waves and brazen skies,
Appalling landfalls in the depths of gulfs of ochre brume
Where serpents eaten from within by parasitic flies
Plunge from the twisted trees in clouds of black perfume.

I would have liked to show the children manatees
Born of the blue waves, the golden fish, the fish that sing.
Flowers of foam have rocked this argosy
And sometimes secret winds allowed me wings.

Sometimes, a martyr weary of the globe and north and south,
The sea whose lamentation sweetened my sea-road
Would offer me its shadow-flowers with yellow sucker-mouths
And like a penitent I knelt, and waited there and prayed . . .

I was almost an island. My walls were stucco'd with the crap
That pale-eyed fractious cackling sea-birds dripped.
When once more I went scudding on, across my ropes
Drowned men arose and then sank backwards into sleep.

Thrown by the hurricane into the birdless ether,
I, a vessel lost among the tresses of the coves,
I, whose sea-drunk carcass neither *Merrimack* nor *Monitor*
Nor Hanseatic brigantine would ever think to save;

Free and smoking, rising from the purple haze,
I who pierced the red sky like a wall beyond which can be got
A delicacy poets will be anxious to appraise
In which the lichens of the sun combine with sky-blue snot;

I who ran on, speckled with electric lunulae,
A raving plank, plus honour-guard of sea-horses in mourning,
When under hammer blows from cruel Julys
Blue heaven was a crater left perpetually burning;

I who trembled when I felt from fifty leagues away
The roar of rutting behemoths and tidal bores,
Interminable mover through blue immobility,
I yearn for Europe and her ancient belvederes.

I have seen star-archipelagos! And isles
Where the delirious skies lie open to the sailor. Can it be
That in those unfathomable nights you sleep your exile's
Sleep, O million golden birds, O power of futurity?

But truly I have wept too much, heartbroken by the dawn
And every cruel moon and bitter sun.
And love has bloated me with torpor. Oh, then,
Let my keel split and let me sink into the ocean.

Bathed in your weariness, O waves, I can no longer
Follow in the wake of cotton-boats, nor stand the brassy sulks
Of navies' flags and banners in the offing, nor
The dead-eyed gaze of loathsome prison-hulks.

If I long for European waters, it is for that pool,
Pitch-black and freezing, where at scented twilight
A child will come and crouch, brimful
With sorrows, and send out his fragile boat.

Michael

I see you often in your later phase –
A refugee from 1954,
Black-suited ascetic, destitute priest
With a flute in a carrier bag,
Having only the clothes you lay down in.

Today you stood among the crowds
Where Grafton Street meets College Green
And waited for the lights to change.
Do up your coat. And where's your scarf?
We don't want you to catch your death again.

The Landing-Stage

For Derek Mahon

Like one surprised yet tolerant,
You walk out of the darkness now
To speak to those you cannot see
Or quite believe in, though the place
Is stowed to bursting with the crowd
Who are, like foreign policy,
Especially concerned with you.

Now that you take the floor at last
We see it is a landing-stage, new-built
For the Odyssean returnee –
Port in a storm or final anchorage
No one can tell but you perhaps
Who even as you speak to us
Take care to keep your counsel still.

In our unheroic age
You have sustained a northern clarity
Enriched with the harmonics of the south,
And learned to voice whatever is the case
For wisdom's and its own sweet sake
As music, intimate and vast.
You let the grave itself unstop its mouth.

You tell the language that your love
Endures, whatever you have undergone
Of shipwreck or dry-docked disorder:
Wave-wanderer, beachcomber, far-flung
Singer with a shell for Nausicaa, at home
Nowhere and everywhere, but here and now,
And straddling the border once again.

Dinner at Archie's

i.m. Archie Markham 1939–2008

This place, the world, as you have more than once remarked,
More than once in fact tonight
Over this mound of roast lamb-with-no-veg and over the rim
                                              of your glass,

This world as we find it consists
Of two sorts of people: those here in the room and the rest,
On the one hand those present and then the great herd

Of the – how shall you put it – the *dim*
Who are not present to protest,
That one for instance, and *her*, and God help us, *him*;

Us and the rest, on the one hand the illuminati
And as you may at one time or another perhaps have remarked
The utterly and irredeemably endarked

Whom fortune and folly have somehow permitted
To be for the most part (catastrophically) in charge,
A theme upon which you are not normally slow to enlarge.

Have you mentioned this ever? Why, yes.
– Because, as you point out, coming back with more lamb
And in case there's a need an additional bottle of red,

It is of course something that every so often *needs* to be said,
And the likes of us – we happy few – have to come to the help
                                              of the party,

Be it never so small and the truth elusive,

And expulsion – you look at me narrowly – rather more likely than not,
While as for the others, at times they are almost enough,
One must confess, with their blather and rot,

To make one grow frankly abusive, alas,
And if that would be casting pearls before swine,
For example those toadies and gibbering no-marks in Administration,

Well somebody's got to set an example and do it.
– And yet, though the day is sufficiently evil, no doubt
We shall somehow contrive to get through it

By means of a diet of lamb-with-no-veg and red wine,
Not to mention our native good humour
And sheer bloody genius, shan't we?

Of course we shall, Archie, of course,
For who could deny that it's fruitless to argue
With one like yourself who contrives to combine

The attributes of the immoveable object
With those of the irresistible force.
More lamb? More wine? No veg. Why, Archie, of course.

Porteriana

Transported back to demi-Paradise –
Via Port Said to aid comparison –
You note down all your city's names with care,
From Bongi-Bo to Heal's and Frognal (though
You draw the line at Haslemere), likewise
The Jacobean scorch-marks left
On pages from the *A–Z* where miniskirts
And lycanthropes have gone in hot pursuit
Of wisdom through the bars and galleries.
The ugly rich resemble gods; the poor
Are no one but themselves; the streets are paved
With unconsoling instances, and while you work
In that high room among the holy notes,
Between the rooftops dusk stands like belief
To lead us on but not to bear our weight.
Then there are landlords to be gratified.
In time all this will help compose
The epic Bach and Arthur Mee have hinted at.
The scratches on the ceiling of the tube,
Pontormo's murdered God, those things with shears,
The whole of death and loss, are to be reconciled
In 'music's huge light irresponsibility',
When in the garden in the square the dead
Are helped into the day and spoken with afresh
Across the long white tablecloths
Where bread and wine are eagerly supplied
By teams of deaf-mute journalists and critics. There
It will be always afternoon, the taxis purring
Calmly at the gates, the oratorio delighted
To possess its soul in patience, while inside the hall
The Berlin Philharmonic longs for your arrival.

Leavetaking

In memory of Peter Porter

In a draughty terrace bar
Beside the *cave* at Château Ventenac,
And lapped by the green Midi canal,
I take my leave, old friend,
By raising *une pression* and not
The Minervois that you would recommend.
Bad news prefers its poison cold and long.
The news has not improved so far –
So, keep the decent bottle in the rack
For later, for the 'decent interval'
That death like a bureaucracy requires.

Or maybe neck it in the midnight heat
Up at the house when everyone's in bed,
At one end of the huge white tablecloth,
At which a Nazi colonel also sat
To sample the warm south
While waiting for the war to end –
The kind of fact you would absorb
For later, but there is no later now.
Flute-playing psychopaths all must
Like cats and poets come to dust,
But I will not be reconciled.

The evening boats slide in,
Last autumn's leaves still piled
Along their guttering and in the seats
Of plastic chairs left out on deck
In token of a former merriment

In which I am required to believe
When the *patron*, a rugby star
From some time back, limps past
To put another freezing glass beside the last,
Then fire the oven up with grubbed-up vines
And stand admiring its crimson speech
As though like alcohol it were
A kind of poetry. My friend,
Is there sufficient detail for you yet?
You'd know much faster than I ever could
The point at which the orchestration starts
And evening is converted into art.

La patronne with her brutal crop
And wide-girl suit comes out
To criticize the styling of the blaze.
The grinning barman comes by bicycle
And finds their bickering, the bar,
The voices from the dim canal, the flicker
Of the bunting's spectral tricolores
A stage to serve his wordless drollery:
These are perhaps our characters, but where's
The crowd to fill the choruses
Of black-edged pastoral?

The world, you'd say, exists
Not to be understood
But to demand conviction. I assent,
As if it matters, and the dancers have arrived,
Cool, pink-pastelled blondes who
In another life have raised
A *parapluie* at Cherbourg, squired
By lupine George Chakirises in black.

This is the world, or part of it.
They do not think themselves Shakespearean,
Although you might, were we to sit
Beside the water here, me with *une pression*
And you among the quiet notes you will transform
Into a poem in the high nine hundreds.
I have not learned your lesson yet.
Work is good, like love and company,
But these so-courteous deaths, who sweep
Their maidens up and down the shore
In perfect silence on their light fantastic feet
(When did the music stop?) insist
That they are quite another thing,
Sent from a place less beautiful than this
But just as carefully designed,
The shade beyond the trees and the canal,
Where evening ends, and songs likewise,
And there is no one left to sing.

The Heat of the Day

Deep in the restaurant afternoon, we share
The hypnagogic drowse of smoking cooks,
Their seething pans, the far white gaze of fish
Awaiting resurrection by the night.
Some days we think at first it's tinnitus,
But then, for those civilians who can't take
The noise itself or face its jealous glare,
These proxies of the sun evoke our roaring star,
Its gold and black, its cruel command.
Cicadas have to scratch their itch en masse,
Each breath the friction of a Lucifer
Against the empyrean. Fuming skeletons
Botched up from old cicada-wrecks,
Then dipped in phosphorus and set ablaze
Before the god who never calls or writes,
No wonder if they're mad to keep the faith.
Like nudist zealots on the harbour wall
Who want their shadows scorched into the rock,
In time it might be possible to learn
How not to dwell on ice-cubes or the dark,
But atheists are indoors having sex
By thunderous air-con, while we're marooned
Beneath this blinding canvas, hard at work.
The sun is not quite real, nor this white heat,
Nor the cicadas in their adoration.
We're Northerners. We need rehearsals first,
Improving views of Hell from time to time,
The heat deferred into the grave, the fact,
We like to think, beyond imagining.
So then, let's drain this burning glass
And try with incandescent tolerance to catch

The waiter's lizard eye and beg a light –
A sip of petrol? No, but please, the bill,
Though our incinerated voices,
Flaring white with eager terror, sound
Far distant, like the tinnitus of gods.

Tables and Chairs

'the innocent walls and light'
ROY FULLER

The tables and chairs, 'the innocent walls and light',
Would be nowhere without us. Enter this house
At the edge of a field, where two unnumbered roads
Converge and part across a ridge of silver birch.
The mirrors and the ornaments survive
The almost-hush of the unopened air; the figures
In the photographs look back in smiling disbelief
From the Town Hall steps. Those were the days.
So what are these, these silences that never cease
To fall between darkness and darkness,
That we cannot interrupt with speech
Or gestures or routine or love? What shall we gain
By witnessing the pathos of a ewer
Standing in an old stone sink,
As faithful and attentive as a dog? If we should
Scrutinize the cracked glaze of a tile
Left lying on the window-sill, and then pass on
To emulate the windows' wall-eyed stare
At ordinary emptiness, a yard, the gate
Ajar to take us back where we began
And see us off the premises,
What margin of endurance do we think
We'll find, between necessity and chance?

Aspects of the Novel

1. Chapter 16

In which the action pauses for an hour
To let the characters rehearse their manias
And share a glass there in the poisoned glade.
Time passes? It does not. Time flies.
The reader cannot wait for homicide.
The danger is this may be only literature,
Whose love is all for means and never ends,
Whose very rhetoric confers
An immortality of sorts, a long
Engagement, not a zipless fuck.
But these are monsters we have come among.
A line of Nietzsche turns to three of coke,
To reminiscence. Anyone might think
Their past was real and likewise their regret
For everything that led them here
To this green silence (no birds sing) to drink
Gall to the lees and rave into the night.
Their leisure is an index of anxiety.
Their watches throb like ulcers. Sticky cushions
Rub against the women's legs. When can it be
If not tonight the worst suspicions
Voice themselves? If not tonight, when shall we
Care about these passions? Wait and see.
For him the problem is ontology, for her
The inability to read the signs that what
This evening holds must be a dripping axe,
And, for their friend, the difference
Between the crimson notion and the fact.
Time they were going, though, high time

We parted at the turning of the page
To meet our ignorance afresh,
And leave them in their papered catacomb
To lie and dream themselves awake, and yet
We wait, we wait, and evening turns to ash.

2. Want of Motive

You detect a want of motive here
But don't you find motive
Is what you become on the way,
O seeker after knowledge,
Truth and beauty, equipped
With disposable income? No?

Don't you sometimes find
That history's at work
In you as in the rest,
The living and the dead
And the imagined?
Or perhaps you don't.

Fare forward then, traveller!
Into the white-gold hinterland
Devoted to Apollo,
Right-angled rectitude
Clear sightlines, God's truth
And nobody, nobody there.

3. The Uninvited Reader

'There was no one I could identify with'

It was unwise to come here looking for a friend
Among the long-established enmities
Assembled on this summer night to mark
The marriage of the dim to the perverse
With shadowy foretelling and asides
Among the ha-has and the sheds:

For what this cast of characters requires
Is an audience, the formal kind
That servants or a governess would once supply –
The help, essential but unheard, their tiny love,
If love it was, less unrequited
Than ignored. You do know this?

Perhaps in fact it's why you came
And keep on coming, not so much to feel
That what you feel goes unrewarded as to learn
With a succinct, addictive pain, like so,
That here, since no one at the party cares,
It ceases to exist. Now get your coat.

The River on the Terrace

Time after time, the river of light
Flows down the broad steps of the terrace
Between the white walls and blue shutters

And under the carob and grapevine, coming on
In slow gold blinks, in indigo and rust,
Minting coins to sink among the shadows

It discards as it conceives them,
Folding clean sheets out of nothing,
Wheeling then pausing minutely as if

On the unbroken skin of itself.
Its depth is the authority it wields
To hold us to this wager, sliding past our feet

Over the plain of cracked paving-stones,
Onwards to the terrace-end, then out and down
Into the burning mezzogiorno air.

The river sinks into the rock. It never was,
Until a breeze comes up the valley
And the water re-awakes. Again we watch,

Like travellers halted at a ford,
Beside this force that seems to be anxiety.
What is it like, what is it like,

Unpassing epoch-afternoon, dry bed
Through which the river fades, then flows?
Like love, and like anxiety, like this.

Narbonne

The sound of a train is the sound of the wind
In the narrow streets, is nowhere, is a train
Not taken, though I see its swaying corridors
Framing the sun's flight second by second
And wake to a scattering of rain at the glass,
To streets I have been dreaming, still and wet,
From which the sound has only now
Yet therefore utterly departed, which is why
I go on listening anyway, until
The silence too exhausts itself and once again
The wind sings in the eaves and campaniles.
I know that when we lie at rest
You listen too, that you are not afraid
If clearly we shall have to live forever
In this state of perfect ignorance, new-born
To these familiar conditions that will once more
Exalt the heart in breaking it. Come close.
No atlas could describe the distances that sound –
The train, the gust among the tiles and attics –
Offers us for nothing as it fades, the wind
Into itself, the train into its schedule – an express
Importantly imagining the north for those
Who long to go or dare to stay or never
Think of going anywhere at all. Come close.
What business can it be of ours
To feel this way, as though both honoured
And arraigned, to have to give this sound
That might be nothing but the wind
Our tribute of attention till it's gone?

On the Toon

Canto I

O fairest of the northern waters, river-god, great Tyne, I asked,
Flow through this language now, hydrate the tongue
Afresh, abolish drought and thirst
And let me drink you in to learn
The meaning of our history, and what must be.
Send me a guide from your deep source,
A water-sprite, a river-girl, to go with me.
'The clue you're looking for at thirteen down,'
She said, 'is river-stairs, and learning that
Will cost you. Mine's a turquoise WKD.'
I looked up. There she sat along the bar
In the unmoving reaches of the afternoon
Among the far-gone gadgies in the Crown Posada,
Bold as brass with long black hair, green eyes,
A tiny dress of shifting emerald and jet.
I put the paper down and fetched her drink
And as she raised it to her lips it seemed
We stood beside the Tyne by night, no moon,
A black tide licking past, ourselves alone.
A boat was waiting, moored beneath the stairs.
She led me down, took up the oar, and as we stood
Upright, *traghetto*-style, she swung us out
Beneath the great arch of an unknown bridge
And on into the secret Hell of Tyne.
First came a labyrinth of flooded passageways
With dead men labouring waist-deep in ice
To win the coal that never reached the light.
I saw them crushed between the jaws of tunnels
Only to unearth themselves and then resume

Their labours with a passion whose futility
They knew but would not bow to. No one spoke.
As we moved off, the echo of their picks came
After us a little way until the stream grew broad again
And steered us to a subterranean Sargasso,
The breaker's yard of all the ironclads the Tyne
Had launched for the engagements at Tsushima,
Jutland and the rest. Among the showers of sparks
The welders moved like surgeons, opening
The rusted ribs of battleships still glowing red
From their exploded magazines. Released
Into the smoky air, the drowned men sealed belowdecks
Slid and flopped along the quays as though alive.
Then silent gangs with carts would haul away
These levies to augment Golgotha's pyramids.
'What does this mean?' I asked my guide. 'Bad faith,'
She said, 'to know and not remember; to remember
In a lie; to claim to want the lost world back. Bad faith
Can have no history, only sentiment.' She could have been
A girl from Scotswood, Byker, Wallsend, Shields,
And yet she said these things. Then she slipped off
Her tall red shoes. 'Massage my feet,' she ordered
While our vessel slid among the burnt-out staithes
And over reefs of sunken cars where twockers
Gazed back disbelievingly as fish went stitching
Deftly through the sockets of their eyes. 'We're nearly there –
Although you're not exactly dressed for clubbing.'
'Smart but casual,' I said. 'Aye, in your dreams.
Stay close, say nowt and dee what I dee, right?'
A wall of smoke arose before us, warehouse windows
Speaking bursts of flame as wooden tenements
Consumed themselves and everyone inside,
While firestorms tore down the city's spires
And night ran red and black and gold

As in a biblical comeuppance. Vast
Explosions in the riverbed threw gouts
Of mud and bones around us, yet the girl betrayed
No fear, but brought us to a cobbled ramp
That seemed to tunnel upwards through the fire,
And at its head a pair of vast red doors
Stood open, guarded by a triple-headed bouncer,
All immaculate in black, who chewed his wads
With the ferocity of Alex Ferguson.
'We're on the list,' she said. He waved us in.
Beyond, there lay a wilderness of mirrorwork
And false lights framing ever more exclusive rooms.
The whole place sweated heartless noise, to which
Dog-headed dancing-girls performed
In leotards of black and white, while slabs of lard
In dandruffed suits rewarded them with absolute
Unsmiling concentration, feeding powder
Up their ruined noses as a timeless duty
Princes of the city deign to undertake. So here's
Where money came to waste itself. 'Let's stick
To lemonade,' she said. 'It took them centuries
Of violent integrity to bring
Geordismo to perfection: here's the fruit,
They like to claim, of all that grim endeavour:
Samurai of self-indulgent crap, who bloom
Like cherry-blossom: so. Now let them die.'
On giant screens by the Olympic pool of schnapps
The match was on – was that Gigg Lane? – but
No one watched, since even here at Pleasure Central
Everybody knew the game was up: tonight
Was next time as foretold, tonight was fire.
And as I thought this, flames burst from the pumps
And lard-men's mouths, a final utterance
That kept the faith with all that proud extremity
And had no breath to waste on content after all.

Canto II

'We've seen enough. Now take my hand and run.'
She led me up a granite spiral in the dark
Pursued by screams and smoke, produced a key
And turned it in a cobwebbed lock and let us
Out into a graveyard in the dawn. We sat there
Smoking reefers on the doorstep of the crypt
Of some forgotten liberal benefactor,
Watching the sunrise come up Westgate Hill
Like one more too-familiar promise made
To all those dwellers in the sky whose promised streets
Have fallen off the map of possibility.
'So what have you to say to them?' she asked
And gestured at this city of the poor, whose life and death
Among the towers and tombs seemed interchangeable.
I shook my head and she shook hers and said,
'If nothing else, let dreams be competent. If not
Don't be surprised to see the Swastika take root
Among these boneyards fed on disappointment.'
Then as her sentence ended we arrived
By Cowen's monument. 'It was from here,' she said,
'The citizens of Newcastle drove Mosley's thugs
Clean off the street. As for the BNP, I've shat 'em.'
She walked me on along the southern edge
Of Grainger Town towards a secret library,
And as I entered I became a book, half-sealed
With smoke, high on a shelf beside the dome
Of that great reading room. I knew the simple fact
That I spent decades unconsulted meant
That there were those below who eyed me jealously
For pulping. From inside the volume next to me
She said, 'And this is what it's like to be
The general good – neglected first and then

Uncomprehended, finally despised. It takes
Less than a lifetime to renew the ignorance
This public mind was built here to dispel.
Now tell me this, whose interest is served
When people can no longer concentrate but find
Their history's best left to the eccentric few
To whom no one need listen? *Cui bono* then?
Who owns the angel at the gate who bids us leave
The earthly paradise of print?' . . . 'Now, pet,
Yer cannat answer that,' the beggarwoman said,
Upon her throne of rags in Charlotte Square,
A hag of sixty holding court among her favourites,
The Gulf War veteran, the methylated Irishman,
The dead-eyed gluey couple with the dog.
All rose and spoke in chorus at her sign:
'See, Fenkle Street was Fennel Street and fennel is
A vegetable sacred to Apollo, god of light
And reason. He it is who animates the mind
To build the city as his monument, set noble curves
Along its hills, see justice done in arch and pediment,
Cut stone that stores the light like lamps, and raise
High windows for the guardians of sense.
Of course the likes of us could only ever be
The citizens of edge and underside,
Cartographers of Grainger Town's decay
From the Enlightenment by way of two world wars
Into the grip of cheque cashiers and glum arcades
Where those with next to nothing give it back
In coin or else in kind upstairs. We speak the truth
And for our knowledge we are flayed alive
Like Marsyas, today and every day.' With this
They raised their cans in tribute and were gone.
I sought my guide along Back Stowell Street
And found the poets' Tower open to the rain.

The time ran on so fast a winter night
Had fallen as I reached St James's Park,
Whose pitiable interregnum stretched
Unhindered to infinity. The lights were out
But slipping through a turnstile I could sense
An eerie glow, and when I reached the pitch
I saw that this was caused by freezing fires
That leaked from all the tombs crammed in
Beneath that sacred turf, some sealed, some with their lids
Rived off, as though grave-robbers searched
For pieces of the past that they could sell,
As if the spirit were a thing. A corpse stood up
Behind his stone and showed his scarf: 'I wore this
Man and boy,' he said, 'since first my father fetched me
To the match among the thousands, where I learned
To praise the arts of Gallagher and Milburn and the rest.
For here was the ground of our being: here!
But someone has been selling off our dreams.
I cannot sleep. Will you release me from my bond?'
I did his bidding, donned the scarf, and once more
Fled in search of my lost guide, the river-girl.
But now her face appeared on posters everywhere,
As missing child and teenage runaway, one face
For all those we have carelessly mislaid, the photographs
Dissolving as I followed where they led,
Until beside a muddy tributary I found
A locked-in boozer called The Sacrifice.
The iron door swung open at my knock.

Canto III

Inside, a Cyclops with an attitude
Gave me a narrow look and weighed a pool cue

Thoughtfully. 'Why is it called The Sacrifice?' I asked.
'Depends who's asking, pal,' he said, and smiled
At all his radgie fellow revellers
Who nodded to a steely one-chord motorik
And wore their thirsty heads beneath their arms
Like honours claimed in some unceasing war
In which it seemed the enemy tonight was me.
'No, leave him, Poly,' said a voice I almost knew.
The naiad's older sister stood behind the bar
Dispensing speed and snakebite to the crowd,
Clan-mother to the dead, Medusa-haired
With tiny spitting snakes in black and white.
She handed me a Ziploc and a pint and said,
'This is the very bottom of the night, the last
Redoubt of proletarian bacchanal.
It's where the Fat Slags get the jump on Dionysos,
Rend him limb from limb, then fall asleep
And come the foul-tongued dawn remember nowt
But feel they might have spoken out of turn.
This is a place of endings-up. Your missing guide
Might well have come to grief down here,
Had she not chosen otherwise. Her disappearance
Was a test. Go out the back. You'll find her there.'
Then as I stepped outside into the dark
The pub descended like a lift into the earth
And I could see across the snowy ground
The naiad beckoning impatiently. The tide
Had filled the muddy ditch, so we cast off
Into the blizzard's freezing dark. I put my hand
Upon her arm. She turned and stared at me
Till I removed it. 'All I meant,' I said,
'Was that I do not even know your name.
Who can you be, to wake such fearful care
That I've pursued you to the back of night?'

'I have no name, although you know me well.
My name, you see, is all the town might yet become.
Now watch again to learn if night will end
Or if this underworld of history must be
The grave and sum of all the labour and the love
The ordinary citizens have given here.'
And as she spoke, a curving line of light appeared
And we sped upstream on the tide to pass
Beneath the eye that blinked for us, then swung to rest
To let the early walkers cross the Tyne.
It seemed the day must be some kind of festival,
So many passed and waved to see our little craft
Commanded by the river-girl. Then, looking back,
I saw it was a fleet they welcomed in,
The tall romance of ocean-going sails we seemed
To herald, hundreds crowding from the globe,
Swan-sure and rigged like promises,
To moor along the packed sea-thirsty quays.
The day was fine. The early sun struck galleries
And concert halls, the courts and prison vans alike.
It reached the weather-vanes and tower blocks
And made the walkers in the canyons by the quays
Stare up past empty offices into a sky
That for this hour looked like common property.
All this the water-engine of the Tyne sustained.
We gazed on through the arch of the great bridge,
Beyond the city to the double springs
Where we begin and re-begin, in work and love –
Or so it seemed, borne on that bracing tide of light
And possibility, whose name I think was Paradise,
Since for a moment that was what I seemed to hear
The gathered host declare as one free city-state
Of equal citizens who served the common good.
And then the word was spoken and the crowd

Moved on into ten thousand conversations
And the faces I had seen along the way emerged
A moment and then blended with the rest.
Now while I had been gazing, she had moored
Where we set out and so we climbed the steps
Into the ordinary day, where all the girls like her
Came out to sport their finery and claim
Their portion of the pleasures of the Town.
'You mustn't think that we've arrived,' she said.
'That place waits in the permanent conditional
That's yet to find its time. Time I was gone as well.'
She kissed me on the cheek. 'Take care now, pet.'
She smiled and stepped into the crowd
And disappeared, and all the jostling girls
Were river-girls, and she was all of them.
My eyes grew cloudy then. I felt my way
Towards the Crown Posada, where I sat
Once more inside the shade of afternoon
And tried to grasp the vision while it fled,
Though all I had about me was a biro
From the bookies and a *Chronicle* to write on. O
Great Tyne, I was unworthy of the task.
I lacked the gifts required to convey
The terror and the pity and the hope
I witnessed on my night out on the Toon.
But here it is. So pick the bones from that. 'I think
We need another tense for dreaming in,' I said,
Which made an old drunk shake his head and smile.
And if we dreamed? I couldn't say, but caught
The barman's eye and turned to thirteen down.

Notes

Notes on 'The Underwater Songbook'

'Songs from *The Drowned Book*' was written as part of *The Book of the North*, a project in which writers and visual artists collaborated on an alternative history of the North. The songs were set to music by Keith Morris. 'Songs from *The Black Path*' are part of a radio play, *The Black Path*, in which the prose dialogue was co-written with Julia Darling. 'Songs from *Downriver*' is from a jazz musical co-written with Keith Morris.

Notes to *Inferno*

CANTO III

60. *Pilate who refused his word*: Pontius Pilate, Roman procurator of Judea AD 26–36. Faced with demands for the crucifixion of Christ, according to Matthew 27.24, Pilate 'washed his hands before the multitude, saying, I am innocent of the blood of this just person: see ye to it.' Pilate is among a number of figures suggested as the subject of this line. He is certainly the most familiar to modern readers. The most popular candidate with commentators, however, is Pope Celestine V, a contemporary of Dante, whose abdication in 1294 (known as 'The Great Refusal') made way for the corrupt papacy of Dante's enemy Boniface VIII.

78. *Acheron*: one of the linked rivers of Hell, with Phlegethon and the Styx, which fall into Cocytus, the pool at the bottom of Hell.

84. *An ancient white-haired man*: Charon, the ferryman, who transports the shades of the dead over Acheron into Hell proper. He appears in the *Aeneid*.

19. *Phlegyas*: set fire to the temple of Apollo at Delphi, in furious revenge for Apollo's rape of his daughter Coronis. He was condemned to punishment in Tartarus, the part of Hell reserved for those who offend the gods. Dante converts Phlegyas into a ferryman to rival Charon. Phlegyas's fury is apt to the Fifth Circle, that of the Wrathful, in which his boat operates.

32. *A figure thick with mud*: Filippo Argenti, a Florentine contemporary of Dante. 'Argenti' since he was said to have his horse shod in silver, according to Boccaccio, who described him as the most irascible of men.

68. *The city known to men as Dis*: Dis is the Roman name for Pluto, god of the underworld.

70. *its mosques*: in medieval Christian terms, Hell is comparable to a city of infidels – i.e. Muslims and Turks.

82. *angels*: those of Satan's party who fell with him from Heaven after their defeated revolt against God.

CANTO XIII

10. *Harpies*: bird-shaped monsters with claws and women's faces, the Harpies drove Aeneas and his crew from the Strophades, islands in the Ionian Sea.

33. *The trunk cried out*: Pier della Vigna (c.1190–1249), poet and chancellor of the Italian realms under the Emperor Frederick II; disgraced, imprisoned and blinded 1249; committed suicide; widely thought to have been the victim of a plot.

115–116. *The one in front . . . / The other*: the spendthrift Arcolana da Squarcia di Riccolfo Marconi, killed near Pieve del Toppo; and the brutal and reckless Jacopo da Santo Andrea, murdered.

CANTO XVII

1. *the monster*: Geryon is the embodiment of Fraud, the subject of the two subsequent cantos. His hybrid form is produced by untrustworthiness and illusion.

35. *another group*: the usurers. Each wears a pouch bearing the device of his family.

85. *quartan*: a form of malaria.

107. *Phaëthon*: son of Helios, the sun god, borrowed his father's chariot but proved too weak to control the horses and nearly incinerated the earth. Jove killed Phaëthon with a thunderbolt and sank him in the River Po.

CANTO XXII

47. *the sufferer*: unidentified.

81. *Fra Gomita*: a Sicilian friar who sold public offices and was later hanged.

CANTO XXV

2. *the fig sign*: an obscene gesture made with the fist, the thumb being inserted between the fore and middle fingers. A Pistoian fortress featured two marble arms aiming this gesture towards Florence.

25. *Cacus*: said to have stolen cattle from Hercules and concealed them unsuccessfully under the Aventine Hill in what became Rome.

43. *Cianfa*: a Florentine, a member of the Donati family, a thief.

95. *Sabellus and Nasidius*: in Lucan's *Pharsalia*, Sabellus is a Roman soldier whose body putrefies following a snake-bite; Nasidius, also a soldier, was also bitten, swelled up and died.

98. *Cadmus and . . . Arethusa*: in Ovid's *Metamorphoses*, Cadmus killed a dragon sacred to Mars and was turned into a snake (IV, 76–89); the nymph Arethusa, pursued by the god Alpheus, was transformed into a fountain (V, 53–58).

140. *Buoso*: not certainly identified.

148. *Puccio Sciancato*: Puccio Galigai, nicknamed Sciancato, 'lame', a renowned thief.

150. *Francesco Cavalcanti*: a Florentine, murdered by the villagers of Gaville, who are said to have been almost exterminated when the Cavalcanti family took their revenge.

CANTO XXVI

8. *what Prato craves*: the city of Prato, under Florentine control; or Cardinal Niccolo da Prato, who excommunicated the citizens of Florence in 1304.

34. *he who was avenged by bears*: the prophet Elisha.

35. *Elijah's chariot*: its departure was witnessed by Elisha.

54. *Eteocles and his brother*: Eteocles and Polynices, sons of Oedipus, killed each other in single combat. So intense was their hatred that the flame of their funeral pyre divided into two.

55–63. *Ulysses and Diomedes*: Homeric heroes, they lured Achilles to take part in the Trojan War, against the wishes of his lover Deidamia. They stole the Palladium, a wooden image on which the safety of Troy depended. Ulysses was one of the Greek warriors concealed in the wooden horse by which Troy was taken. The fall of Troy brought about the departure of Aeneas, and, by inference, the ultimate foundation of Rome.

75. *a stranger's language*: traditionally the Greeks looked down on speakers of other tongues as 'barbarians'.

91. *Circe*: the enchantress, who lived on the island of Aeaea and changed the shipwrecked Ulysses's crew into swine. Ulysses, protected by the magic root, moly, made her reverse the change. He lived with Circe for a year and she bore him a son, Telegonus.

92. *Gaeta*: a seaport north of Naples. It is said to take its name from that of Aeneas's nurse, whom he buried there.

108. *his markers*: the Pillars of Hercules, at the exit of the Mediterranean into the Atlantic.

13. *Count Ugolino*: intrigued with both Guelfs and Ghibellines in pursuit of power. Betrayed by Archbishop Ruggieri, he was imprisoned with his sons in July 1288.

32. *Gualandi and Sismondi and Lanfranchi*: powerful Pisan Ghibelline families.

82. *Capraia and Gorgona*: offshore islands belonging to Pisa.

118. *Fra Alberigo*: a *frate godente*, a member of the Guelf Manfredi family. At a family dinner he used the instruction to 'let the fruits come' as a signal to assassins to kill several of his relatives.

124. *Ptolomea*: the third part of Cocytus, named after Ptolemy, King of Egypt, who murdered his guest, the fugitive Pompey, or the treacherous Pompey of Jericho, whose story is told in Maccabees 16.11–17.

126. *Atropos*: one of the three Fates. Clotho spun the thread of life; Lachesis measured it; Atropos severed it.

137. *Branca D'Oria*: murdered his father-in-law, Michael Zanche, at dinner.

Note to *November*

Cahiers du Cinema. Karl Malden does not in fact appear in *The Battle of the Bulge*. But clearly he should.

Index of Titles

A Coffin-Boat 352
A Corridor 147
A Donegal Golfer 113
A Little Place They Know 367
A Master 57
A Matinee 96
A Northern Assembly 222
A Provincial Station 186
A Rarity 168
A Secret 188
Abendmusik 399
Acheron, Phlegethon, Styx 210
After Laforgue 152
After Rilke: To Hölderlin 401
After This Poem 87
Air 7
Amerika 260
Amours de Grimsby 202
An Ordinary Evening in New Holderness 146
Anne-Marie, the Flower Girl 13
Arcadia 406
Aspects of the Novel 465
At the Gate 218
At the Wellgate 120
Autumn Begins at St James's Park, Newcastle 167
AWOL 179

Ballad of the Lit and Phil 141
Baltica 228
Before 105
Beginning 243

Betweentimes 127
Biographer 192
Blizzard 405
Blue Night 397
Boundary Beach 117
Bridge 389
Bruges-la-Morte 448
By Ferry 350

Cahiers du Cinema 419
Canto I 470
Canto II 473
Canto III 475
Canto III, The Entry to Hell 291
Canto VIII, Crossing the Styx 297
Canto XIII, The Wood of the Suicides 302
Canto XVII, Geryon; the Usurers 308
Canto XXII, Escape 314
Canto XXV, Snakes and Metamorphoses 320
Canto XXVI, Ulysses 326
Canto XXXIII, Ugolino 332
Cantona 195
Chapter 16 465
Cherchez la Femme 388
Cities 237
Civilians 60
Clio 21
Closed 443
Cold 131
Counting the Rain 438
Cousin Coat 89

Dedication 341
Dinner at Archie's 456

Drains 351
Dundee Heatwave 122

Eating the Salmon of Knowledge from Tins 348
Elegy 429
Entertainment 114
Envoi 86
Essay on Snow 174
Europeans 428
Ex Historia Geordisma 271

Fantasia on a Theme of James Wright 379
Fiction and the Reading Public 92
Fireweed 411
First Time Around 440
Fishing 123
Football! Football! Football! 258
For Lowell George 27
from Sports Pages 212
from The Go-As-You-Please Songbook 271
From the Narrator's Tale 44
from The Poems of Mercedes Medioca 272
From the Whalebone 135

Geography 102
Grey Bayou 361
Grimshaw 395
Gun Law 36

Hatred of Libraries 111
Heatwave 38
Here You Are 391
HMS Glasshouse 129
Homework 191

Horizontal (Bobby Smart) 248
House 175
How Ryan Got His Start in Life 76

In a Military Archive 53
In Madre Maria 95
In Residence: A Worst Case View 126
In the Head 25
In the Other Bar 109
Indian Summer 232
Infernal 447
Inheritance 387
Interior 161

Jazz 26
Jeudi Prochain 412
Josie 417

Kanji 234
Kingdom of Kiev, Rios das Muertes 98

Lament 245
Last Orders at the Fusilier, Forest Hall 220
Late 39
Latinists 178
Le Départ 9
Le Voyage 189
Leavetaking 459
Lines on Mr Porter's Birthday 264
London Road 71
Lost Song of the Apparatus 385

Marine Siding 442
Michael 454

Midsummer's Eve 31
Mission Impossible 121

Narbonne 469
Naughty Ron 139
Nineties 211
No One 181
Noonday 263
Not Sending Cards this Year 33
Notes on the Use of the Library (Basement Annexe) 125
Novembrists 436

Of Origins 177
Of Rural Life 384
On a Blue Guitar (Lulu Banks) 248
On Not Being Paul Durcan 198
On the Piss 133
On the Toon 470

Paradise 196
Paysage 190
Poem for a Psychiatric Conference 274
Poem Written on a Hoarding 173
Porteriana 458
Postcards to the Rain God 265
Praise of a Rainy Country 403
Proem 254
Propaganda 115
Proposal For a Monument to the Third International 371

Quiet Wedding 40

Railway Hotel 393
Railway Lands 446

Railway Songs 183

Rain 171

Ravilious 221

Reading Stevens in the Bath 200

Reasonable Men 390

Revenants 160

Riding on the City of New Orleans 230

River-doors 346

Rose 396

R=U=B=R=I=C 204

Ryan and the Life to Come 83

Ryan at Home 77

Ryan's Farewell 84

Ryan's Rebirth 81

Ryan's Vocation 79

Salisbury Street 416

Serious 137

Serious Chairs 382

Seriously, Like 273

Sheol 365

Six Railway Poems for Birtley Aris 387

Sleep 427

Smoke Signals (Bobby Smart and Sailor Chorus) 250

Somebody Else 157

Something to Read on the Train 193

Song of the South 67

Songs from *Downriver* 207

Songs from the Black Path 243

Songs from the Drowned Book 239

Special Train 163

Station Song 8

Stories 12

Summertime 61

Sunday in a Station of the Metro 441
Sung Dynasty 384
Sunk Island 415
Symposium at Port Louis 368
Synopsis 269

Tables and Chairs 464
Terra Nova 69
The All-Night Afternoon 170
The Allotment 64
The Amateur God 49
The Apprehension 342
The Beat Goes On 28
The Brighton Goodbye 119
The Brochure 19
The Captain's Pipe 47
The Citizens 414
The Dampers 54
The Disappointment 15
The Drunken Boat 450
The Eavesdroppers 219
The Genre: A Travesty of Justice 283
The Grammar School Ghost 236
The Hand 400
The Head Man 100
The Heat of the Day 462
The Ideology 215
The Iron Hand 244
The Island 444
The Lamp 41
The Landing-Stage 455
The Lost Book 432
The Lost War 362
The Mechanical Toy Museum 74

The Mere 357
The Middle 187
The Name 18
The Next Meeting 30
The Olympics 256
The Origins of Sport from Ancient Times 255
The Park by the Railway 11
The Plain Truth of the Matter 439
The Police 16
The Politics Of 166
The Railway Sleeper 277
The Realists 58
The Red Hospital 62
The River in Prose 355
The River on the Terrace 468
The River Road 358
The Seaside Specialist 35
The Snowfield 3
The Thing 380
The Uninvited Reader 467
The Widower 34
The Yard 90
Thom Gunn 381
Three Facetious Poems 322
Three Lighthouses 359
Thrillers and Cheese 107
Tides 42
Time on yer Beer Now (The Company) 252
Timor Mortis 363
To the Unknown God of Hull and Holderness 149
Transport 398
Trespass 66
Two Finger Exercise 46

Unregistered 68

Valedictory 376
Valentine 182
Vérité: Great Junction Street 418
Victims 43
Victorians 14

Walking 5
Want of Motive 466
Water-Gardens 344
Welcome, Major Poet! 209
White Enamel Jug 426
Why The Lady 384
William Ryan's Song in July 24
Working on the Railway 136

Yellow Happiness 388
Young Howard 55

Index of First Lines

A blue light is hung in the house 31
A poster in a newly opened shop professes to preserve 420
After eating with friends, after music and wine, 61
After the whole abandoned stretch, 115
After this poem, perhaps it is evening. 87
All afternoon, the streets are deaf with snow, 98
And when his speech was done, the thief flung up 320
Arcane and absolutist aunt 21
As every mag along the front reveals 35
As I walked out on London Road 71
As schoolkids know, the modern games began 256
As though between performances, the 'varnished waves' of
        seats are gone, 419
At ten p.m. it starts. We can hear from the bar 171
At this hour the park offers only 129

Before the poor are working I am here, 48
Beneath the great white horse's one green eye, 221
'Beyond me lies a city full of pain. 291
Blue night. Enormous Arctic air. Orion's belt. 397
Build me a city all builded with brick 243
Built for bracing airs above the sea, 19
But all this has been stolen – all the light, these dustmotes in the
        beam, 425

Check the gas and hide the back door key. 438
Clocks, clocks, what about clocks? 285
Come for a walk down the river road, 358
Consoled by the dead with their tea-things 33
Contraceptives crisp with frost 77
Correct. You can't go back. But then we saw the gate, 416

Damp gravel on the landscaped bombsites 268
Damp weather wrings its yellow hands, 54
— Dark as Edgar Wallace in his Albany of death. On every floor 423
Deep in the restaurant afternoon, we share 462
Do we live in small murderous towns 283
Down to that area of retired water, among gridlocked stone 355
Dreamed I sat on Daddy's knee 248
Drifting ashore on a salt-cracked book-box, 368
Duke Ellington was very strict upon it 250

Farewell, supreme foyer where it was always afternoon! 422
For half my life I tried to learn from you. 57
Forever a winter too old, 109
From ancient days until some time last week 254
From the bomb-damaged slates 175
From the Crescent City slowly 230

God of blind corners and defunct commercial premises, 149

Hand me that banana now. 272
Here's where the far-gone Irish came to die 432
Here's winter now – the first frost on the field, 220
Hinny, make wor a stotty cake, 241

I am in love with detail. Chestnut trees 5
I am the one you've been looking for, 286
I apologize: I have by heart the names of clouds 342
I came back to municipal Arcadia 406
I have put a blockade on high-mindedness. 12
I have seen cavalry break camp before, 314
I once loved a boy with an iron hand. 244
I play my last arpeggio, 46
I remember the girl leaning down from the sunlight 417
I see you often in your later phase – 454

I shall be writing you until I die, 7
I should have seen you all the time, you ghosts, 8
I step from the wardrobe unblinking. 81
I was dreaming in a station of the Metro. 371
I was dreaming underwater 241
I was never strong on navigation 248
I watched her coming through the park 25
I wrote a cheque out in the snow 36
In a draughty terrace bar 459
In fact you are secretly somebody else. 157
In late afternoon, when the snow began, 69
In my book even golf is sinister, 113
In studied southern dialects 114
In the beginning was all underwater, 239
In the mechanical toy museum 74
In the rented rooms above the bay 39
In the small, the final, town of X, 269
In this compartment you discover 387
In which the action pauses for an hour 465
Inside, a Cyclops with an attitude 475
Into the pit go all Estates, 363
Invalids, perverts, and chambermaids born to be duped, 117
It could be true. There might just be 13
It is Newcastle at evening. It is far 200
It is so simple, being lonely. 3
It is to you, my dear, I owe 26
It strikes you: you are here. It's quite a sight — 447
It took you forty years to reach this empty room. 341
It was different then, oh you cannot imagine 365
It was unwise to come here looking for a friend 467
It will not feature streetlamps, gable-ends 200
It would be sacrilege to put a word 389
It's four o'clock, an autumn Sunday, 160
Its poplars and willows and sludge. Its gnat-clouds. 357

It's time now let's have your beer 251
It's under the X where the viaducts met. 168

Just round a corner of the afternoon, 429

Lay the cold boys in the earth 245
Let me be the first to admit it: 198
Let me continue. Long before we neared 297
Let us be serious now, says the teacher, 136
Let's drift again in these vast solitudes, 211
Like one surprised yet tolerant, 455
Like sluggish electrons 50
Like youth, this language has forgotten you. 427
Listen now, how far back sports began, 255
Look at this frosty red rose leaning over 232
Look away just for a moment. 411

Make over the alleys and gardens to birdsong, 105
Most men hire out their lives 34
My good right hand, farewell to you. 400
My lover tells me that when autumn comes 384
My sporting life (may I refer to me?) 258

Name me a river. 240
No cigarettes tonight. No tea. The spoon 443
No one believes them. Their windows get broken. 16
No one, you must wait in all these rooms, 181
November – Copper beeches bare – The gates 395
. . . Novembers, Decembers, you smoke-haunted Fifties: lead me 173
Now it's time to pull yourself together. 192
'Now see the monster with the pointed tail, 308
Now they're bricked over and leaking 210
Now we are in Europe let us take 428
Nowadays 264

O fairest of the northern waters, river-god, great Tyne, I asked, 470
— O Muse of Cinema, who taught us waking sleep, who warned 423
On the edge of the light from the tea-bar 123
One touch, then turn, then open the defence, 195
One weekday afternoon when we are dead, 418
Or else on a road between roads in warm darkness 86
Our island is full of detectives, 444
Over these moss-padded sleepers 446

Perhaps you are still awake now 170
Pigs. Chickens. Incest. Murder. Boredom. Pigs. 384
Pluvius shelters under the hawthorn 265

Rejoice, O Florence, that you are so great 326
River-doors are not sea-doors. They open 346

See 239
She represents the rose and universal hope; 384
She stands for a moment in the florist's window 266
She stares down the dead straight mile, at a walk, 415
Sites of municipal vaticination, 351
Six cranes where Baltic vessels come 68
Slowly, these evenings, it warms to its business, 41
So here we are now in the library, wasters. 111
So, then, let's strike a northern light 222
Some of them like zealots seek 43
Summer for me has always been August, no other. 24
Suppose that the summer is ending tonight, 146
Suppose you lived in Bruges-la-Morte: this brown murk would be
        blue – 448

That girl isn't doing her homework. 191
That's him finished, halfway down the hall, 187
The A66 in Cumbria was blocked for several hours today by early
        medieval warfare. 271

The bank on the corner of our street 267
The brutalized youth has returned 186
The centaur had not crossed the stream again 302
The chestnuts take their shadows in 38
The child in love with maps and lithographs 189
The clank of supernatural machinery 76
The cold eases over my wrists. I'm at home 64
The Corps of The Royal Flying Headers 121
The curved platform of Cullen Station, 1963. 385
The downlands, private under drizzle, 66
The fat-fingered leaves of the chestnuts 179
The ferry, *The Waverley*, churns on the sandbar. 350
The field is much bigger than when you arrived. 269
The fields and 'the wooded escarpments' 161
The final rusty flourish of the mountain ash 442
The globe was spinning when I left the room, 236
The house has been up for sale for months. 267
The middle-distant roar of trains 177
The mirror on this corridor 53
The Muse, your ex, Miss Jeudi Prochain, 412
The narrow brick foot-tunnel under the railway 267
The news is old. A picket line 61
The night has built a district of its own. 107
The open drains began a long way off 348
The other life, the properly narrated one 182
The pages of water are always revising themselves, 228
The painting over the luggage rack – 388
The pillars in the ruined church of steam 441
The popular song that first season, remember, 403
The priest and the police chief are in the back room. 95
The Principal's other edition of Q, 124
The radio's remembering 28
The ring of fire in Act Three should actually 380
The rotundas of the mercantile retired 122

The rows. Remorse. The birthday guilt 58
The saved were all ingratitude, 362
The service ran only on Sundays, 163
The shops, the banks, the bars are shut. 96
The shoulder-high tiles in municipal green, 147
The sinner looked up from the brutal meal 332
The sky becomes mother-of-pearl, 15
The snow will bring the world indoors, the fall 405
The sound of a train is the sound of the wind 469
The subtleties are wasted on the Yanks. 260
The sultry back lane smells of fruit and shit 263
The tables and chairs, 'the innocent walls and light', 464
The train stopped this evening. I looked 62
The vast indifferent river carried me, and in a while 450
The yellow lamps hang underneath the smoke, 79
Their speechless cries left hanging in the cold 120
There are miners still 379
There are no trains this afternoon. 219
There are tides in the paper that lies on the desk. 42
There are two tribes this world can boast – 439
There is an hour waiting in between. 128
There isn't much in this town to compare 188
There used to be a white enamel jug, 426
There's ground you cannot farm or build on. 83
These evenings I step from the Whalebone 135
They are reasonable men, 390
They have opened the holds of the trawlers, 131
They want it right now, do the serious drinkers. 133
This dark-eyed goddess, warm as breath, remote as a Czarina 421
This evening, Rilke at the harmonium 399
This is the air of another planet. 398
This is the flat with its absence of curtains. 126
This is the open gate to summer, beckoning 218
This is the place we imagine we live, 119

This is the room that reminds you 391
This isn't the way to the airport. 40
This must be where I came in, gaberdined 436
This place, the world, as you have more than once remarked, 456
Those living and those yet to be 376
Time after time, the river of light 468
To get these eclogues written I must sleep 190
To say that the sessions are long is to call 366
To take ship. 268
Tonight the blue that's flowing in 102
Tonight the summer opened like a park 84
Tonight's the turn of Mrs Mac 30
Trains cry in the night across fields 388
Trains go past. Their effigies do likewise, 183
Transported back to demi-Paradise – 458
Trewartha, Gerald, Felix, Windy, 178
Two aunts in garish rosy prints 55

Under the arc, the Toon Army tsunami, 167
Upright, blue-cushioned, with curved wooden arms, 382

Vlad the Impaler, the torturer's horse, 18

Water looked up through the lawn 344
We are entering *L'Angleterre profonde*, which does not exist. We 277
We change our cars and eat our meat. 67
We change the river's name to make it ours. 414
We have been here before, but not often, 174
We have sat here in too many poetry readings 209
We may not stay, not even with the most familiar things. 400
We set out to explore the poison root, 381
'We've seen enough. Now take my hand and run.' 473
What are cities made of? Steam vents. Blue light. Murder. 27
What fills the heart is felt to make amends, 27

When I return to Grey Bayou, the mud-kingdom 361
When I walk by your house, I spit. 166
When I went in that afternoon 141
When Marsyas the satyr played and lost 274
When Naughty Ron said middle age 139
When the lights fail at a tunnel's mouth 193
When the poem sneaks up on itself – 215
When the sway of the exotic overwhelmed 202
When their history's over, 359
When you are in the swimming bath 268
Where should we meet but in this shabby park 11
Whether it happens upstairs or on Pluto 44
White heads, white hats, in garden chairs, 14
White overflow, white wall. 90
Why this hotel, and this town and this province of X 393
Winter again with the forces of Northern reaction, 273
Wish you were here, though I never arrived. 234
With echoes drowning 266

You are my secret coat. You're never dry. 89
You are trying to work but you sit 136
'You can, now that she's qualified. 12
You could make me believe with your fine tongue 440
You detect a want of motive here 466
You read, and then you go to sleep: 92
You say that you are poor but you are happy 196
You say you've been back for a look. 100
You sit in your shed in the rain. 269
You sit there watching August burn away 396
You've been leaving for years and now no one's surprised 9

ACKNOWLEDGEMENTS

The poems in this volume were originally published in the following books:
The Indoor Park (Bloodaxe, 1983), *The Frighteners* (Bloodaxe, 1987),
HMS Glasshouse (Oxford University Press, 1991), *Ghost Train* (Oxford
University Press, 1995), *Downriver* (Picador, 2001), *Rivers* (Fremantle
Arts Centre Press, 2002), *Inferno* (Picador, 2006), *The Drowned Book*
(Picador, 2007), *Night Train* (Flambard, 2009) and *November* (Picador, 2011).
A number of poems were also included in *Penguin Modern Poets 5*
(Penguin, 1995) and the pamphlets *Boundary Beach* (Honest Ulsterman
Publications, 1989) and *The Ideology* (Smith Doorstop, 1997).
To the publishers of these works, acknowledgement is made.